Canto is a paperback imprint which offers a broad range of titles, both classic and more recent, representing some of the best and most enjoyable of Cambridge publishing.

D1580623

Genius Explained

In *Genius Explained* Michael J. A. Howe addresses the commonly held belief that genius is born not made. Controversially, he suggests that genius is not a mysterious and mystical gift but the product of a combination of environment, personality and sheer hard work. The exceptional talents of those we call geniuses are the result of a unique set of circumstances and opportunities, but in every case they are pursued and exploited with a characteristic drive, determination and focus which the rest of us rarely show. Michael Howe develops these ideas through a series of case studies focusing on famous figures such as Charles Darwin, George Eliot, George Stephenson, the Brontë sisters, Michael Faraday and Albert Einstein in this fascinating and accessible book.

Michael J. A. Howe is Professor of Psychology at Exeter University. He is a Fellow of the British Psychological Society and the author of numerous articles and books including *The Origins of Exceptional Abilities* (1990) and *IQ in Question: The Truth about Intelligence* (1997)

Genius Explained

Michael J. A. Howe

CAMBRIDGE
UNIVERSITY PRESS

PUBLISHED BY THE PRESS SYNDICATE OF THE UNIVERSITY OF CAMBRIDGE
The Pitt Building, Trumpington Street, Cambridge, United Kingdom

CAMBRIDGE UNIVERSITY PRESS
The Edinburgh Building, Cambridge CB2 2RU, UK
40 West 20th Street, New York, NY 10011-4211, USA
477 Williamstown Road, Port Melbourne, VIC 3207, Australia
Ruiz de Alarcón 13, 28014 Madrid, Spain
Dock House, The Waterfront, Cape Town 8001, South Africa

http://www.cambridge.org

First published 1999
Reprinted 2000
Canto edition 2001
Reprinted 2001 (twice)

Printed in the United Kingdom at the University Press, Cambridge

Typeset in Plantin 10/12 pt in QuarkXPress™   [SE]

A catalogue record for this book is available from the British Library

ISBN 0 521 00849 2 paperback

Cover illustration: Albert Einstein. Computer illustration of the German-
American physicist Albert Einstein (1879–1955) seen with an astronomical
artwork and equations including $E=mc^2$. In this famous equation, E stands for
energy, m for mass and c for the speed of light. In 1905 Einstein published papers
on the photoelectric effect, Brownian motion (the random movement of
suspended particles) and, most significantly, the special theory of relativity
which included the equation $E=mc^2$. In 1915 he published the general theory of
relativity. His paper on the photoelectric effect won Einstein the 1921 Nobel
Prize for physics. Credit: Mehau Kulyk/Science Photo Library

Contents

For Jordan

Preface

I learned about geniuses at school. They were, I discovered, a race of godlike individuals quite unlike ordinary people, possessing marvellous and practically boundless capabilities that the common run of men and women could never dream of.

After some years my conviction that geniuses form a breed apart began to waver. There were too many unanswerable questions. The idea of a class of intellectual giants who are inherently superior to everyone else seemed just about conceivable, but what about near-geniuses, or creative inventors and discoverers who are regarded as geniuses by some people but not by others? If there could be differing degrees of genius, and no clear dividing-line between them and others after all, how could geniuses possibly be a separate breed? And if they were not, could there really be genuine grounds for believing that geniuses are fundamentally set apart from those ordinary men and women who make themselves exceptionally capable by their own strenuous efforts?

Despite these difficulties, many people are reluctant to relinquish the belief in geniuses as a kind of super-breed. There is a suspicion that once these wonderfully creative individuals are perceived as being not altogether unlike ordinary people, geniuses will start to seem less fascinating and less admirable than we want and expect them to be. Stripped of their aura of apartness, geniuses might cease to be the exotic figures whose wondrous feats dazzle and astonish us, adding to the quality of our own lives.

There is no need for these fears. Having spent some time exploring the early lives of a number of geniuses, directing my attention as much towards the ways in which they resemble other and unexceptional people as towards their extraordinariness, I find that neither my admiration for them nor my astonishment at their creativity has diminished at all. These individuals really are amazing: their achievements are often quite wonderful, and far beyond anything that most of us could dream of doing. The fact that they spring from the same flesh and blood as everyone else makes geniuses all the more impressive, not less. Their triumphs are the achievements of individuals who have been able to shape formidable capabilities from the same basic materials that millions of people are born with. Discovering how that has happened is often difficult but invariably fascinating. It is heartening and invigorating as well. Geniuses are often heroic figures, and finding out how they became what they were is truly inspiring.

Of course, my view that geniuses began their lives made from much the same basic materials as all the rest of us is one that not every reader will be easily persuaded to share. Some time ago I began to scrutinise the evidence relating to the more common belief that people who do exceptionally well in various spheres of expertise – including science, mathematics and the arts, and also numerous sports – do so largely as a consequence of having been born with special gifts or innate talents. At that time I was working, with my friends John Sloboda and Jane Davidson, on a research study investigating the backgrounds of young musicians. Among the hundreds of parents, music teachers and young people we talked to, the majority were (and still are) firmly convinced that a few children are born with an innate gift for music, and that only those who possess such a gift stand a chance of excelling as musicians. That account is perceived by numerous people as being straightforwardly factual, no more debatable than the Pope's Catholicism.

Yet although those who hold that view do not question its truth, they can rarely produce positive evidence in support of it. Believers in innate talents may observe that people are very different from one another, which is undeniable, but hardly a convincing reason for concluding that some must have been born with special gifts. They may also remark that they cannot think of alternative reasons for individuals becoming as different as they are, especially when young people have been brought up in the same family and have attended the same school. But the logic behind an insistence on special innate gifts being the cause of genius, in the absence of independent evidence of the existence of such gifts, amounts to no more than asserting:

1 I cannot think of an alternative explanation to mine.
2 Therefore, my explanation must be the correct one.

In reality, however, the truth of a theory is never confirmed by someone's inability to think of alternatives. My failure to provide a better explanation for the presents that appear on Christmas Day is not a sufficient reason for anyone sharing my belief that Father Christmas brought them down the chimney. With geniuses, the idea of their being born with special gifts is a plausible possibility, but, as we shall see, there are alternative explanations that are more convincing.

Writing is always a solitary activity, but plenty of people have given me help, assistance, advice or encouragement, and I am grateful to all of them. Listing names is always potentially embarrassing. As when making a list of wedding guests, one is painfully aware that the more who are included the larger the number of others who might feel pained by their exclusion. So, taking a coward's approach, I shall keep the list very short. Howard Gruber first made me aware that psychologists do not have to be Freudians in order to have profound insights into genius. John Sloboda and Jane Davidson have been closely involved in the investigations of young musicians to which I have contributed. It has been good to work with them. Among those researchers investigating expertise and high abilities who have been especially helpful and encouraging, Anders Ericsson has been particularly inspiring, and he and Andrew Steptoe, Steve Ceci, Bob Sternberg, Andreas Lehmann, John Radford and Joan Freeman have all aided my efforts by inviting me to write on issues that are explored in this book. At Cambridge University Press my original editor Catherine Max and her successor Pauline Graham gave plenty of encouragement. Friends and colleagues at Exeter University have also been very generous with their support. Finally, but not least, my thanks to Sylvia.

1   Introduction

Genius appears to be a mystery, immune to scientific analysis. Unlike the mundane kinds of expertise that ordinary men and women gain through training and practice, genius is seen as a quality that is bestowed from above on particular individuals who are chosen to receive it. For the eighteenth-century German philosopher Immanuel Kant, genius was an incommunicable gift that cannot be taught or handed on, but is mysteriously imparted to certain artists by nature, and dies with the person.[1] That view is still widely shared today. Confronted with the challenge of explaining the purity and perfection of Mozart's music, the editor of a book on genius insists that the task is impossible, adding that, 'We can only answer, "because he was a genius", which is tantamount for saying that we do not know. For in each age and in each art, genius is that which defies analysis.'[2]

Should we even try to argue with that conclusion? It is undeniable that the greatest human achievements leave most people spellbound. Listening to a recording of *Così fan tutte*, I feel pressed to concede that the causes of genius must always remain mysterious. We can admire genius, wonder at it, be moved, dazzled and amazed by it. But *explain* genius? That seems to be another matter entirely. Our best efforts to understand its origins may fall flat, and perhaps we would be foolishly lacking in humility to think otherwise. Genius is a magical quality that resists understanding, it seems. Its origins will always resist our efforts to fathom them, and that's that.

Yet many people would dearly like to know more about the circumstances that create geniuses. They intrigue us. Their achievements touch our own lives. Galileo and Newton changed the world by transforming mankind's understanding of the earth's physical existence. So did Darwin and Einstein. Numerous men and women have had their minds uplifted by great artists and musicians. Writers like Shakespeare and Dante have altered the very languages in which our thoughts are rooted. There is no lack of reasons for making strenuous efforts to uncover the influences that have made certain individuals exceptionally creative or inventive.

[1] Quoted in Norris (1989), p. 154.   [2] Murray (1989), p. 1.

A number of practical concerns fuel the desire to know more about geniuses. What are the origins of remarkable accomplishments? Where do exceptional capabilities come from? Is it possible to deliberately manufacture a genius? We would benefit in a number of ways from having a better understanding of genius and its causes, not least by becoming better equipped to encourage today's young people to be more creative.

Confronted with the strength of opinion insisting on genius being a mystery, it is hardly surprising that many people have assumed that efforts to explain it must end in failure. But is that pessimism justified? It is certainly not helpful. Starting out with the belief that something is inherently mysterious creates extra barriers to understanding.

How might progress be made? I begin by proposing that the disciplines of biography and psychology form the two main sources of evidence that can help us to discover how and why children turn into the particular men and women they eventually become. The need for biographical information is obvious enough. Biographers are attracted to what is distinct and unique about a person: they take on the job of tracing and putting into perspective the events that mark a young person's progress towards maturity. By 'psychology', I refer to the scientific field of study in which researchers explore the ways in which people are influenced by their biology and their experiences. Research-based inquiries into children's development have helped to illuminate the effects of childhood experiences. Researchers have also studied the acquisition of expertise, drawing attention to the kinds of knowledge and skill that set apart especially capable men and women from those who are less competent.

It is easy enough to assert that psychological evidence is just as essential as biographical knowledge, but can we be confident that the findings of psychological research really will help us to understand how and why someone becomes a genius? Readers may be sceptical, and perhaps conscious of the limited extent to which light was cast on creative accomplishments by the psychodynamic psychology permeating those 'psychobiographical' accounts of great artists' and thinkers' lives that blossomed in the middle of the twentieth century. So just claiming that psychological science can make a contribution is not enough: we need convincing that it really does. Has research actually provided genuinely new insights? Do they help remove the mystery about geniuses? We can make a start towards answering these questions by applying research findings to the investigation of some early feats by Mozart, a genius whose stupendous accomplishments present some especially thorny puzzles. Can psychological investigations help untangle them? Ascertaining that will be a good test of their value.

Here are three facts about the young Mozart that appear to defy explanation. First, he began to compose music when he was no more than four. Second, by the time he was six or seven Mozart was such a brilliant performer on both harpsichord and violin that the young prodigy and his older sister were able to travel around Europe demonstrating their talents on money-making tours. Third, Mozart had an amazing memory for music, and it was reported that at fourteen he wrote out the complete score of a lengthy multi-part musical composition, Allegri's *Miserere*, after hearing it performed on just a couple of occasions.[3] All three of these feats are remarkable by any standards. They certainly appear quite mysterious. It is hard to see how they can be explained without appealing to magic or miracles. Perhaps he was born possessing some innate gift that made him totally different from other children. It seems impossible to imagine any other way to account for Mozart's dazzling childhood accomplishments at composing, performing, and memorizing music.

Can psychological research help to provide alternative explanations? Let's start by looking at the young Mozart's composing. He did indeed begin creating music at an exceptionally young age. But by the standards of mature composers, Mozart's early works are not outstanding. The earliest pieces of all were probably written down by his father, and perhaps improved in the process. Many of Wolfgang's childhood compositions, such as the first seven of his concertos for piano and orchestra, are largely arrangements of works by various other composers.[4] Of those concertos that only contain music original to Mozart, the earliest that is now regarded as a masterwork (No. 9, K. 271) was not composed until he was twenty-one: by that time Mozart had already been composing concertos for ten years. Similarly, Mozart's first symphonies, written in the style of J. S. Bach's son Johann Christian Bach, who helped and encouraged the nine-year-old boy when they met in London in 1764–5, consist of movements lasting no longer than four minutes and have been said to be almost copies of J. C. Bach's.

So Mozart only started producing the distinctive music that we associate with him after a lengthy period of training. The same is true of other great composers. An investigation by John Hayes, who examined the output of seventy-six well-known composers, established they *all* took a long time to reach the peak of their capabilities.[5] With seventy-three of the seventy-six, Hayes discovered that no major work was produced prior to the tenth year of their composing career. (The three exceptions were Shostakovich and Paganini, who each composed a substantial work after only nine years, and Eric Satie: *Trois Gymnopédies* was written in his ninth

---

[3] Sloboda (1985). See also Gardner (1997).   [4] Weisberg (1998).
[5] Hayes (1981). See also Simonton (1994).

year of composing.)[6] In Mozart's case, none of those compositions that are sufficiently original to be included among his major ones appeared prior to the twelfth year of his musical career.

It is of course extraordinary for a young child to be composing at all, and Mozart's early career as a composer was undeniably phenomenal. But knowing that even Mozart did not begin creating original masterpieces until he had been receiving serious training for a substantial number of years encourages us to challenge the assumption that his early attainments are impossible to explain without recourse to magic or mystery.

But what about Mozart's extraordinary early performing? That, surely, must be inexplicable, even if his early composing is not. Yet, here again the findings of recent psychological research suggest that whilst Mozart's precociousness was remarkable enough, it was not miraculous. That is evident from the results of investigations examining links between musicians' performing standards and the training they have undertaken. The research findings make it clear that in all performing musicians, high levels of skill depend upon large amounts of daily practice. In one study, for instance, researchers estimated the number of hours of formal practice notched up by German student violinists in their early twenties. By the age of twenty-one the best students in the performance class of a conservatoire had accumulated around 10,000 hours, and the less accomplished violinists (who were training to be violin teachers rather than performers) had practised for around half that time. There was not a single case of a player reaching very high standards without practising frequently and regularly over a period of years.[7] Further investigations by John Sloboda, Jane Davidson and myself have confirmed that the best performers accumulate more practice than less capable ones. It might have been expected that a few gifted young players would advance through the successive musical grade examinations much more easily than the others, but there was no evidence of that happening. In order to move ahead by a fixed amount, the most promising players spent as much time practising as the others did.[8]

It would be absurd to claim that practice is the *only* cause of success as a performing musician. Yet the sheer amount of formal practising appears to be the best single predictor of a player's level of accomplishment,

[6] Hayes' method for deciding if a particular musical composition meets the criterion of being a 'major' one was simple but ingenious. He looked in current catalogues for items that are available in several recordings, the reason for insisting on the availability of more than one version being to exclude immature compositions that could have been recorded simply for their novelty value.   [7] Ericsson, Krampe, & Tesch-Römer (1993).
[8] Sloboda, Davidson, Howe, & Moore (1996).

despite the fact that the measures of practising available to researchers are rough-and-ready ones, unreliable because they are largely retrospective, and taking little or no account of either the quality or the appropriateness of young people's practising activities. Practice and preparation are equally vital in other fields of achievement. For instance, around ten years of sustained training are needed for a chess player to reach international levels, and it takes comparable periods of time to reach the highest standards in mathematics, the sciences, tennis, athletics, and a number of other sports. As in music, although it is widely believed that certain gifted individuals can excel without doing the lengthy practising that ordinary people have to engage in, the evidence contradicts that view.

Returning to Mozart, are we now any the wiser about his precocious performing skills? Nobody knows for certain how much time the young Wolfgang Amadeus Mozart actually spent practising, but it is clear that his father, Leopold Mozart, subjected him to an arduous and unusual regime. From the child's earliest years much of the boy's time was devoted to musical activities. There were few opportunities to play outdoors or make friends with other children. Leopold Mozart, a capable violinist and a highly ambitious music teacher, went to great lengths to make his son into an outstanding musician, having had considerable success at teaching Wolfgang's sister, Nannerl. The father was anxious to display his children's abilities (and his own teaching skills) in the best possible light, and he was not above subtracting a year from their ages on the posters advertising their public performances.

Let's assume that Mozart's father made his son practise for an average of three hours a day from the age of three. In that event, by the time the child was six (when he and his sister were first taken around Europe on the musical tours in which they displayed their talents), Mozart would already have practised for a total of around 3,500 hours. That is roughly as much time as the typical young performer today takes to reach the standard of a good amateur player. In Mozart's day it was (as it still is) unusual for a young instrumentalist to have already practised for more than 1,000 hours by the age of six. So if the young Mozart had experienced substantially more training and practice than that, this would largely account for his standard of performing being superior to anything his audience had previously observed in a child of his age.

Lacking the knowledge we now have about the likely consequences of prolonged practising, it would not have been at all surprising if spectators watching the youthful Mozart's performances could not give a rational explanation for the feats they were witnessing. They would have seen nothing like them. But we, unlike Mozart's contemporaries, can perceive that there was no real mystery involved. These days, it is by no means unknown for children to reach the same levels of performance as the young Mozart did. Most of today's instrumentalists begin later than Mozart, but among those who do start musical training unusually early some young players achieve appreciably higher degrees of expertise than his at the equivalent age.[9] In the hundred or so years following Mozart's birth, piano sonatas became more technically difficult, requiring more demanding playing techniques, and there has been a definite tendency for music prodigies of generations later than Mozart's to play music that is increasingly difficult.[10] Compared with the most precocious young performers of the eighteenth century, the skills of more recent prodigies are more advanced.

So the task of explaining Mozart's childhood feats as a musical performer, like that of accounting for his early composing, is not the impossible one that it first seemed to be. Impressive as his early accomplishments were, they can be accounted for in the same ways that help explain the developing capabilities of hundreds of other young musicians who have patently not been geniuses.

There remains the third of Mozart's exceptional early abilities, his memory for music. This, like his composing and performing, appears at first to be a complete mystery. But can that feat too be explained in terms of the same processes that lead to high levels of competence in unexceptional young people?

In fact, accounting for Mozart's memory feat is surprisingly straightforward. There now exists a substantial body of research findings demonstrating that a person's ability to recall information about a particular topic is closely tied to that individual's existing knowledge and interests. Almost anyone who has a strong enthusiasm finds it easy to remember new information that is related to it. For instance, every Saturday afternoon many British soccer enthusiasts can recall all the scores from the league match results after hearing them just once.[11] To anyone who does not study the football results that may seem a remarkable feat, and up to a point it is, and yet week after week thousands of ordinary people manage it. Similarly, chess experts can remember huge amounts of information about moves in games of chess. Comparable feats of memory are not uncommon in connection with other fields of knowledge, with numerous ordinary people whose jobs or interests encourage them to gain specialised information finding it easy to remember new facts that can be linked to whatever the individual already knows.

Mozart's relative youth at the time he performed his feat of musical

---

[9] Lehmann & Ericsson (1998).   [10] Lehmann & Ericsson (1998).
[11] Morris, Gruneberg, Sykes, & Merrick (1981).

recall would not have been a handicap, because the increased remembering that specialised knowledge makes possible transcends age differences. Although adults do better than children at most tests of memory, the reverse is true when the task involves information that children, but not adults, can connect to their existing knowledge. For example, in a study in which ten-year-olds who were good chess players were given a memory task that required them to recall chess pieces arranged in legitimate positions, the children performed better than adult participants who were not expert players. But items that were unconnected to the children's special interest were recalled more accurately by the adults.[12]

For all that, Mozart's memory feat still seems remarkable, and it *was* remarkable. To a non-musical person, a memory feat like Mozart's seems to involve recalling an immense sequence of separate notes. But imagine the unusual everyday life of the young Wolfgang Amadeus Mozart. He inhabited a world of music, hour after hour, day after day, in the company of a father who was an expert teacher. By adolescence, the sheer amount of Mozart's musical knowledge would have been enormous by most people's standards. He would have recognised many familiar structures and patterns, eliminating the need to recall each note separately. As a result, compared with a non-musician Mozart would have perceived the task very differently, with the information that needed to be remembered being meaningful and interconnected. And although Allegri's *Miserere* is a lengthy composition, it is one that happens to contain a great deal of repetition. For a person as knowledgeable as Mozart, that would have lightened the burden of remembering.[13]

We can now see that it is entirely possible that all three of Mozart's remarkable early feats could, after all, have been achieved through the operation of mental processes that were broadly the same as the ones that give rise to the more modest skills and achievements of ordinary people. It no longer appears inescapable that Mozart must have begun life with some mysterious special gift of genius. Of course, what we have achieved by unravelling the likely causes of certain of Mozart's early feats falls far short of a full accounting for his creative achievements. I have not even begun to sketch out the uniquely creative powers that enabled a masterpiece like *Don Giovanni* to be forged. But a start has been made, and it is a

---

[12] Chi (1978).

[13] A complicating factor is that our capacity to assess the magnitude of the memory feat is constrained by the impossibility of knowing whether or not Mozart's recall of the music really was as accurate as it has been assumed to have been. The evidence verifying Mozart's accuracy at remembering rests on the statement of one singer, who had no opportunity to assess the precise match between Mozart's version and the original score. Minor discrepancies from the original would probably have gone undetected by Mozart's audience.

fruitful beginning because it gives revealing glimpses of the ways in which a young person might have gained certain of the qualities that made the creation of works of genius possible. There is no denying that the eventual accomplishments of an individual like Mozart are quite superior to anything that most people are capable of, and yet it begins to seem conceivable that the underlying capabilities Mozart depended upon may not have been fundamentally different in kind from ones that are shared by numerous men and women with no claim to genius.

One way to make progress towards explaining the human attainments that result in their creator being seen as a genius is to discover how a person masters the knowledge and mental skills that make those accomplishments possible. That is the approach taken in this book. The creative activities that are most directly involved in the construction of masterpieces will not be neglected, but my primary aim is to trace the routes by which a few outstanding individuals gained the capabilities their achievements have depended upon. Charting individuals' early advances is, I think, a particularly effective way to help reveal the origins of genius.

I am convinced that it is indeed possible to understand genius and its causes. A major aim of the present book is to unearth the influences that have helped make a few rare individuals capable of remarkable feats of imagination and discovery. When that has been achieved, providing us with some understanding of the contributing factors, the absurdity of appealing to mystical forces will be evident. There is simply no need to believe that mysteries or miracles are involved.

Our efforts to account for genius will run into numerous difficulties, of course, if only because explaining how a young person becomes the adult individual he or she turns out to be is never easy. But although it is possible that with those men and women whose lives and feats are the most striking of all the barriers to understanding will be especially daunting, and that the problems that have to be overcome in order to discover how certain children grow up to be geniuses are vastly more challenging than the ones involved in charting the progress towards maturity of an ordinary boy or girl, there is no compelling evidence that this must be so. I am not convinced that there is anything about the lives and achievements of geniuses that is in principle less amenable to explanation than the lives and achievements of other people. The children's writer Enid Blyton was no genius, but explaining how she was able to turn out the thousands of words she produced every single day is as much of a challenge as accounting for the accomplishments of authors who were far more creative. That geniuses are special is undeniable, but the view that they are special for reasons that are mysterious needs to be challenged.

It would be immensely difficult, and perhaps impossible, to delineate each and every one of the events that had to take place in order for, say, the young Mozart, or the young Einstein, to become capable of their achievements, and then go on to create them. I do not attempt that feat. Some readers may feel that any investigation that stops short of such exhaustive documentation must fail to provide an adequate explanation. My own view is that this is rather like insisting on believing that although Joe Bloggs has admitted making the crop circle that appeared last week in his neighbour's field, the one that appeared yesterday must have been created by aliens from a distant galaxy, or like saying that even though most of the tricks performed by Mr Uri Geller are within the capabilities of skilled conjurors, his claim to possess mysterious special powers must nevertheless be believed. In each case the more reasonable assumption would be that where insufficient evidence exists to fully explain a new event, an explanation that is based upon observed causes and broadly follows the lines of one that accounted for a similar event in the past is preferable to one that invokes unverifiable causes or mysterious special powers.

There are gaps in what is known, but these create problems rather than mysteries. That distinction between problems and mysteries is a crucial one. A mystery is a state of affairs surrounding some phenomenon that resists any explanation in terms of known causes. A problem, in contrast, is a state of affairs in which there exists uncertainty about the explanation for something, but in which there is every reason to believe that one can be found, provided that the necessary resources are available. For me, discovering the best railway route between Madrid and Vienna would be a problem. It is not a mystery, since I am confident I can find the answer, as long as the missing information is forthcoming.

In the chapters that follow I show that the challenges involved in arriving at a full understanding of the achievements of geniuses belong within the category of problems rather than mysteries. In principle at least, there are no points at which explaining human accomplishments becomes impossible except by resorting to miracles or magic. The qualification 'in principle' is needed because in some instances it will never be possible to obtain all the information that a full account would need to draw upon. For instance, we shall never discover how William Shakespeare became the genius he was, if only because we know too little about his early years.

The creative undertakings of a genius involve two broad (and overlapping) stages. First, there is the matter of acquiring those capabilities the person draws upon. Second, there are the inventive activities that directly contribute to masterpieces. In most of the present book's chapters the emphasis is on the former stage, and I explore the ways in which a number of individuals have gradually acquired the exceptional capabilities that equipped them for their achievements. How, I ask, did certain men and women become capable of their remarkable feats?

We must take pains to be sure that any explanations arrived at are ones that genuinely illuminate and extend our understanding, rather than being pseudo-explanations. It is important to be aware that clues about possible causes of genius that are encountered in commonsense wisdom, can actually impede understanding rather than adding to it. One widespread belief, hinted at in Kant's suggestion that genius is a quality which nature endows in certain people, is that the causes of individuals' exceptional attainments take the form of special gifts or innate talents.

That claim is not necessarily false, of course. It is entirely conceivable that geniuses are indeed born with special characteristics that partly account for their outstanding achievements. And irrespective of whether the claim is true or false, the fact that many adults are convinced that only those young people who are born possessing special gifts can thrive in fields of expertise such as music has momentous practical implications for numerous children. However, for it to be legitimate to conclude that innate gifts really are an influence, there would need to be independent evidence that they do actually exist. In the absence of that evidence such a conclusion would be groundless. What often happens, however, is that simply because someone is exceptionally able, in the absence of an obvious alternative it is *assumed* that the person must have been born with a special gift or talent. Subsequently the person's (unverified) possession of that innate gift is invoked as the cause of the outstanding ability. Creative attainments are assumed to be 'explained' by the assertion that their creator possesses special inborn powers, although the person's achievements provide the sole basis for believing in the existence of those special powers. This reasoning is entirely circular: appearances notwithstanding, nothing is actually being explained. So when it is introduced in this way, the notion of an innate gift and talent is no more than a kind of 'magic ingredient', which provides no more than the illusion of an explanation, as in,

Question: What is the reason why X is so fat/thin/ill/healthy/clever?
Answer: Because X was born with a special quality that makes a person fat/thin etc.

The explanatory powers innate gifts may appear to have, in the absence of independent evidence of their existence, are similarly imaginary rather than real.

Deciding whether or not there are solid grounds for believing that innate gifts and talents do actually exist is a complex issue, and I explore it in Chapter 9. But unless their existence can be verified, all that is achieved by invoking special inborn qualities as the cause of genius is to create the kind of pseudo-explanation that attributes events to the presence of some or other kind of magic ingredient.

A not uncommon view that is sometimes linked to the belief that genius is a consequence of a person being endowed by nature with a special gift is that it is only possible for someone to become a genius as a consequence of being designed in advance to be one. That assertion is easily rebutted. The reasons for questioning it are not unlike the arguments with which Darwinian science has refuted the claim that the human species could never have come into being except through some form of 'design from above'. Darwin's theory contradicted that belief by demonstrating that it was indeed possible for humans to be created as a consequence of evolutionary processes, in the absence of any designer. Our species did not have to be planned in advance.

Nor did the lives of individual geniuses. The processes that enable an individual's capabilities to be acquired through learning and experience are very different from the ones that enable new species to evolve. However, the learning and training experiences that creative people undergo obviate the necessity for their accomplishments to depend upon being designed in advance just as convincingly as evolution makes design from above unnecessary for the emergence of new species.

Before going any further, we should try to decide what a genius is. Precisely what do we mean by the term? A straight answer to that seemingly simple question is not at all easy to find. For better or worse, there is no straightforward specification or definition of genius. Even listing the defining attributes turns out to be impossible.

Why do these difficulties arise? The essential reason is that whilst saying that someone is a genius appears to be a statement about the person's qualities, it is actually not. What is really being achieved by calling a person a genius is to acknowledge or recognise their *achievements*. The word 'genius' is ours, not theirs, and it is a kind of accolade that has been bestowed upon certain individuals, usually not until well after the person has died.

The term 'genius' has a long history, but until fairly recently the most common use was not for describing a person but for identifying the supposed reason for someone being capable of creative accomplishments. A person's genius was seen as working in broadly the way that a poet's muse was believed to function: genius was envisaged as a partly external spirit that gave a helping hand. Not until the eighteenth century did the practice of referring to a person as a genius become common. The modern meaning of the word comes partly from the Latin word *genius* which stems from *gens*, meaning family, but also from the Latin *ingenium*, denoting natural disposition or innate ability.

We can call a man a giant because he is very tall, but there is no single attribute of a person that justifies saying that someone is a genius. Describing a person as a genius is not like stating that he or she is tall, or even intelligent or clever. The word is never introduced solely as a description of an individual: it always denotes a recognition of outstanding accomplishments. If you are unconvinced about that, try to think of someone who is widely regarded as having been a genius but who never produced highly valued creative work: I suspect that you will fail. There have always been men and women who were exceptionally intelligent, wise, artistic, sensitive, incisive and so on, but unless they have produced major achievements, other people have not called them geniuses. Whenever someone is widely regarded as having been a genius, we can be sure that the person has made a contribution which is valued. If a baker is someone who makes bread, a genius is a man or woman who produces masterpieces or discoveries that greatly impress other people.

The difference between being immensely capable or creative and being regarded as a genius is not totally unlike the difference between being exceptionally brave and winning a medal for bravery. To win a medal, you undoubtedly do need to be brave, but you have to be a little fortunate as well. The bravery must have positive consequences, and it must be observed by someone who is in a position to report it. Similarly, in order for someone to be regarded as a genius, that person not only has to be exceptionally able but also must achieve something that is appreciated by others, and whether or not that happens will be partly outside the person's control. As we shall see, success often goes not to the individual who is most intelligent or capable in absolute terms, but to the man or woman who happens to possess just those skills or qualities that are needed in order to solve a particular problem at a particular moment in history. So the accolade of genius is bestowed on a person for creating something that others admire, rather than for being outstandingly clever.

By and large, creative individuals are more likely to be regarded as geniuses if their achievements are not too recent: few of those who are widely acknowledged to have been a genius died less than a hundred or so years ago, Einstein being a notable exception. It also helps if the person's different accomplishments are linked rather than being too diffuse. Sir Richard Burton (1821–90) was one of the most dazzling of all Victorians. As well as translating the *Arabian Nights* into English, he led expeditions of discovery, translated other poetry and folklore, mastered around thirty languages, wrote poetry of his own, contributed to archaeology, ethnology, anthropology, and the study of swordsmanship, and also made discoveries in botany, zoology and geology. Yet, largely because his achievements were so scattered, few have thought Burton to have been a genius, for all his brilliance.

The fact that the word 'genius' is used more as an accolade than as a description helps make it the useful term it is, but creates some difficulties as well. One limitation is that introducing the term does not actually help to account for a person's attainments. We should not be fooled into thinking that anything is being clarified by a statement such as 'She produced a great novel because she was a genius'. All that is really being said here is that the individual who wrote her great novel was a person acknowledged to be capable of doing just that.

Another problem is that there is no objective procedure or hard-and-fast criterion for categorising people as geniuses or non-geniuses. A limited number of individuals are very widely regarded as having been geniuses: Archimedes, Plato, Aristotle, Dante, Copernicus, Galileo, Michelangelo, Newton, Darwin, Bach, Beethoven, Mozart, Shakespeare, Rembrandt and Einstein would be placed in that category by most educated people in the English-speaking world, as might some others, perhaps including Dickens, Schubert, George Eliot, Tolstoy, Tchaikovsky, Balzac, van Gogh, and Flaubert. But what about Trollope, Coleridge, Renoir, Monet, Manet, Degas, Turner, and Jane Austen? And should we include Emily Brontë, Benjamin Franklin, Marie Curie, Puccini, Verdi, Brunel, Charlotte Brontë, Elizabeth Gaskell, Edgar Allan Poe, or James Joyce? As soon as we move on from a surprisingly small number of creative people, most of whom have been dead for a long time, agreement on who deserves to appear in a definitive list of geniuses becomes impossible, even though there are certainly hundreds and possibly thousands of individuals for whom a serious claim can be made. Charles Darwin's cousin Francis Galton tried to introduce a degree of objectivity by referring to one in a million individuals as 'illustrious' and one in four thousand as 'eminent', but in the absence of clear rules for deciding how to select particular men and women, even that approach to categorising outstanding people could never have worked.

To complicate things, reputations wax and wane. In common with other circumstances in which accolades are bestowed, the matter of whether or not a particular creative man or woman acquires the reputation of being a genius depends on factors outside that individual's control. Chance can play a role. Had Albert Einstein or Michael Faraday lived thirty years earlier or thirty years later than they did, the particular skills and qualities they possessed might have had less impact. Conversely, there are other scientists whose importance might well have been greater had they lived at a slightly different time, or in a different place. Fashion too can play a role, and just as people's reputations can wax and wane, so can views about whether a certain person merits being called a genius. Someone whose work is little valued in one century may be regarded as a genius by citizens of a later era. For us, Bach was a genius, and perhaps Botticelli too, although earlier generations either ignored them or judged them far less favourably than we do now. As recently as 1941, when Edmund Wilson wrote about Charles Dickens in *The Wound and the Bow*, that author's reputation was not what it is today.[14] It is pointless to ask, 'Was Botticelli (or Dickens) a genius or not?'.

Yet another complication is revealed by the necessity to decide whether, if someone 'accidentally' creates a masterpiece, that person should be called a genius. Questions like this surface in connection with occasional individuals such as Gregor Mendel (1822–84). He made a monumental contribution to the science of genetics, but perhaps without ever quite recognising the significance of what he was doing.[15]

So the problem of deciding who should and who should not be counted as a genius is impossible to resolve. I sidestep the issue by being willing to consider any individual whose claims to the status of a genius have received a substantial measure of support. Restricting our attention to just those very few people who are universally regarded as having been geniuses would create severe practical problems, if only because of the rarity of individuals for whom we have substantial information about their early lives. It would be fascinating to trace the childhoods of, say, Archimedes, or William Shakespeare, or Isaac Newton, but the necessary factual evidence has been lost. Even with a relatively recent genius like Schubert, available knowledge about critical life events can be remarkably sparse.

What are geniuses like? What kinds of people are they? They are hugely diverse, but a few characteristics are shared by virtually all of them. The first is an intense curiosity and dedication to one's work. A second and perhaps more surprising trait possessed by most geniuses is the capacity to acquire a variety of different human qualities.

Geniuses are usually sure about what they want to do, single minded, committed, and they have a firm sense of direction. They often work with a ferocity and intensity, even when impeded by doubts and frustrations. They also share a capacity for sustained diligence. Isaac Newton said that he discovered the law of universal gravitation by thinking about it continuously; Charles Darwin attributed much of his success to a capacity to

[14] Wilson (1941).   [15] Brannigan (1981).

reflect for years on an unexplained problem; Einstein asserted that curiosity, determination, and hard work were vital ingredients of his effectiveness, and the great English painter J. M. W. Turner, asked to reveal the secret of his success, gave the straight reply 'the only secret I have got is dammed hard work'.[16] Isaac Newton was described by a contemporary as having concentrated so hard that had it not been for the fact that the practical aspects of undertaking experiments forced him to get some relief from thinking, he would have killed himself through studying. He displayed an impressive doggedness at persisting in the face of difficulties. Struggling to comprehend the mathematics in Descartes's *Geometry*, Newton just kept on trying. He 'read it by himself when he was got over 2 or 3 pages he could understand no farther than he began again & got 3 or 4 pages farther till he came to another difficult place, than he began again and advanced farther and continued doing so till he had made himself Master of the whole.'[17] The capacity to keep persisting is as essential in music and art as in science and mathematics. Perseverance is at least as crucial as intelligence. An interesting and perhaps surprising research finding is that, compared with assessments of young children's intelligence, indications of their capacity to delay gratification and avoid acting too impulsively are better predictors of future competence. Clearly, a young person's temperament is hugely important. This raises an interesting possibility. If, as seems likely, inherited differences between individuals contribute to the fact that individuals differ in their eventual achievements, the most crucial inherent differences may be ones of temperament rather than of intellect as such.

It is especially advantageous to be able to keep trying. As the eighteenth-century British artist Joshua Reynolds remarked about facility at drawing, it, 'like that of playing upon a musical instrument, cannot be acquired but by an infinite number of acts.'[18]

The second way in which many geniuses are alike is in their ability to bring a number of different qualities to their enterprises. It may sometimes appear that remarkable intellectual or artistic capacities, combined with fierce determination, form the sole all-important ingredients of creative accomplishments, and there is no denying that geniuses tend to be single-minded individuals. They typically exhibit a sharp awareness of the direction in which they intend to move and a degree of indifference to other things. They can appear to be narrowly obsessed by one particular goal, as they fiercely concentrate on their work for long periods of time. We can readily picture Mozart totally absorbed in his work, or Isaac

---

[16] Hamilton (1997), p. 128.   [17] John Conduit, quoted in Westfall (1980), p. 111.
[18] Hamilton (1997), p. 23.

Newton neglecting his visitors while he sits wrestling with mathematical problems on the floor of his cellar, and forgetting the wine he is supposedly fetching, or Albert Einstein, thinking only of his work and disregarding ordinary activities like putting on his socks. And yet on closer examination it is clear that geniuses can rarely afford to be too narrow. Even when the actual achievements for which someone is acclaimed are fairly specific, a broader range of qualities is likely to have been necessary in order to create the circumstances that enabled the person to move ahead.

Take Charles Darwin, for instance. He is seen in the popular imagination as a reclusive scientist, preoccupied with his poor health, rarely straying from the house he lived in for almost forty years, and protecting his privacy by building a high wall and lowering 170 yards of the adjoining lane. Yet Darwin would never have enjoyed the success he earned were it not for the fact that in addition to the intellectual capabilities, fierce determination, and single-mindedness that he possessed in common with other geniuses, he also had some impressive diplomatic skills, as well as courage and a marked ability to get on with others. People who knew Charles Darwin liked and respected him. He needed all these personal qualities for dealing with a series of characters whose cooperation he depended on, including a sometimes difficult male parent, and, later, the prickly and short-tempered Captain Robert Fitzroy, with whom Darwin worked hard at maintaining a harmonious working relationship on board the tiny HMS *Beagle* during its five-year voyage. Then there were the various scientists who served Darwin as mentors in his early days and collaborators and disciples later on. Darwin also assembled a network of individuals who were helpful to him because they knew about breeding and the domestication of species. He cooperated with many collectors, veterinarians, horticulturists, and numerous animal and plant breeders, amongst whom were pigeon and poultry fanciers, rabbit raisers, beekeepers, rose growers, livestock men, nurserymen, silk-growers, farmers, horse-trainers, botanists and practical gardeners. A glance at *On the Origin of Species* demonstrates that Darwin counted on the aid of these practical experts for much of the immense body of evidence that was needed to buttress the theory of evolution and make it invulnerable to the sharp attacks that he knew would be directed at it.

At various points in his life Darwin was able to seize chances that would have been missed by someone lacking his impressively broad capabilities. In childhood, his older brother (by four years) Erasmus found Charles mature enough to engage as a helper in scientific experiments, with the result that by the age of thirteen Charles Darwin had gained a useful grounding in practical chemistry and biology. The opportunity that came

his way when he was twenty-two to take part in HMS *Beagle*'s voyage happened only because Darwin had been noticed as a young man whose
judgement as well as knowledge outstripped his years. He was 'the very
man they are in search of', the Regius Professor of Botany at Cambridge
University told him. That Darwin could grasp that opportunity was only
possible because when his father proved awkwardly opposed Charles had
the wit to take the only course of action that could have induced the
parent to drop his veto. Later, it was because of Darwin's well-deserved
high reputation that when the theory of evolution finally appeared in 1859
it was sympathetically examined by his fellow scientists (rather than
encountering the instant rejection that had greeted other evolutionary
ideas) and quickly seen to be as sound as it was revolutionary.

Darwin was by no means unusual or unique in having to call upon a
variety of human qualities. Even Albert Einstein, although often seen as
an isolated thinker, leaned heavily upon his communication skills and his
capacity for friendship, and Thomas Edison would have achieved very
little were it not for his impressive organisational powers.

In trying to understand how certain men and women became geniuses,
how can we most effectively combine psychological research and biographical expertise? My views about the desirable characteristics of an
approach which achieves that will become clearer in later chapters, but
two features need mentioning here. First, an effective approach needs to
be largely *descriptive* and not overburdened with theoretical dogmas. That
does not mean denying the importance of explanatory theories, but since
it is rarely possible to explain *how* something happened without knowing
precisely *what* it was that took place, it is essential to begin by tracing in
some detail the lives of particular men and women. Researchers can get
into difficulties by failing to appreciate the necessity to start with good
descriptions. The tendency to construct detailed theoretical speculations
from flimsy supporting evidence was a weakness of the psychodynamic
theories underpinning psychobiographical explorations of people's lives.

It is a mistake to regard the act of describing what happens as being no
more than a preliminary, 'pre-scientific' stage of an investigation. Careful
descriptions actually achieve much more than that. Once a really good
descriptive account exists, the job of explaining observed facts may be
more than half done, as good theorists like Darwin have always known. Of
course, it is often helpful to have hunches and intuitions about why things
happen, but at times it is just as necessary to keep a rein on one's theoretical views, because they can all too easily act as blinkers rather than aids.
Holding on to one point of view can blind us to others. If someone has
become convinced that the only conceivable reason why Mozart became

a great composer is that he was born with a special gift for music, the chances are that the person will fail to discern alternative explanations. In common with a young woman who, asked for directions to a neighbouring town, told me 'You cannot get from here to [nearby] Helensburgh: you'll have to start somewhere else,' those who are rigidly committed to one explanation may have their minds opened up by being encouraged to examine things from an alternative perspective.

It is helpful to think of a person's life as being like a kind of journey, one that follows a particular route which is unique to that individual. Biographical accounts make it possible to trace the temporal patterns of events and consequences that take place as a person develops, and plot the very different routes by which young people move through the time that structures their lives. Once we gain a detailed knowledge of the events of a person's childhood, it is likely that we will begin to discern how and why the child gradually turned into the adult he or she eventually became.

In tracing such a route and trying to identify the various experiences and events that collectively make a child into an adult, an essential facet of the person's development involves the expansion of their capabilities. Everyone's expertise has to be acquired, and so do their likes and dislikes, their interests and their preferences. That is just as true of geniuses as it is of people whose accomplishments are unexceptional. Like the skills and abilities of ordinary men and women, the more remarkable capacities of a genius are gained more or less gradually. Especially rare or impressive capacities build upon a foundation of more commonplace ones. When the path can be charted towards the extraordinary attainments of, say, a grandmaster at chess, or a concert pianist, it is usually found that the person's itinerary through the earlier stages of expertise is broadly similar to that of other people. The exceptional individual goes further, and may move ahead faster, but always there is a route to be traced. There are no gaps or inexplicable leaps. If there *appears* to be a gap, the chances are that when we look closer we will discover that what is being identified is a hiatus in our own knowledge, not a discontinuity in the person's progress.

The analogy between a person's early life and a journey or a voyage can be misleading if pressed too far. The voyage metaphor may appear to suggest that people forge ahead along a single track, with the implication that the first step towards exposing the causes of genius is just a matter of identifying a person's special capability and seeing how it was nurtured. In reality, it is more accurate to envisage the trajectory of someone's life as involving a number of linked but partly independent strands, all of which contribute to the person's progress.

Tracing the events of someone's formative years involves getting close to the individual concerned. The need to do that makes it important for our approach to have a second aspect. That involves placing emphasis on trying to lay bare the actual *experiences* of the men and women whose early lives are examined. Having continuous records that cover substantial parts of people's lives helps to make this possible. Such records illustrate the uniqueness of each life, making it easier to see why different people do not react in the same way to identical events or similar opportunities. What really matters is not simply what happens to a person – as an observer might record it – but how the particular individual actually experiences life's happenings.

It is important to avoid confusing experiences with environments. People are directly affected by their experiences, but only indirectly influenced by their environments. Surprise is sometimes expressed at the fact that two children brought up in the same family environment can turn out very differently, but there is nothing very remarkable about that, since the children may have experienced events in constrasting ways. The key distinction here is between events as seen from the outside and as perceived from the unique vantage point of the person concerned. We may know a great deal about someone's physical environment, but that knowledge will not necessarily provide much insight into that person's actual experiences, and it is the latter rather than the former that have a direct influence on an individual's life.

Although we can never duplicate someone else's experiences or reconstruct their unique point of view, it is worth striving to get as close as we can to doing that. Individual children and adults are often affected by the happenings that make up their lives in ways that no outsider could begin to perceive without knowing about the person's unique life and character, temperament and personality. But when some of that knowledge *is* available, the actual significance of events in someone's life becomes clearer. It is possible to see, for example, why apparently destructive events can have benign consequences. Thus for the seven-year-old H.G. Wells the ostensibly disastrous accident of breaking a limb had a happy outcome, because it encouraged him to spend more time reading, with immensely positive personal consequences. We can now also understand why, as Charles Dickens reported, he too benefited from illness in childhood, by being stimulated to read books.

In the following chapters I shall trace the early lives of a number of geniuses, attempting to discover how and why each individual became capable of their remarkable accomplishments. Deciding which men and women to concentrate upon could have been difficult, but two constraints guided my choices and made selection easier. First, relatively detailed accounts of the person's formative years had to be available. Second, there were obvious advantages to be gained from making sure that at least some of the chosen individuals had enough in common with one another for comparisons to be made and parallels drawn, as is possible when people have belonged to the same era and have shared a common culture. With these considerations in mind, and having decided that my main subjects would include Charles Darwin and John Stuart Mill – choices influenced by the fact that the documentation of their childhoods is unusually full and informative – I saw some advantages in concentrating mainly on individuals whose contributions were made in roughly the middle half of the nineteenth century.

That was a fruitful time for geniuses. In Britain alone there were a number of major novelists, including George Eliot, Charles Dickens, Elizabeth Gaskell, the Brontës, William Thackeray and Anthony Trollope (who were all born between 1810 and 1824), and Mary Shelley. Benjamin Disraeli wrote well-received novels as well as being a statesman. There were some great engineers, among them Brunel, the two Stephensons, and Joseph Locke. The poets of the time included Robert and Elizabeth Barrett Browning, Christina Rossetti, Robert Southey and Alfred Tennyson (who was born in the same year as Darwin and Gladstone: Abraham Lincoln shared with Darwin his actual day of birth in 1809). The ageing Wordsworth lingered on until 1850. Also, there were artists such as John Everett Millais, Dantë Gabriel Rossetti and J. M. W. Turner; scientists including Charles Darwin, Michael Faraday, Sir John Herschel, Charles Lyell, James Clerk Maxwell, Alfred Wallace, Charles Wheatstone, William Whewell and Charles Babbage, and numerous other thinkers and writers, amongst whom were John Stuart Mill, Thomas Carlyle, Thomas Macaulay, Harriet Martineau, William Morris, John Ruskin and Herbert Spencer.

Across the Atlantic a number of innovative writers and artists were at work, including Emily Dickinson, Ralph Waldo Emerson, Oliver Wendell Holmes, Henry Longfellow, Nathaniel Hawthorne, Herman Melville, Edgar Allan Poe, Henry David Thoreau, Walt Whitman and James McNeill Whistler. Benjamin Franklin's long life had recently ended and the equally lengthy one of Thomas Edison had begun. Mark Twain was starting his career.

The many creative individuals living on the European continent at that time included novelists such as Honoré de Balzac, Gustave Flaubert, Alexandre Dumas, Victor Hugo and Stendhal, a number of major composers including Berlioz, Bizet, Brahms, Liszt, Mendelssohn and Wagner, painters such as Courbet, Degas, Delacroix and Manet, and various major poets including Charles Baudelaire. Among the numerous

European scientists, mathematicians and thinkers of the period were André Ampère, Claude Bernard, Auguste Comte, Gustave Fechner, Karl Freidrich Gauss, Heinrich Heine, Hermann von Helmholtz, Alexander von Humboldt, Friedrich Kekulé, Sören Kierkegaard, Karl Marx, Georg Simon Ohm, Friedrich Schelling, and Arthur Schopenhauer. In Russia, Gogol and Dostoyevsky were active, and as Pushkin approached his premature end Tolstoy's life was beginning.

In the following two chapters, I direct the bulk of my attention to a great scientist, Charles Darwin, and a great railway engineer, George Stephenson, an inventive genius who made an enormous contribution to developments that revolutionised transportation and passenger travel, despite starting life with a childhood of grinding poverty, in which he never had a single day of schooling. Chapter 4 examines the remarkable early life of another great scientist, Michael Faraday. Chapter 5 looks at a number of families in which a parent has made a more or less deliberate attempt to 'manufacture' a genius. This chapter includes a discussion of the education of John Stuart Mill, whose reputation as a child prodigy preceded his mature accomplishments. In Chapter 6, which examines a number of child prodigies, I take an excursion from the mid-nineteenth century in order to provide an account of Albert Einstein's childhood. That diversion is justified by his enormous importance, together with the fact that his early life is a mine of useful information concerning the formative experiences that contribute to scientific creativity. Chapter 7 deals largely with the acquisition of expertise in writers, including the Brontës, George Eliot, and Charles Dickens. That chapter, which stresses the importance of childhood writing activities and explores some ways in which early experiences have been drawn upon by imaginative novelists, concentrates on the similarities rather than the differences between exceptional and less remarkable authors in the manner in which their expertise was acquired and extended. Chapter 8 provides a more direct examination of the creative activities that are involved in the actual making of discoveries and inventions, and the production of masterpieces. It introduces a variety of discoverers and inventors, ranging from the Wright brothers, who achieved the first powered flight, to the twentieth-century discoverers of the structure of DNA, Francis Crick and James Watson.

Chapter 9 examines some ideas and theories that have been put forward in order to account for geniuses and their accomplishments. This final chapter examines genetic as well as environmental influences on human capabilities. It takes a critical look at commonsense views about human abilities and their causes, showing that even those ideas that are almost universally accepted and seen as 'obviously' or self-evidently true can be entirely wrong. I establish, for instance, that there is no firm scientific justification for the widely accepted belief that high abilities are made possible by certain individuals possessing innate gifts or talents. I also question some common views concerning the manner in which genetic variability exerts its effects on people. Mistaken beliefs about the origins of exceptional capabilities are pernicious, and can lead to faulty decisions being made, with damaging consequences to immense numbers of young people.

2   The young Charles Darwin

We enjoy being told about those geniuses who amaze us with feats that are especially spellbinding. Without them it would be harder for people to cling to the belief that geniuses are a special breed, akin to the magicians and dragons and fabulous giants that populated the mythologies of past generations. So we prefer geniuses to be sharply different from ordinary people, and preferably a little eccentric. Einstein makes an ideal genius. It is frustratingly hard to understand his discoveries, let alone imagine a more conventional person emulating them. Mozart too has a special mystique, fuelled by most people's inability to even imagine the possibility of creating anything that could move us in the way his music does.

Darwin is different. Nobody doubts his theory's monumental power or disputes its immense influence, but the principle of natural selection has the disturbing quality of being easy to understand. At its core is a transparently simple idea: in a species whose members are not identical, those individuals that are the best adapted to their environments are the most likely to procreate and pass on their inherited characteristics. That elementary but elegant principle accounts for the evolution of all species.

For some critics of Darwin the discovery of natural selection has too much of the air of an accidental encounter with something that has been waiting to be found. It is the kind of idea that, once articulated, seems to be plain obvious as well as being right. Like the invention of the wheel, the theory of evolution is an advance that left people asking themselves why nobody had hit upon it earlier. As soon as Thomas Huxley learned of Darwin's theory he wondered why he had been so stupid not to have thought of it himself.

Detractors have found additional excuses for withholding admiration from Darwin. Some have suggested that since *artificial* selection of domestic animals had been an established fact of life for many generations before Darwin, only a small mental leap may have been needed in order to arrive at the principle of *natural* selection. Other critics have seized upon the sheer implausibility (as we see it today) of creationism – the Genesis story that the world was created in 4004 BC – as a rival account of the origin of life, suggesting that even in Darwin's time no genuine scientist could have seriously entertained the possibility of creationist alternatives to evolution. Also, denigrators of Darwin have had their doubts fanned by knowing that at least some of his insights were shared by Alfred Wallace, the co-discoverer of natural selection, and also by Patrick Matthew, a Scottish botanist who included the major elements of a theory of evolution in a book he wrote on the subject of trees.

Yet, even if it were true that the theory of evolution did not involve such a vast creative leap as some other scientific discoveries, the sheer immensity of Charles Darwin's achievement would be enough to justify our hailing him as a great scientist. Of all the Big Ideas in science, natural selection is possibly the most momentous. It compels us to see the world differently. It explains how complex life arrived. It renders expendable the ancient shibboleth that the only way to account for the existence of plants and animals is to believe that they were placed on our planet by 'Design from Above'. The principle of natural selection has established that it is entirely possible for the human species to have evolved without supervision by all-knowing deity. Darwin demonstrated that complex species gradually emerge from primitive forms of life. There has been no necessity for an overseeing Great Designer to take charge of the creation of species.

A number of complications made the feat of forging the theory of evolution a far more difficult accomplishment than Darwin's critics have appreciated. For a start, the creationist accounts that were believed in his time to provide adequate rival explanations were far from being as simple-minded as the bald statement that the world was created six thousand years ago makes them seem to be. Nineteenth-century creationist theorising was highly ingenious, to the extent that until early in that century accounts rooted in creationism had still seemed capable of explaining much of the available scientific evidence. Only then did it become incontrovertible that processes of gradual change were responsible for the present state of the world.

A second obstacle faced by Darwin was that in his time there was harsh and active opposition to evolutionary ideas.[1] There were political as well as religious reasons for this. From the perspective of many people in positions of authority in the middle years of the nineteenth century, the very thought that evolution might have taken place threatened the established order of things. The concept of an established order was central to a social (and mental) framework in which the existing divisions of wealth and power were regarded as being a natural and inevitable state of affairs.

---

[1] A careful discussion of the responses evoked by evolutionary thoughts in the early nineteenth century is provided by Desmond & Moore (1991). See also Newsome (1997).

Each person had been allotted to their particular station in life. Interfering with the established social system was unnatural and dangerous. Above all, evolution was contrary to the will of God.

That way of thinking created in the minds of those who subscribed to it a moral climate in which evolutionary views were condemned and those who actively promoted them were persecuted. Even speculating about evolution was considered dangerously subversive. For those in power, the established system of Church and State, privilege and poverty, existed because that was the way the Christian God had appointed things, and it was important for that view to stay unchallenged. The belief in a God-given natural order propped up the whole system. Without it, nobody could have gone on maintaining the pretence that there were ethical reasons for the rich hanging on to their wealth and opposing changes that might benefit the poor, and insisting, as they repeatedly did, that the injustices of an oppressive status quo were necessary and unavoidable. Powerful individuals saw belief in the natural order as the only effective bastion against dangerous social viruses such as democracy and anarchy, two equally terrifying evils that threatened to plunge Britain into the turmoil so recently seen in France, across the narrow English Channel.

A few brave and determined thinkers had arrived at evolutionary theories and succeeded in having them published, despite the prevailing climate of oppression. But another barrier to the creation of an adequate explanation of evolution remained, and mastering this further obstacle would take far more than courage alone. Only a thinker with quite extraordinary mental resources would be capable of overcoming it.

The problem Darwin faced was that he was at the same time having to describe the evolutionary changes that had taken place and also provide an explanation for them. Rather than simply having to explain known facts, it was also necessary to simultaneously discover what was being achieved by evolution. Darwin was placed in an exceedingly difficult position. He had to discover the causes of biological changes without having a proper account of the precise nature of the changes that needed to be explained. It is immensely hard to explain something when there is considerable uncertainty concerning what it is that requires explaining. Nevertheless, Darwin succeeded in doing just that.

The reason why Darwin was confronted with such a confusing state of affairs was simple. Almost nothing was known about genetics. Had accurate knowledge about the principles of inheritance been available to Darwin at the time when he was working, the task of teasing together an evolutionary theory explaining how species adapt and change would have been a relatively straightforward one. But in his time the way in which organisms reproduced themselves seemed to be a complete mystery, and that situation did not alter until the end of the century, well after Darwin's death, when Mendel's findings concerning the inheritance of genetic characteristics became known. At the time Charles Darwin was grappling with the theory of evolution, biologists knew practically nothing about the passing-on of characteristics between generations. Today, it takes an effort to comprehend just how little was known then about elementary truths about inheritance that ten-year-olds now take for granted. Yet in Darwin's lifetime nobody even knew what was actually transmitted from one generation to another. Until the beginning of the nineteenth century it had not even been verified that people inherited anything from their mothers at all. It was widely believed that inheritance took place exclusively via the semen of the male.

Because of these barriers to evolutionary thinking, enormous intellectual effort was needed in order to arrive at the theory of evolution by natural selection. So despite the simplicity of the principle that accounts for evolutionary change, Darwin's achievement was far from being an easy accomplishment.

There may be no such animal as a 'typical' genius, but most can be placed reasonably comfortably within one or other of a number of categories, on the basis of shared attributes. Darwin cannot. Most geniuses were remarked upon as being precocious while still children. Darwin was not. Many geniuses have had to struggle in order to make a living. Darwin never had to. When we begin to investigate the events of Darwin's life that enabled him to become capable of his great work, it quickly becomes evident that his early circumstances were not at all like those of certain other geniuses. Charles Darwin came from a wealthy family. There was no lack of educational opportunities in his formative years. There was no need for Darwin to keep striving in order to escape poverty and ignorance and extend his horizons, since he was born privileged.

Because he was born to wealth, it was possible for Darwin to add to his capabilities during the course of his early life in a manner that was measured and unhurried, even stately. A wealthy young person had the luxury of being able to afford to waste time, make bad decisions, and vacillate, before eventually getting started on a course of action that would lead in a meaningful direction. Thus Leo Tolstoy, for example, did not have to settle into writing until he had gambled away a fortune and arrived at middle age. In Darwin's case, likewise, there was no necessity for an arduous battle against the odds. And he did not lack the kinds of social connections that could ease a young man's path. The adult Darwin was fiercely committed to his work, and he was as diligent and determined as anyone, but these qualities were never imposed upon him. Circumstances did not require Darwin to be as forceful as some geniuses have had to be, in order to stand any chance of getting ahead.

We know about numerous aspects of Darwin's life. Many letters to and from him have been preserved. There are descriptions of him by relatives and friends, and two versions of a brief autobiography. Reading the Darwin correspondence is a joy, and it provides many glimpses of a deeply sympathetic individual who cared for his family and friends and whose warm feelings for them were strongly reciprocated. Despite that, he was often highly anxious and not infrequently unhappy.

Enough information exists for it to be possible to trace in some detail the course of Darwin's early years. We know about many of the events and the people he encountered, and the books he read and the lectures he attended. There are plenty of cues that help reveal how he experienced his days and made use of the various opportunities that came his way as he developed into a scientist. In Darwin's case, plotting the route of his movement forward reveals a lengthy, very gradual, but steadily rising course. We see a child who appears to be remarkably ordinary, lacking any obvious talent or special gift, slowly extending his capabilities, little by little. Eventually, a point is reached at which it becomes evident that, without anyone noticing, the very ordinary boy has become an extraordinarily able young scientist, exceptionally well-positioned to take advantage of any opportunity that presents itself.

Darwin was a complicated man, and discovering the ways in which he steadily achieved those advances in his capabilities that prepared him for his most momentous work is a less straightforward matter than charting the routes via which others have pushed themselves ahead in their different ways. There were always parts of himself that Darwin kept hidden from others. He was not secretive except when he had good reasons for hiding things, but he carefully guarded his privacy. Having discovered as a child that keeping his own counsel was a good way to protect himself from the intrusive demands of adults and older sisters, he was reluctant to correct people when their perceptions of him were inaccurate. In particular, during the crucial years immediately preceding the voyage on HMS *Beagle* that was to establish his reputation as a mature scientist, Darwin encouraged his relatives to persist in an increasingly inaccurate view of him and regard him as being less determined, less mature, and less committed to science than he really was, and considerably more naive and indecisive.

Even with his sisters, whose love and affection he enjoyed and valued, the good-natured Darwin was happy for them to continue regarding him as their error-prone and somewhat ineffectual younger brother, well past the point when it was clear to those who knew of his work that he was actually an exceptionally capable young biologist. His father, especially, regarded the young Charles Darwin as being somewhat aimless. Biographers have concurred with this assessment, depicting Darwin as being drifting and lacking in ambition until he was well into his twenties. But that view of him is inaccurate. By the age of twenty he was determined to be a leading naturalist, and although his family did not know that a few of his friends already did. At least one friend, John Herbert, foresaw Darwin's future eminence. In making him an anonymous gift of a microscope, the prescient Herbert, a fellow undergraduate at Cambridge, included a note saying that Darwin's acceptance: 'will give particular gratification to one who has long doubted whether Mr. Darwin's talents or his sincerity be the more worthy of admiration, and who hopes that the instrument may in some measure facilitate those researches which he has hitherto so fondly and so successfully prosecuted.'[2]

Well before he wrote that in 1831, Herbert had been given the opportunity to see that beneath Darwin's self-effacing air of modesty lurked a steely resolution that few others had detected. It had never dawned upon either Charles' father or his sisters that the younger son in the family was at all determined or clear about his ambitions, or that he even had any firm ambitions at all. Yet Darwin's correspondence to his friends provides firm clues to the seriousness of his intent. The tone of much of the correspondence between Darwin and his fellow enthusiasts during the 1828–30 period contradicts Darwin's own rather dismissive autobiographical account (written many years later, but unquestioned by most of his biographers) of his approach to natural history at that time.

An indication of the young Darwin's real attitude can be gleaned from a typical letter to Herbert, composed in 1828 when Darwin was still not twenty. After a characteristic apology for imposing on his friend for the favour he is requesting, followed by the placatory gesture 'you cannot imagine how much you will oblige me' and a somewhat uncharacteristic boast (to stress the importance of what he is requesting) that he has taken some of the rarest British insects, Darwin issues his friend with detailed instructions that have an air of remarkable authority for one so young.

But now for Business: **several** more specimens if you can procure them without much trouble, of the following insects. The violet black coloured beetle found on Craig Storm under stones, also a large smooth black one, very like it: a bluish, metallic coloured, globular, dung beetle, which is *very* common on the hill sides: Also, if you *would* be so kind as to cross the ferry, & you will find a great number under the stones on the waste land of a long smooth jet black beetle. . .

---

[2] Note from John Maurice Herbert to Charles Darwin, early May 1831. P. 122 *The correspondence of Charles Darwin, Volume 1.* Burkhardt & Smith (1985).

After continuing in this vein with some further detailed descriptions of insects, Darwin stresses, 'These 2 last insects are excessively rare: & you will really will extremely oblige me by taking all this trouble pretty soon: Remember me most kindly to Butler, tell him of my successes, & I daresay both of you will easily recognise these insects.'[3]

A letter like this one is not the effusion of an aimless boy. The imperious tone is only partly jocular. The nineteen-year-old Charles Darwin was already a determined young man, even if his determination was sometimes hidden under a diffident air. Like most creative people, Darwin drew heavily on qualities of temperament and personality as well as his intellectual powers. But the attributes Darwin needed most were very different from those which some other geniuses have depended upon. The life which the young Darwin enjoyed within his wealthy family gave him many experiences and opportunities that helped to prepare for his eventual career, without enormous strain. There was no necessity for the Herculean exertions that some other scientists of the time, such as the celebrated chemist Humphry Davy and his brilliant assistant Michael Faraday, had been obliged to make in order to learn under adverse circumstances.

Charles Darwin reported in his autobiography that he began to be interested in natural history before he was eleven years old, and he remained enthusiastic throughout his childhood and adolescence. This state of affairs produced ideal conditions for the gradual accumulation of a foundation of organised knowledge and skills. Compared with the intense childhood regime of someone like Mozart, the circumstances that brought about Darwin's increasing competence were less formal and deliberate, and less competitive. Yet there were similarities. In common with all individuals who have achieved exceptionally high levels of expertise, Darwin was able to devote many hours of concentrated attention to the field in which he eventually excelled. Doing that would have been crucial to his success, even if for much of the time he would not have been making a deliberate effort to learn. Despite the fact that Darwin was unusual among geniuses in being neither a prodigy nor even the least bit precocious as a child, he did benefit from the fact that his early interests, together with the opportunities he was given to develop them, combined to ensure that over a lengthy period of time he was able to gain capabilities upon which he could draw later. The result was that he was able to enjoy advantages that would normally have been available only to someone who had been precocious as a child.

---

[3] Letter from Charles Darwin to John Maurice Herbert, 13 September 1828. Pp. 64–65, *The correspondence of Charles Darwin, Volume 1*. Burkhardt & Smith (1985).

Darwin often needed to be able to count on the cooperation of other people. He always could, but only because he was known to be dependable and helpful himself. For someone whose main accomplishment was as earth-shattering in its implications as the theory of evolution, he made remarkably few enemies. The personal resources necessary to overcome the most alarming of Darwin's challenges included a combination of moral strength and good judgement. As he became increasingly certain that natural selection was the explanation for evolution, he also had to face up to the fact that his views would arouse bitter controversy, and he worried about that endlessly. He knew that because the theory contradicted some of the apparent certainties which many people's peace of mind depended upon, it would provoke angry hostility. That did prove to be the case, although the preparatory work that Darwin had undertaken between assembling the theory and announcing it to the world ensured that its acceptance in scientific circles was relatively swift and painless. Thanks to the efforts of Thomas Huxley and other friends, less vituperation was directed towards Darwin himself than he had expected, and the effects on his family were not so destructive as he had feared.

Charles Darwin was born in Shrewsbury on 12 February 1809. He had two colourful grandfathers. One was Erasmus Darwin, an imaginative polymath famous for his long scientific poem *The Botanic Garden*, which gave a comprehensive account of botany in the form of lively rhyming couplets. Erasmus Darwin speculated on evolution in a series of volumes on organic life, entitled *Zoönomia*. The other grandfather was the celebrated potter and industrialist Josiah Wedgwood, whose successful business made him extremely wealthy. Darwin's two grandfathers had many shared interests and were close friends. Both were enthusiastic members of the influential Lunar Society, a group of enlightened individuals who met in Birmingham to discuss scientific, philosophical and humanitarian issues. Among other prominent members were Joseph Priestley, the chemist, and Matthew Boulton, who in partnership with the Scottish engineering genius James Watt (another member) had masterminded many of the improvements in the efficiency of steam power that made passenger trains a practical possibility. Erasmus Darwin happened to be one of the very few eighteenth-century writers to predict this eventuality.

When Josiah Wedgwood died in 1795 his daughter Susannah inherited £25,000, a fraction of his large fortune. The following year she married Erasmus's Darwin's son, Robert. Susannah was forty-four when she gave birth to their second son, Charles, the fifth of her six children. Charles' father, Robert Darwin, prospered as a physician with a mainly rural practice, but the bulk of his large income came from mortgaged property: he was a kind of one-man building society. The Darwins were gentry, like other wealthy and well-connected families living in the country, although lacking a large estate they could not be described as landed gentry in the usual sense.

Unhappily, Susannah Darwin died when Charles was only eight, after a painful illness. The adult Darwin had only a few memories of his mother. In the years after her death Charles' older sisters had rarely talked about her: it was too painful for them. Some biographers have suggested that an outcome of this understandable if regrettable reaction was to prevent Charles from properly mourning his mother and coming to terms with the death, thereby contributing to the frequent physical maladies and feelings of depression he experienced as an adult. The evidence is too sketchy for that interpretation of events to be either confirmed or refuted.

Even before his mother's death, two of Charles' sisters, Caroline (born in 1800) and Susan (born in 1803) were helping with his schooling and that of his younger sister Catherine. The older sisters had a strong interest in the new ideas about education that were being promoted by educational thinkers like Guizot and practitioners such as Pestalozzi.[4] Later they set up a small infant school of their own. From many of their letters to Charles that have been preserved, as well as numerous letters from Charles to them, it is clear that Caroline and Susan always cared very deeply about Charles and his younger sister Catherine (the youngest child in the family, born eighteen months after Charles). There were times in Charles' early childhood when he chafed at his older sisters' attentions, and their letters display a certain well-intentioned fussiness, which he sometimes found irritating. But Charles was always grateful to Caroline and Susan for their kindliness in his childhood.

Darwin believed that his younger sister Catherine had been quicker than him and more advanced for her age. Being the fifth of sixth children is not an enviable position within a family, and Darwin recalled occasional childhood incidents in which he behaved outrageously in order to gain attention, and then felt foolish after getting into trouble and receiving the inevitable reprimand. But even if he sometimes wanted more attention than he was getting, he never felt unloved. As Caroline recalled as an old lady in her seventies, far from being a naughty or stupid boy, he was 'particularly affectionate, tractable and sweet tempered, and my father had the highest opinion of his understanding and intelligence'.[5] That was not the invented sentiment of an elderly person: much earlier,

---

[4] For differing views concerning the effects on Charles Darwin of his mother's early death, see the biographies by Bowlby (1990) and Browne (1995).
[5] Quoted in Brent (1981), p. 23

she had told him in a touching letter written when he was a seventeen-year-old student at Edinburgh University, 'I think when you & Catherine were little children & I was always with you or thinking about you was the happiest part of my life and I dare say always will be.'[6]

Darwin first went to school early in 1817, when he was just eight. A recollection by a schoolmate suggests that Darwin's mother was taking a close interest in his education, despite the fact that her health was seriously affected by the illness that killed her later that year. The schoolmate, who was later to be one of the many naturalists with whom Darwin corresponded, said that Darwin, who had brought a plant from home for the small garden of the school, told him that his mother 'had been teaching him how by looking into the interior of a blossom he could ascertain the name of the plant'.[7]

A year later Darwin was moved to Shrewsbury School, a long-established institution which under its headmaster, Dr Butler, was thought to be among the best dozen schools in England at the time. Darwin was a pupil there for seven years. Despite the fact that the school was very close to Darwin's home, his father made the sensible decision that Charles would board, and thereby avoided placing him in the awkward position of being a day boy in a boarding school. This arrangement worked out well. Unlike most of the other boarders Darwin often had time to make brief visits home, and his early days at the school were made a little easier by the fact that his brother Erasmus, four years older than Charles, was already a pupil there.

Despite these advantages Darwin did not shine at Shrewsbury School. His schoolwork was never more than average. He later became highly skilled at shooting, but at school he never made an impression at any sport. He was certainly not disliked: schoolfellows recalled him as kindly, friendly, gentle and popular, and were intrigued by his knowledge of natural history. But his formal school achievements were not in the least distinguished.

In the early education of a modern scientist we would expect to find some relationship between the individual's scientific progress and his successes in other subjects. Nowadays, it would be surprising to find a young scientist as enthusiastic and capable as Darwin making little impression at school. But matters were arranged differently in Darwin's day, because science as a school subject simply did not exist. It seems remarkable to us that a hundred years after Newton's death, at a time when Faraday, Ampère and others were producing the stream of discoveries that would make electrical power a practical possibility, and many other scientists were making radical innovations, the headmaster of a prestigious school could see no reason to give his pupils even the most rudimentary scientific education. But Dr Butler was not just indifferent but actively hostile to the idea of encouraging boys to learn something about science. The headmaster's response to discovering that Charles Darwin was spending time collaborating with his brother Erasmus on scientific experiments in a crude laboratory they had set up at home was crassly negative. Butler's contribution to the age of science was to drag Charles Darwin in front of the whole assembled school and denounce him as a 'stupid fellow' who 'will attend to his gases and his rubbish, but will not work at anything useful'.[8]

Darwin's own opinion of the usefulness of his school curriculum was as negative as Dr Butler's views about science. On a number of occasions Darwin wrote that his formal education had been largely a waste of time. He was adamant about this: 'Nothing could have been worse for the development of my mind than Dr Butler's school', he said; and 'The school as a means of education to me was simply a blank'.[9] That sweeping dismissal may have been a little harsh. Another scientist such as Michael Faraday, forced by circumstances to provide himself with an education through his own efforts, might have thought Darwin's condemnation one-sided. Even a curriculum that is singularly ill-suited to a pupil's interests and aspirations can help a young learner to gain useful knowledge and skills, and perhaps some effective working habits as well.

What *did* Charles Darwin learn at Shrewsbury School? He recalled that the curriculum was strictly classical and that he was taught nothing else except a little ancient geography and history. Although Darwin probably gained more from his studies at school than he realised, he was correct in thinking that a large part of his time there was wasted. Much had to be learned by heart, to be instantly forgotten as soon as the dreaded class was finished. The stranglehold of the classics ensured that Darwin received a great deal of instruction in the Greek and Latin languages, as well as ample amounts of Greek and Roman history. He became familiar with some of the works of a substantial number of classical authors, including Plato, Aristotle, Thucydides, Juvenal, Homer, Horace (whose odes he came to enjoy), and other dramatists, historians, philosophers, and rhetoricians. There were also lessons in history, geography, philology and scripture, as well as some lectures on the geometry of Euclid, one of the few school subjects which Darwin actively liked.

Dr Butler held the belief, popular then and not uncommon now, that certain 'mental disciplines', and in particular the classical languages, are

---

[8] Quoted in Brent (1981), p. 32
[9] *The Autobiography of Charles Darwin*. Barlow (1958), p. 27.

especially valuable because they create 'trained minds', enabling students to think more rationally and consequently be equipped to deal with any of a variety of mental challenges. The idea is that by studying the classics a pupil 'learns to think'. That view may seem plausible enough, but it does not stand up to rigorous testing. Research findings provide very little support for it. The evidence makes it clear that only to a very restricted extent will a recently learned capability 'transfer' to new learning tasks or to problems arising in contexts different from the ones in which the learning originally took place.

Transfer to new circumstances only occurs when the already-acquired knowledge or mental skills are directly applicable to the novel task. Hence, the knowledge that two plus two makes four will be useful in a range of circumstances, but the feat of learning to decline a Latin verb will not have comparably broad applicability. By and large, research suggests that the effects of training are typically more specific and less generalisable than is usually appreciated. For example, in an investigation that was conducted over a period of years, the researchers discovered that ordinary people could eventually gain the ability to memorise lists of items that were many times longer than the maximum list length that could be recalled prior to training. However, the training only succeeded in improving memory for the particular kinds of lists used in the practice sessions.[10] Consequently, someone who, as a result of lengthy training, was able to memorise lengthy lists of digits would be no better than other people at recalling new lists of letters or words.

But even if the idea of mental training as a kind of cerebral muscle-building is largely misguided, the belief that studying certain disciplines can have useful consequences is not totally wrong. That is because there are other useful outcomes of having to study an academic discipline. For example, as a result of learning from one's own experience that performance eventually improves when one keeps striving at a subject, a young learner may become more conscious of the value of studying, and also more confident about his or her capacity to learn in the future. Also, a person who studies regularly will tend to get into the habit of studying, and acquiring such a habit can be extremely valuable in itself. Gaining a firm habit of regularly engaging in study activities does much to help make it easier for a learner to get down to an arduous new task. Someone who has established regular study habits will be at an advantage when faced with a situation in which it is necessary to keep concentrating and persisting when things get difficult.

Despite the fact that Darwin's education as a scientist was largely

---

[10] See, for example, Ericsson (1985).

unconnected to his schooling, it started at roughly the same time, although in the initial years it would never have occurred to him to apply the term 'science' to the collecting activities that his scientific training began with. Far from regarding those activities as being educational, Darwin as a child was in no position to argue with the prevailing view that his interest in natural history and his enthusiasm about collecting were no more than signs of natural indolence. Collecting has always been attractive to children, and like many young boys and girls Darwin gradually progressed from more or less indiscriminate hoarding of any objects that caught his fancy to collecting activities that reflected a more informed interest. This was encouraged by his mother, who urged Charles to share her fascination with plants. She was keenly interested in gardens and impressed the neighbouring gentry with the beauty and variety of shrubs and flowers she introduced. She had brought to the house a number of books on botany that had belonged to her father, Josiah Wedgwood. His interest, as it happened, had been encouraged by Darwin's other (paternal) grandfather, Erasmus Darwin.

By the age of ten, when Darwin first went for a three-week holiday on the Welsh coast, his collecting activities were already beginning to be specialised and well-informed. By then he had become especially enthusiastic about collecting beetles, a passion that endured. He was also keenly collecting butterflies, moths, and other insects. Even at ten, he knew enough to notice that there were moths to be seen on the Welsh coast that were not found in Shropshire. He was also an enthusiastic birdwatcher. That interest was stimulated by encountering Gilbert White's *Natural History and Antiquities of Selborne*, which he first read at around this time. Darwin's school friends were already noticing that in contrast to his mediocre performance at lessons he knew a great deal about natural history and was good at identifying the objects they brought to him. Even at school, much of his spare time went into collecting. Throughout his childhood there were always opportunities for collecting objects. With curiosity about the natural world being almost a family trait, he had no need to be a solitary naturalist, and it was not hard for him to find friends who shared his interests.

By adolescence, what had begun as a child's hobby was becoming a way of life. There never seems to have been a point in Darwin's childhood at which he was other than keenly interested in natural history. The nature of his collecting activities altered considerably as his knowledge increased and his observational skills were sharpened, but there was no abrupt leap from indiscriminate collector to informed naturalist, or from a strictly 'amateur' naturalist to a serious scientific biologist. The changes in his activities and interests were gradual, reflecting his steadily deepening knowledge. The butterflies and beetles that fascinated him at ten still fascinated him at twenty, albeit for different reasons. He had gradually become something of an amateur expert, but without ever having had to make a sudden commitment to studying natural history as an academic subject. His activities as a naturalist in training sometimes involved fatigue and hardship, and yet his efforts would always have been directly fuelled by his own purposes and interests. Unlike a young person from an impoverished background, the young Darwin was lucky enough never to be in a position in which the vague and distant goal of self-improvement had to serve as the main incentive for persevering at hard studies in unfavourable conditions.

More holidays in Wales followed, offering plenty of opportunities for collecting. At eleven (in 1820), Charles had been on a riding tour with his fifteen-year-old brother, Erasmus. The year after that, once more with Erasmus and also on this occasion with two of his Wedgwood cousins, he went on a more ambitious tour in which they covered 250 miles in ten days, going as far as Bangor. From there they went to see one of the engineering wonders of the day, Thomas Telford's suspension bridge that was being built across the Menai Straits to link the island of Anglesea with the mainland. (It was completed in 1826, and was joined in 1850 by a railway bridge that had been built by George Stephenson's son Robert, who spent a brief period at Edinburgh University in 1822–3, two years before Darwin arrived there.) In the following summer Darwin enjoyed at least two further riding tours. He was now thirteen, and beginning to find delight in beautiful scenery, a source of pleasure throughout his life.

Charles' brother Erasmus was a companion on most of his childhood holidays. Considering the four-year gap in their ages Erasmus was generous to Charles, lending him books and including him in the older brother's activities. Most biographers have taken at face value a comment by Charles that because their minds and tastes were very different he did not think that he owed much to Erasmus intellectually. The two brothers were indeed very different, but Erasmus had a much bigger influence on Charles' development than has been recognised. When Charles was sixteen he and Erasmus had a year together at Edinburgh University, where they were both studying medicine; they lodged together, read the same books, and they not only spent a good deal of time in each other's company but shared a number of interests and enthusiasms. Even more importantly for Darwin's early progress in science, when only thirteen, he and Erasmus (who was then studying at Cambridge) set up a simple chemistry laboratory in a toolshed in the Darwins' garden. Ostensibly, Erasmus was in charge and giving the orders, with Charles a mere assistant. But the actual day-to-day arrangements for setting everything up and running the experiments were left entirely in Charles' hands.

A number of surviving letters from Erasmus to Charles make it clear how this cooperation at a distance worked in practice. What strikes the reader most forcefully is that Erasmus never doubted for one minute that his thirteen-year-old brother was sufficiently competent and responsible to make all the necessary arrangements. Some of these were highly complex or demanded considerable initiative on Charles's part; others required him to become involved in negotiations or search for abstruse information. Charles was being trusted to get on with the job of implementing some fairly elaborate plans. By putting Charles in a position in which it was taken for granted that he was mature and capable enough to undertake some complicated tasks, Erasmus was not only recognising his younger brother's competence but also, perhaps unwittingly, doing much to help Charles learn how to act independently. Erasmus encouraged Charles to develop an ability to organise things on his own. For a boy who was the fourth of five children, and whose siblings were too prone to cast him in the role of the immature younger brother, the opportunity that he was being given by Erasmus to take responsibility for the organisation and running of a potentially dangerous laboratory would have been a godsend. At the same time, Charles was also receiving a valuable chance to learn about practical chemistry. Whatever Dr Butler might have thought, for Darwin all this was 'the best part of my education at school'.[11]

Because he was a sensible and agreeable young person, neither too conceited nor too shy to be a good companion, Darwin usually got on well with other people. That enabled him to take advantage of openings that would have not been on offer to someone less personable. The young Darwin was not a charmer – men were not dazzled by his conversation and women did not swoon in his company – but people did seem to enjoy being with him. Adults found him likeable. That was partly because he was sensitive to other people's needs and prepared to listen to them, as well as exhibiting a youthful enthusiasm that was already coupled with the lively curiosity that was to stay with him until his death. Even his Wedgwood uncle (named Josiah like his more famous father), who was considered to be a taciturn and rather forbidding man, took a keen interest in Charles' activities. Consequently, he was able to be of enormous help to his nephew some years later, at a crucial point in Charles' life. It was Uncle Josiah who, in 1831, persuaded Darwin's father to drop his opposition to the idea of Charles taking part in the five-year voyage of HMS *Beagle*.

[11] *The Autobiography of Charles Darwin*. Barlow (1958), p. 46.

Darwin learned to shoot (an activity which for ten years or so was one of his main sources of pleasure) from another local landowner, William Mostyn Owen, whose estate at Woodhouse, about twelve miles from Shrewsbury, was regularly visited by members of the Darwin family. The Darwin correspondence includes sixteen letters written to Charles by Owen's high-spirited youngest daughter, Fanny, the first love of Darwin's life. Some of these letters contain messages from William Owen himself, saying how he is missing Charles or looking forward to his next visit. Another adult to be impressed by Charles' lively curiosity and enthusiasm was the historian Sir James Mackintosh, who Charles met when staying at Maer, the Wedgwood family's estate. 'There is something in that man that interests me', said Mackintosh, who was then writing his *History of England*, but died a few years later, in 1832, before he could discover just how percipient his remark had been.[12] And later, when Darwin was a university student, at both Edinburgh and Cambridge, he encountered a number of distinguished scientists who were sufficiently impressed by him to take him seriously, and found him congenial enough to deserve their companionship. As a consequence, he spent a good deal of time at both universities in the company of active scientists who were the ideal mentors for him: these men had an immense influence on Darwin's future career.

The young Darwin was often away from home. As well as boarding at school and going for holiday expeditions in the vacations, he often went to stay with his Wedgwood cousins at Maer, close to Stoke-on-Trent in the Potteries region towards the centre of England, about twenty miles from Darwin's home, or at Woodhouse with the Owen family. Apart from the various experiences travel provided and the opportunities to see relatives and make new friends, spending time away from his own home had the further desirable outcome for Darwin of getting him away from the sometimes oppressive company of his father.

Dr Robert Darwin was no ogre. He was considerate to his patients, fair to his tenants and kind to his servants. He had suffered some tragic losses: his mother had died when he was only four, his older brother died from septicaemia as a medical student at Edinburgh after cutting his finger at a post-mortem on a child, and he was devastated when his wife Susannah died. He had an active and enquiring mind and numerous interests, and became a Fellow of the Royal Society, an influential scientific institution in Britain. He was in many respects an excellent parent, caring deeply about all his children, and his decisions were usually wise. He was devoted to Charles. As Caroline Darwin recorded, 'My father was very

---

[12] *The Autobiography of Charles Darwin.* Barlow (1958), p. 55.

fond of him & even when he was a little boy of 6 or 7, however bustled & overtired, often had Charles with him when he was dressing, to teach him some little thing such as the almanack – and Charles used to be so eager to be down in time. Charles does not seem to have known half how much my father loved him.'[13]

But Dr Darwin was not an easy parent to live with. Tall and fat, with an incongruously high-pitched voice, he was somewhat overbearing, with a tendency to hold forth at great length. When not listening to his own voice he liked to know what everyone else in the room was saying. A consequence of this was that younger members of the family, who might have preferred to relax and gossip over a quiet game of cards, were forced to endure long evenings of stiff conversation. Family and guests complained that the atmosphere in the Darwin house was not so free or spontaneous as that at Maer, the Wedgwood home, or at Woodhouse, where their friends the Owens lived.

In a wealthy family such as the Darwins' it was possible for all the children to get away from time to time on visits to other houses, and Charles also took advantage of the fact that in the 1820s it was easier for a son than a daughter to find reasons for being absent from home. He was usually able to maintain a cordial relationship with his father, but he soon discerned that doing that was easier at a distance. From the time he was sixteen or so his periods of staying at home were usually brief.

Some biographers under the influence of Freud have been convinced that Darwin's professed love and affection for his father concealed an unconscious hatred. That seems unlikely. Warm feelings predominated, although Darwin's view of his father was balanced and realistic rather than idealised. Charles Darwin was perfectly aware that his father could be an awkward customer and a bit of a bully, with plenty of faults, and had on a few occasions been unjust towards himself. But Darwin also knew his father as a kindly and deeply caring parent, a man of many enthusiasms and a source of amusing anecdotes. As an adult, Darwin chose to make numerous visits to his father that could easily have been avoided. In his *Autobiography*, written when he was getting old, Darwin writes about his father with transparent good spirits. He rambles on and on, as one story reminds him of another, dragging himself away from his pleasurable memories of his parent only when the time to return to the narrative of his own life is well overdue.

There were family resemblances and shared concerns within the Darwin family, the most striking being the deep interest of both Charles Darwin and his grandfather Erasmus Darwin in evolution and its possible

[13] Quoted in Brent (1981), p. 23.

causes. Inevitably, questions about genetics arise. What did Charles inherit from his forebears? To what extent could his extraordinary capabilities have been genetically inherited? Could he have inherited an interest in natural history?

There will be a more extended discussion of genetic influences on people's capabilities in Chapter 9. At this point it must simply be said that none of the above questions can be answered with complete confidence. Despite the advances that have been made in the science of genetics (which, as we have noted, did not exist at all in Darwin's lifetime) frustratingly little is known about the part played by genetics in the causation of exceptional human accomplishments. It is certain, however, that the commonsense view that complex human traits are straightforwardly inherited from a parent, in the way that simple physical characteristics such as eye or hair colour are, is simply wrong. So assertions such as 'she inherited her mother's sense of humour', and 'he inherited his father's love of animals' are (if meant literally) invariably unfounded. In order for complex human attributes like these to be directly inherited, it would be essential for there to exist a distinct gene or a set of genes determining, say, a person's sense of humour, or love of animals. But genes do not operate like that. Nor, contrary to a common view, do genes work as a kind of blueprint, invariably causing someone who has inherited a certain set of genes to have a particular kind of personality or to act in a specific way. With a few exceptions, such as blood group, human traits are never entirely fixed by a person's genetic materials. Little is known about the extent to which genetic influences contribute to particular individuals becoming exceptionally capable men and women. Whilst it is definitely possible that genes make a substantial contribution, the actual manner in which they do so is not at all clear, and the genetic influence, assuming it exists, is almost certainly far from being simple or direct. Even when genetic mapping becomes more advanced than it now is, it is by no means certain that it will be possible to identify genetic materials that inevitably make a person unusually intelligent or creative. What is certain is that there is no distinct single gene or set of genetic materials that makes a person a good scientist, or a fine musician or a great novelist.

A new phase of Darwin's life began somewhat abruptly at the age of sixteen. His father could see that his son's failure to do well at Shrewsbury School was partly due to that establishment being an unsuitable learning environment for Charles. Robert Darwin wisely decided to let Charles go to Edinburgh University, where his brother Erasmus was intending to study for a medical degree, after some years at Cambridge. At that time it was not extraordinary to begin university at sixteen, and Erasmus could be counted upon to keep an eye on his younger brother and ease the transition. Edinburgh then was one of the liveliest of Europe's universities. It was the obvious choice for someone wishing to study science (including natural history) or medicine. Charles had regularly accompanied Dr Robert on his visits to patients, and had quickly found himself becoming interested in the work. Father and son convinced themselves that Charles had the makings of a successful physician. Dr Robert himself (whose brother died at Edinburgh) had qualified at Edinburgh University, and Darwin's uncle, the second Josiah Wedgwood and his two brothers had all studied there.

Darwin, at the age of sixteen, was not so unpromising as he appeared to his headmaster, and there were signs of future strengths that seem to have been unnoticed at the time. He was a decidedly enthusiastic young naturalist, and within that field of interest he was unusually knowledgeable for his age. He had also acquired a keen interest in science, and was eager to learn more, even if there was nothing very remarkable about his early achievements. But if there is any truth at all in the view that Charles Darwin possessed some kind of inborn talent, it certainly was not evident at this point in his life. Darwin had been given plenty of opportunities, and on the whole he had used them well. He had been encouraged by his father, his sisters and his brother. His family background was amply supplied with two crucial ingredients that help nourish a young person's growing mental powers, intellectual stimulation and, equally importantly, the presence of support and structure that can be provided by other members of the family.

Modern research investigations have provided some valuable insights into the ways in which the family background can affect a young person's progress. Mihaly Csikszentmihalyi, an American psychologist, has undertaken a series of investigations aimed at discovering why it is that whilst some able young people in their early teens have considerable success at extending their abilities in the succeeding years, others, who appear to be equally promising, fail to do so.[14] How, Csikszentmihalyi asked, do those teenagers who do succeed differ from the ones who do not? He noted that one difference was that the former, but not the latter, spent substantial periods of time engaging in the study and practice activities that are essential if a person is to do well. That comes as no great surprise, but Csikszentmihalyi took the investigation a stage further, asking why it is that some young people find it possible to concentrate on the studying and practising that is necessary in order for a young person to make good progress, whilst others seem incapable of doing this.

Csikszentmihalyi looked at young people's own perceptions of the

---

[14] Csikszentmihalyi & Csikszentmihalyi (1993).

studying and practising activities that are so essential for success at difficult skills. One important aspect of such activities is that they demand continuous concentration and may appear arduous or repetitive, and therefore, not obviously attractive to most teenagers. Also, study and practice tasks normally require the individual to work in solitude, without the companionship that most young people enjoy. Consequently, most adolescents do not like practising and studying. They do not like doing difficult things on their own, especially when these require sustained concentration. They would rather spend their time in other ways, such as hanging out with their friends or watching television. In short, studying is generally disliked by young people, because it involves activities that they do not enjoy and excludes ones they do enjoy.

One implication of these findings is that, other things being equal, those young people who like studying most, or dislike it least, will be more successful in extending their talents and abilities than other youngsters. So it would be useful to know how those young people who do not particularly dislike studying differ from those who do. To answer that further question, Csikszentmihalyi collected information about the teenagers in his study. He asked them to supply data about the extent to which their family backgrounds contributed resources that would encourage an adolescent to have high aspirations and act responsibly and independently.

In particular, two measures of the participants' families were obtained. First, the family backgrounds were rated as being more or less stimulating. This measure referred to the extent to which parents provided opportunities to learn and had high educational expectancies. Second, the families were rated as being more or less supportive. This measure indicated the amount of assistance and structure available in the individual's home. For instance, a family in which there were clear guidelines, and clearly allotted tasks, and in which individuals could depend upon one another, would be rated as highly supportive. Young people in these families know what was expected of them and get on with it, and know that they could count on help if it was needed. A family which was assessed as *lacking* structure and support tended to be one in which young people spent a lot of their time arguing or complaining, or negotiating with each other and saying things like 'it's not fair' or 'it's not my turn'.

Next, Csikszentmihalyi identified those adolescents in his sample who had the least dislike for studying. To do this he had to invent a method for assessing how individuals actually experience what they are doing at any particular time. He developed a neat technique that involved adolescents carrying around with them a small bleeper. Ten times every day, on randomly timed occasions, the bleeper would sound. Every time that happened, the adolescents would get out a small booklet they had been issued with and answer some questions about their activity at the time, for example, what they were doing, where they were, whether they were alone or in company, and so on. One of the questions asked was whether the person was *enjoying* whatever it was that he or she was doing. Another question asked how *alert* the person felt at the time when the bleeper sounded.

When Csikszentmihalyi asked the adolescents how they felt about activities other than studying, such as talking to friends or watching television, their responses were generally positive, and differences in family background had little effect on the answers. But there was a very different pattern of responses if the bleeper sounded when an adolescent was studying. First, answers to the questions about enjoyment and alertness tended to be negative, with participants usually reporting that they were *not* enjoying studying, and *not* feeling alert or attentive. Second, on these occasions the answers given were strongly affected by the participants' family backgrounds. One group was very different from the others; that was the group whose family backgrounds were both supportive *and* stimulating. These young people, but not the others, were generally positive about studying. They enjoyed it more than the others did, and when they were engaged in study on their own they reported being much more attentive and alert.

Essentially, certain of the young people observed by Csikszentmihalyi were perceiving their studying activities very differently from the other teenagers, and the differences in the way they experienced studying were closely related to their home backgrounds. Perhaps this was because young people whose families were both stimulating and supportive had learned to get on with the job of working at a study activity and had acquired the habit of doing so. Because they were happier about studying they devoted more time to it and because they were more alert and attentive they learned more. Those individuals who were not so well-prepared for practice and study activities by their family backgrounds may well have caught up later, but temporarily at least, they were at a real disadvantage.

The findings of Csikszentmihalyi's investigations encourage us to believe that Darwin's supportive and stimulating family background would have made him better equipped than most boys of his age to study on his own. And released from the detested school, Darwin did indeed throw himself into his studies at Edinburgh. Settling in was not difficult, and with all the family connections there were plenty of invitations to dine in the evenings. Edinburgh was (and still is) an attractive city and an exciting place to be. Darwin conscientiously attended a number of lecture courses, making detailed notes, and back in the comfortable lodgings which he and Erasmus had found for themselves they devoured large numbers of books, borrowing more volumes from the university library than most students that year. Erasmus, when he first heard in the previous winter about Charles' new plans, had urged that they should 'read like horses', and that is just what they did. They studied books on medicine and anatomy, and other scientific topics, and wrestled with Newton's *Optiks* as well as lighter fare such as Boswell's *Life of Samuel Johnson*.

Diligent as Darwin was in his first year at Edinburgh, it was not long before he found himself wondering whether he was really suited to medicine. A number of bad experiences prompted his doubts, and despite his initial enthusiasm, he could not hide from himself the fact that the lecture courses bored him stiff. With the exception of a series of lectures on chemistry given by Thomas Hope, whose teaching was universally admired, none of the lectures Darwin attended gripped him. He was also put off medicine by watching a couple of surgical operations. Operations, which at that time were conducted without anaesthetics, were horrifying. Screaming patients writhed against the straps holding them down as the blood-soaked surgeons rushed to finish their work. It did not help that one of those operations that Darwin witnessed was on a child. He found the experience unbearable and could not stay to the end.

Two further discoveries fuelled Darwin's concern about whether he had made the right decision in choosing medicine. First, he had become aware (probably from talking to Erasmus) just how wealthy his family was. If the thought that he would need to earn an income had influenced his choice of profession, he now knew that doing that was not strictly necessary. Second, Charles Darwin was finding his mind increasingly drawn away from medicine and towards the scientific disciplines that border natural history. The habit of observing, and then raising fundamental questions, had never left him. He noted in his diary on 18 January 1826 that in the evening he had seen a hedge sparrow creeping into a hole in a tree, and asked himself, 'Where do most birds roost in winter?'. On 9 February he recorded catching a sea mouse. He noticed that it tried to coil itself into a ball when its mouth was touched. At this point his observations betray the fact that by now he has come a long way from being a naive amateur. He remarks that one authority states that the sea mouse has two feelers, whereas Linnaeus says it has four of them. Darwin had never stopped being interested in collecting, and now that he was in a university environment where he was exposed to the enthusiasms of amateur natural historians and could see at first hand the work of serious scientists who were systematically describing and classifying natural phenomena, he could hardly resist having his own interests dragged back in that direction. Among the books he had borrowed from the library during the previous autumn were a translation of Linnaeus's system of classification and books on zoology and entomology. By March 1826 Darwin had begun to admit his misgivings about medicine in letters to his family: it must have been well before then that he first began having doubts, perceiving that his real interests lay elsewhere.

During the remainder of Darwin's two years at Edinburgh much of his time went into natural history. The 1825–6 academic year ended in May, and at the end of that month he returned to Shrewsbury, but he spent much of the summer away from home. He walked with friends in the Welsh mountains, stayed with his Wedgwood relatives at Maer, went on a riding tour with his sister Caroline, and enjoyed the shooting at Woodhouse, where the Owen family always made him welcome. Erasmus had almost finished his studies by then and was temporarily practising medicine, although he still had to take a qualifying examination back at Cambridge University. (Within a few years Erasmus abandoned the profession: he seemed content to be a dilettante without employment for the remainder of his life.)

Darwin returned to Edinburgh in November 1826. He was now seventeen. This year he did not plan to attend many lectures, and enrolled in just two courses. One was in medicine, and the other, given by Professor Robert Jameson, was in natural history. Jameson's course was popular, and involved carefully organised practical classes as well as lectures. A number of his students, some of whom went on to enjoy distinguished careers, commented favourably on Jameson's teaching. (One of them was George Bidder, an inventive engineer and former child prodigy who we shall encounter later, in Chapter 6.) But Jameson did not impress Darwin. He especially disliked Jameson's lectures on geology, describing them as incredibly dull: they were too pedestrian and insufficiently innovative for the young Charles Darwin. Moreover, Jameson's geological views clashed with those of Thomas Hope, one of the few Edinburgh teachers whose lectures Darwin had admired. Perhaps Jameson's lectures were better suited for students who were not so well informed as Darwin would have been. Nevertheless, Darwin did benefit from Jameson's presence at Edinburgh, spending much of his time in the natural history museum that was run under Jameson's direction. It was a well-organised museum, one of the largest in Europe, and held some impressive collections. For a keen young natural scientist like Darwin it made an excellent working environment.

Despite the fact that in his second year at Edinburgh Darwin was no longer the conscientious model student who diligently attended lectures and made careful notes, the activities he did engage in during that time made an enormous contribution to his development as a scientist.

Without his elder brother to constrain him, Charles was always out and about, meeting people, walking with friends, attending the meetings of societies, and, when not otherwise engaged, frequently observing and collecting, and dissecting his specimens. He was keen to learn how to stuff birds, and for two months he took daily lessons in taxidermy from a freed black slave, who entertained him with intriguing accounts of life in exotic places such as South American tropical rain-forests. The accounts of daily activities that are found in Darwin's correspondence show that, at least in the first half of his life, the popular image of him as a withdrawn individual who avoided company and was often unwell is very wide of the mark. Until he was well over thirty, Darwin was almost always vigorously active and outgoing, and usually robustly healthy.

During that year, Darwin became involved in a number of societies at Edinburgh. He went to meetings of the Wernerian Natural History Society, where on one occasion he listened to the great American naturalist and artist James Audubon. He also heard a report, in the course of a lecture by Robert Grant, of some of the first original discoveries made by himself, the speaker's 'zealous young friend Mr Charles Darwin'. He was especially active in another society, the Plinian Society, which attracted a wide variety of students and others. Among its members were a number of radically-minded individuals who challenged religious orthodoxy, believed in democracy, and thought that the world was created by physical causes rather than the events recorded in the Bible. These people were enthusiastic about evolutionary views. By then Darwin was already aware of the possibility that species evolve rather than being suddenly created in their final form, having read (probably during the previous summer) his grandfather Erasmus's *Zoönomia*. He was soon elected to the Plinian Society's council, and became friendly with some of the most radical members. These included William Browne, a lively heretic who was active in anti-clerical politics, and William Greg, who held the daring notion that the brains of lower animals were not fundamentally different from those of humans, and challenged the dogma that morality came from God, not nature.

All this questioning of the established order must have seemed heady stuff to the seventeen-year-old Darwin, but his contact with the Plinian Society gave him his first sharp warning that expressing radical or anti-clerical views could be a dangerous activity. Despite the fact that religious persecution had abated somewhat since Galileo's time, speaking too wildly or too freely could still have dangerous consequences. The particular event Darwin witnessed was a minor one, involving censorship rather than persecution, but it presaged more sinister acts of oppression that he was to encounter later, at Cambridge University. All that happened was that following a much debated talk by Browne, who argued for the materialist view that mind and matter are related (contradicting the traditional Cartesian wisdom), with consciousness being an outcome of the activity of the brain, some members of the society were so concerned about the possible consequences of these views having been expressed that it was decided to strike the record of Browne's proposition from the minutes. It is not known who did this, or what were the precise reasons underlying the decision to make the deletions, but for one reason or another that repressive course of action was judged to be necessary.

Much of Darwin's time at Edinburgh that year was spent working in the field as a practical natural historian, observing, collecting, and gradually gaining more and more of the knowledge and skills that distinguish the expert from the mere hobbyist. Darwin was tireless in his searches for species. He walked along the coast, and sometimes persuaded the captains of trawlers dredging the ocean bottom to let him accompany them. He was looking for sea-creatures, corals, sponges, polyps, leeches, seapens and molluscs, and indeed almost any kind of marine life.

This vigorous activity coincided with his getting to know the prominent zoologist Robert Grant, an expert on sponges who became one of the most influential of Darwin's teachers. Grant was a happy choice as Darwin's first real scientific mentor, because as well as being an excellent scientist whose own research quickly engaged Darwin's interest, he was a man whose broader views about the origins of living things were unusual in being strongly inclined towards evolution. Grant, who had studied in Paris, was an admirer of Lamarck, the great French naturalist (still living in 1827) who was famous for having produced an influential evolutionary theory. Lamarck's theory is based upon the assumption that acquired characteristics can be passed down through inheritance. We now know that this cannot happen, but in an era when no knowledge of genetics existed Lamarck's key assumption was not readily disproved. (In the Soviet Union a variety of Lamarckism was still being advocated by the biologist T. Lysenko in the 1950s.) Robert Grant had also read and admired the discussion of evolution in Erasmus Darwin's *Zoönomia*, an experience that may have contributed to his willingness to be helpful to Charles. Grant was an evolutionist and a freethinker at a time when few scientists challenged the prevailing conservatism. His views would have provoked Darwin to begin thinking seriously about the evolutionary possibilities that had been hinted at in *Zoönomia*.

By guiding Darwin's activities and directing them towards realistic scientific goals, Grant helped to ensure that the energy of the young enthusiast was not wasted. At the same time, Grant, whose own dedication to the practical task of finding specimens was unsparing, gave

Darwin an excellent brief apprenticeship in practical science. In his search for tiny, almost invisible sea-slugs, Grant would spend up to ten hours a day wading through bitterly cold waters. Darwin was impressed by this example, and as he walked and talked with Grant and watched him at work he learned rapidly from him and began making original observations himself. On 27 March 1828 the (just) eighteen-year-old Charles Darwin made the first presentation of his own discoveries at a meeting of the Plinian Society.

With hindsight, it is blindingly clear that Darwin's second year at Edinburgh was a crucial period in his development as a scientist. But the prevailing view at the time, at least within his own family, was that he was wasting his time. As his father saw it, since Charles was not going to complete his training in medicine another profession had to be found. A degree course that would lead to ordination as a minister of religion seemed the best choice. It would then be possible to purchase for Charles a living as a vicar of a country parish.

Knowing what we do now about Darwin, the idea of him being condemned to the routine of a country parsonage seems bizarre, but in fact his father's plan was not as ridiculous as it might appear to have been. As the young Michael Faraday had discovered twenty years earlier, science as a profession still hardly existed (a fact that Darwin's own disciple Thomas Huxley would find to be still true as late as 1850), and Dr Robert had no grounds for believing that his son Charles had any chance of ever becoming one of the extremely few individuals to gain a paid job as a scientist. There were some scientific professors, like Grant, but their numbers were very small. In any case, a large proportion of them were ordained, and Robert Darwin would have known that Charles's working towards a university degree that would enable him to become a clergyman would not close the door on his scientific interests. So Darwin's becoming a country vicar would definitely not have ruled out his taking an active interest in natural history, and it would not even have prevented Darwin from making a substantial contribution to science. After all, Gilbert White, famous for his *Natural History and Antiquities of Selborne*, which Darwin had known since childhood, was a curate, and so were the authors of other influential books. Livings as parish clergymen were not quite sinecures, but such was the state of the Church of England at that period that it was not at all unusual for its ministers to be only mildly concerned about their pastoral and evangelising responsibilities. Of course, had Dr Darwin been able to see into the future he might well have made alternative plans for the final years of Charles's education, but lacking any firm grounds for predicting that his son would become a leading scientist, the proposals he arrived at were entirely sound.

It was decided that Charles would study for a Bachelor of Arts degree at Cambridge University. Cambridge, because of its links with the Church, was the appropriate institution for a British student intending to become ordained. Darwin had left Edinburgh early in 1827, but to prepare himself for his course at Cambridge he needed tuition in some of the subjects at which he was weak, and he did not arrive at the university until the beginning of 1828, around his nineteenth birthday. During the three years he spent at Cambridge Darwin did enough work in non-science subjects to pass his examinations, but as at Edinburgh, much of his energy went into natural history.

At Cambridge, Darwin enjoyed many of the pleasures that appealed to affluent and well-bred young men of his generation. He shot (and consumed) many kinds of birds, hunted, rode, drank, and enjoyed the antics of dining societies. Had it not been for the habitual self-discipline that he had already acquired in his two years at Edinburgh it is quite possible that these diversions would have taken over his life. But by now, thanks largely to the experiences of those Edinburgh years, Darwin was sufficiently mature to be able to organise his time properly and make sure that during his three years at Cambridge he did not just enjoy himself with the friends he made there, but succeeded at his examinations as well, and also found plenty of opportunities for pursuing natural history.

As soon as he arrived at Cambridge Darwin became friendly with a second cousin, William Darwin Fox, who shared his passion for insects and was enthusiastically building a collection of beetles. Being a few years older than Darwin, Fox left Cambridge earlier, but they maintained their contacts through frequent letters. From Darwin's surviving letters to Fox, which are peppered with jokey remarks, it is clear that he gained tremendous enjoyment from entomology (the study of insects). The content of Darwin's letters to Fox and many of his friends jumps unselfconsciously from the personal to the scientific and back again. Here there is a sharp contrast with the correspondence of some other great scientists of the time, such as Michael Faraday. Faraday kept his personal and professional lives separate, but Darwin's letters often contain a delightful mix of warm messages of friendship and scholarly information or requests. For instance, one letter to Fox, written from home in the summer of 1828, begins with the lament 'I am dying by inches, from not having any body to talk to about insects', quickly switches to technical information accompanied by three well executed sketches of beetles, then jumps to the comment 'I am constantly saying, "I do wish Fox was here"' and repeats a previous invitation, adding that 'My Father desired me to say, that he should be at anytime most happy to see you'. The letter next moves to a technical description for another paragraph, mentioning that Darwin has seen 'the Cocc: bipunctata (or dispar) 4 or 5 in actu coitus with a black one with 4 red marks', then asks Fox's pardon 'for sending such a very selfish letter', disarmingly requests Fox to 'remember I am your pupil', asks about Fox's plans for the summer, and concludes with plans for their next meeting and queries about family matters.[15]

Correspondence with a friend often continued for many years. In William Darwin Fox's case, although he and Darwin rarely met after Fox left Cambridge, the two were still writing to each other in the 1870s. When Fox died in 1880 Darwin was too unwell to attend his cousin's funeral, but he poignantly remarked that he could still picture his face and imagine his voice as clearly as if he were present in the room.

Something else that is evident from the contents of Darwin's letters to his cousin, which often concerned birds, beetles, and other species they were interested in, is that Charles Darwin at this time usually knew what he was talking about. Fox must have been taken aback at first to discover that by the time Darwin arrived at Cambridge, this young man who had only just reached his nineteenth birthday was already something of an expert and almost certainly better-informed than Fox himself, who as well as being older than Darwin was devoted to natural history and quite an ambitious collector. Darwin himself was building up a substantial collection, and was prepared to devote considerable time to it, and money too when that was necessary. As in his second year at Edinburgh, he was constantly going on long walks and expeditions, searching for new and rare specimens. He was furious to discover that a supplier whom he was paying to provide beetles was letting another collector have the first pick, and reported to his cousin, 'accordingly, we have made our final adieus, my part in the affecting scene consisted in telling him he was a d---d rascal, & signifying I should kick him down the stairs if he ever appeared in my rooms again'.[16]

As we have seen, Darwin never had difficulty finding mature scientists who were willing to take him seriously. In Darwin's correspondence during his three years at Cambridge there are increasing signs that his skills were admired by his friends, who already included a number of competent scientists. By the time he began his lifelong friendship in early 1830 with Professor John Henslow, the most influential of Darwin's mentors, it was clear that Henslow already regarded him as a very promising young biologist.

John Henslow, Professor of Botany at Cambridge University, is rightly

[15] Letter from Charles Darwin to William Darwin Fox, 12 June 1828, *The Correspondence of Charles Darwin*, vol. 1, p. 56. Burkhardt & Smith (1985).

[16] Letter from Charles Darwin to William Darwin Fox, April 1, 1829. *The Correspondence of Charles Darwin*, Vol. 1, p. 81. Burkhardt & Smith (1985).

regarded as the most influential of all Darwin's teachers. He was enormously helpful to Charles Darwin throughout much of his early career. Henslow had many virtues. On his death in 1861, Darwin wrote to Joseph Hooker, Henslow's son-in-law, 'I fully believe a better man never walked this earth'.[17] As well as being a good scientist Henslow was by all accounts sincere, friendly, helpful, wise, well-intentioned and anxious to encourage young naturalists. Nobody profited from his helpfulness more than Darwin did. But the usual view of their relationship as being one between the wise mature teacher and the naive, unformed apprentice is inaccurate. Darwin had first learned of Henslow's reputation as early as 1823, in a letter from Erasmus. He attended Henslow's lectures and went to parties at his house in Darwin's first years at Cambridge, as well as going on some of the excursions Henslow organised. Yet by the time Darwin got to know Henslow really well and became his frequent companion on walks and expeditions into the countryside, Darwin was within a year of completing his degree. By then he had already gained quite a reputation among his friends and teachers and had convinced them that he was no ordinary naturalist. He had been continuing his vigorous pursuit of natural history, extending the knowledge and skills that had already been considerable by the time he had ceased studying with Robert Grant at Edinburgh.

Ever since he had been a child of ten or so, Darwin had enthusiastically pursued his interest in the natural environment. Year after year he had continued adding to his knowledge and skills. By the time he left Cambridge, at the age of twenty-two, he would have devoted at least several thousands of hours to natural history. The sheer time and effort he had so enthusiastically – and with so much obvious enjoyment – spent on observing and collecting would almost inevitably have equipped him with a level of expertise that went well beyond what was to be expected in those young people for whom natural history was simply an enjoyable hobby. Of course, just being interested in an activity and spending time doing it does not guarantee expertise, as many people who play tennis or bridge every week are aware, but Darwin brought to his collecting activities a combination of curiosity and enthusiasm that would have guaranteed that as well as enjoying his hobby he would actively extend his competence. He also had good access to the scientific books that provided the knowledge he required. Even by the time when Darwin had first arrived at Edinburgh, his earlier work in the chemistry laboratory that he and Erasmus had constructed at home would have provided him with a degree of scientific expertise that would have been unusual in a young person of his age. Consequently, the young man of twenty or so who

[17] *The Correspondence of Charles Darwin*, Vol. 9, p. 133. Burkhardt & Smith (1994).

accompanied Henslow on his walks was no raw youth, but a scholar whom a botanist as perceptive as Henslow would have noticed to be one of the most promising natural historians of his generation at Cambridge, perhaps the most promising. Certainly by the summer of 1831 Henslow saw Darwin in precisely that light. Had he not done so he would never have singled him out as the person who was most fitting to be given the matchless opportunity for a naturalist that was being made available by the voyage of HMS *Beagle*.

It has often been said that *Beagle*'s voyage 'made' Darwin, but that is only true up to a point. The voyage did not present him with evidence that instantly converted him to the view that species evolve by natural selection: there were no sudden 'Eureka!' experiences of that kind. Indeed, as Frank Sulloway has pointed out, some of the most compelling evidence for evolution that Darwin encountered, notably in the Galapagos archipelago which the *Beagle* visited in 1853, was either mistakenly described or labelled, as in the instance of 'Darwin's finches', or not collected by Darwin at all, as in the case of the Galapagos tortoises.[18]

All the same, if Darwin had not had the opportunity to take part in a lengthy expedition it is unlikely that he would have developed into the great theorist he became. As well as exposing him to an immense variety of unfamiliar phenomena that would have sparked new thoughts and new insights in a mind as well-prepared as his, the voyage gave him the leisure and the intellectual privacy to contemplate freely and at length. And by getting away from Cambridge and England he was escaping from a mental climate in which certain thoughts were unthinkable. On the other side of the world, especially during the lengthy periods spent exploring in the South American continent, well removed from the company of the *Beagle*'s ultra-conservative captain, Robert Fitzroy, there was little to constrain Darwin's thinking. So,

Five years on board the *Beagle* taught Darwin to think for himself and allowed him, especially through his geological work, to envision himself as a theoretician with a penchant for far-reaching explanations and universal laws. Once the anxious collector on the *Beagle* was transformed into an increasingly bold geological theorist, Darwin was able to transfer his developing intellectual talents to many other related fields of science. Thus the influence of the *Beagle* voyage transcended any particular scientific field or discovery on Darwin's part. In the process, the voyage provided Darwin with something much more important, namely the opportunity to mature intellectually under highly auspicious circumstances and thereby to become the Darwin that history now celebrates.[19]

Darwin became increasingly confident as the voyage proceeded. At the beginning he saw himself as a collector providing specimens for Henslow

[18] See pp. 145–6 in Sulloway (1985).   [19] Sulloway (1985), p. 146.

and the 'serious' scientists back in Europe. When many months went by
without any of Henslow's letters reaching him (an understandable consequence of the difficulty of communicating by post with a small sailing
craft circumnavigating the globe) he initially became more and more
anxious that he was failing at his duties. Only after Henslow's supportive
and encouraging letters finally reached him did Darwin start to become
sufficiently assured to start thinking of himself as a theoretical scientist in
his own right.[20]

It would be wrong to assume that had it not been for the *Beagle* Darwin
would have become just another country parson who dabbled in natural
history. One can only speculate on what might have happened, but by the
time the opportunity to join the voyage arrived Darwin was set to make a
definite impact, albeit one that might otherwise have been less theoretical
and not nearly so important to science. Even without the *Beagle*, Darwin's
eventual reputation might well have been on a par with the well-regarded
natural scientists of the day, such as Henslow or Hooker.

It is not even true that had it not been for the *Beagle* Darwin would have
been unable to travel in other continents. At Edinburgh, he talked at
length to the freed slave who taught him taxidermy and who had accompanied the naturalist Charles Waterton on his travels in South America.
Darwin was also hugely impressed by Humboldt's account of that continent. He copied out Humboldt's descriptions of Tenerife, with its lush
vegetation and volcanic scenery, and enthusiastically read them aloud to
his friends. Like a number of nineteenth-century naturalists who were
able to go on extensive voyages, including Charles Lyell, Thomas Huxley,
Alfred Wallace, Henry Bates and Joseph Hooker, Darwin was eager for
the experiences that such a voyage could provide, and wealthy enough to
be relatively unconcerned about the cost. In the summer of 1831 Darwin
threw himself into making plans for a scientific voyage to Tenerife. The
intention was that Darwin would be accompanied by Henslow and
several other naturalists. To Darwin's dismay, by early August it was
apparent that the plan would have to be postponed, but there was no
doubt about the seriousness of Darwin's intentions. What this episode
demonstrates is that even if the *Beagle* opportunity had not arisen,
Darwin would have devoted considerable efforts to finding a way to go on
some other scientific voyage to the tropics.

The question has to be asked: Why, when the invitation to accompany
the *Beagle* first arrived towards the end of 1831, was his father so firmly
opposed to the project? If Charles Darwin really was a seriously committed and well-prepared young naturalist by then, why was Dr Robert less

[20] Sulloway (1985).

than enthusiastic? As we have seen, for all his faults Dr Robert had usually displayed considerable sensitivity and judgement on matters connected with Charles's future. So why not now? The answer to that question is interesting because it throws light on aspects of Darwin's character that contributed to his genius.

There was not just one reason for Dr Robert's initial opposition to the *Beagle* plan. Even today, despite the telephones, faxes, cheap travel and electronic mail that make long-distance travel a far less daunting prospect than it used to be, a parent can find it alarming to be suddenly confronted with the prospect of a twenty-two-year-old son disappearing for a period of years to the other side of the world. That would appear especially worrying if the father had recently been very ill (as Dr Darwin had, in the previous November) and the son (as in Darwin's case) had never left Britain except for a short trip to Paris in the company of an older sister. On those grounds alone, there is nothing outrageously insensitive about Dr Robert's initial negativity. But there was another important reason, namely that neither Dr Robert nor the other members of Darwin's immediate family quite appreciated how accomplished and serious and committed a scientist Charles had become. As we have seen, they had persisted with a view of him that was somewhat out-of-date. They had experienced few signs of the ferocious determination with which he could pursue his interests. They were still seeing him as the younger son, able enough, but somewhat immature and aimless, and still in need of the guidance of his family, whether to correct his spelling errors or to keep him from spending most of his time shooting, hunting, and drinking with his friends. To them the prospective voyage of the *Beagle* might well have seemed too much like a dangerous jaunt, perhaps not entirely respectable, and certainly a hazardous prospect for the vulnerable and impressionable (in their eyes) young Charles.

Not being fully aware of his growing reputation as a serious naturalist, Charles's father and his sisters could not at first perceive that, dangerous and uncertain as the prospective voyage undoubtedly was, it was also a marvellous scientific opportunity. Nor did they appreciate the extent to which Charles was being honoured by being chosen. They were not aware that the invitation represented an acknowledgement of the remarkable promise that influential scientists had discerned in this particular young man.

In the event, it only took a brief letter from Dr Robert's brother-in-law to make Darwin's father understand the true situation, and see that his reaction had been too hasty and rapidly change his mind. In this, as in other matters, the much-maligned Dr Robert was neither foolish nor inflexible. But why was it that his family's perception of Charles's prospects had been so inaccurate? To some extent their faulty understanding can be attributed to the not-uncommon tendency for parents and older siblings to persist with out-of-date impressions of a young brother who has grown up and changed in their absence. But part of the reason lay in the behaviour of Charles himself, who, as we have seen, did remarkably little to discourage his family's misperceptions of him. At a very young age Darwin had devised his own way of responding to criticism that he considered unwelcome or unfair. He would grit his teeth and say nothing, and neither argue nor attempt to justify himself to whoever was criticising him, whilst inside his mind he would persist with his own opinions and go on in precisely the same way. As he put it in his *Autobiography*, writing about his older sister Caroline, always kindly but 'too zealous in trying to improve me' when he was a young boy, Charles would often wonder what she would blame him for next, and to protect himself, 'I made myself dogged so as not to care what she might say'.

This practice became a habit, and one that usually served Darwin well. Keeping his head down and retreating into his shell was a good way of dealing with Dr Butler's disapproval at Shrewsbury School, for example. Darwin simply went on concentrating on his own interests, without bothering too much about Butler's opinion. And when his sisters exhorted him to change his habits, or take more interest in religion, or improve his spelling, Charles often thanked them for their well-intentioned advice but rarely followed it.

For Darwin, acting in this way was a way of providing himself with the kind of protective shell which all geniuses require and all make for themselves, but in differing ways. Major creative achievements are only possible when an individual is able to concentrate more or less exclusively and for long periods of time, free from distractions and other concerns, and unconstrained by mundane worries and anxieties. Some kind of private space is necessary, providing a means of gaining privacy and isolation, and a degree of separation from the pressures of other people and their demands.

There are a number of ways to achieve this. Isaac Newton made it possible to devote all his energies to his work by becoming to some extent oblivious to the needs of other people, almost always giving priority to his own interests. Michael Faraday enabled himself to concentrate exclusively on his scientific work through the use of a number of devices, including keeping his professional and personal lives entirely separate, strictly limiting his social engagements, and cultivating a degree of unworldliness and paying little or no attention to external concerns, such as the political crises that filled his most active decades. Other creative scholars and artists have gone to similar lengths to keep their thoughts free from interfering distractions, often neglecting other responsibilities, sometimes acting with monstrous selfishness towards their loved ones, as Dickens did, or using other people shamelessly, as Picasso did, or being childishly irresponsible, as Mozart sometimes was. The good-natured and sociable Darwin, for whom the cooperation and friendship of others was always important, required more subtle ways of holding people at arm's length. Later in life he achieved this through a carefully devised style of living, but in his younger days the practice of keeping many of his thoughts to himself while encouraging others to think of him as they wished served reasonably well. There were occasional blips, however, of which the near-fiasco at the time of his invitation to join the *Beagle* was by far the most serious.

It would be an exaggeration to say that by the time Charles Darwin joined the *Beagle* at the age of twenty-two his career was assured, but he had undoubtedly prepared himself admirably well, in the course of his outwardly unexceptional childhood and adolescence. Within two years of his return to England in 1836 he had worked out the essential details of the theory that was to make him famous. Nobody could have predicted at that time that he or any other young scientist would achieve that. Even so, had detailed information been made available at that time concerning the progress until then of Charles Darwin and the score or so most promising naturalists among his contemporaries, it is not at all unlikely that he would have been picked as the one most likely to become a major scientist.

That is not to say that anyone could have predicted then that Charles Darwin would become known as the great scientist who produced the theory of evolution by natural selection. His succeeding at that achievement still seems remarkable. But the fact that something is remarkable does not justify our insisting that it simply could not happen in the absence of mysteries or miracles, or that it requires the intervention of special genes, or innate gifts that create a distinct breed of geniuses. And there are no compelling reasons to suggest that the kinds of reasons that very adequately explain Darwin's progress until the age of twenty-two or so cannot also account for his later achievements. Even the motivational forces that drove those mental activities that helped Darwin to move ahead are unmysterious. With some geniuses it is hard to understand why they persevered quite so long or struggled quite so hard, but in Darwin's case his obvious enjoyment of what he was doing seems to provide ample justification for the learning activities of his formative years, and, if to a lesser extent, for the more strenuous mental exertions of his later career.

That the Charles Darwin who embarked upon his lengthy voyage on HMS *Beagle* was already a well-prepared young scientist, and not aimless at all, does not detract from the fact the years on the *Beagle* were immensely influential ones. As well as the rich diet of experiences it exposed him to, the voyage gave Darwin time for prolonged and unconstrained ruminations. His careful reading of Charles Lyell's newly-published *Principles of Geology*, which established beyond reasonable doubt that the physical world in its present form came into being as a consequence of gradual change, would have removed any lingering belief in the Genesis story of the earth's beginnings. Darwin, who had already been encouraged to speculate about evolution and its possible causes, was able to see that if Genesis was so utterly mistaken about the causes of changes in the physical landscape, it could hardly be right about the origins of flora and fauna.

The achievements of Darwin's later career were to make heavy demands upon his determination and his courage, as well as involving immense intellectual struggles, but by then he had already acquired a degree of commitment to his work that kept him wedded to the scientific problems that faced him. The fact that following the return to Britain of HMS *Beagle* towards the end of 1836 he received much praise and recognition for what he had achieved during the voyage cannot have been unhelpful. Certainly, the years immediately following his return were a period in which he was furiously active as a scientist. Even then he was distracted by a variety of false leads and unfruitful ideas that delayed his reaching the conclusions that formed the nub of evolutionary theory. It was in 1838, when Darwin was twenty-seven and two years after his return, that it became clear to him that natural selection was the key to evolution, the insight which created a profound revolution in human knowledge when it was eventually published in 1859.

3 The long ascent of George Stephenson

Until the 1830s, travelling conditions in England had improved little since the Norman invasion of 1066, although recent improvements in road surfaces allowed the very fastest coaches from London to reach Exeter, 200 miles to the west, in 16 hours and Manchester, even further in the north, in 26 hours. Then, quite suddenly, the railways arrived. People rushed to take advantage of the new trains, quickly jettisoning their fears about this alarming way of being moved around at amazing velocities. Men and women who a few years earlier would have hooted with laughter at the very idea of humans being transported at much above 10 mph were regularly travelling at four times that speed. Charles Darwin's 1838 diary finds him grumbling like a present-day commuter about late trains and missed connections. The British statesman W. E. Gladstone, another frequent traveller by train, confided to his diary a stream of similar complaints about waiting for late connections and enduring smoky carriages.

Railway travel created exciting new possibilities for those who could afford it. On the afternoon of his wedding in Shrewsbury in January 1839 Charles Darwin and his bride caught a train to London, arriving the same evening. By the early 1840s there were already almost 2,000 miles of railway lines in Britain, and even Queen Victoria enthused about rail. In 1849 a new line through the northern wilds of East Yorkshire allowed Charlotte Brontë (whose brother Branwell had worked for a railway company) to take her ailing youngest sister Anne for what was intended to be a holiday in the seaside resort of Scarborough. Sadly and unexpectedly, Anne died there within a few days. On a dark evening in 1851, a despairing George Eliot enacted a scene that would not have been out of place in *Brief Encounter*. She begged the man she loved to explain his feelings as they waited for her train. The train 'whirled her away very sad,' he recorded, just after he had warned her 'that I felt great affection for her but that I loved E. [his mistress] and S. [his wife] also'. The future author of *Middlemarch* could not foresee that she would soon be setting up house with a different married lover, but she did perceive that with railways now commonplace, the world of her childhood – Jane Austen's unchanging England – had been left behind.

These revolutionary changes were made possible by the efforts of a self-trained colliery worker, George Stephenson, who in sharp contrast to Charles Darwin was born in poverty and never had a single day's schooling. Because of Stephenson, Britain was the first country in the world to have passenger railways. The Victorians called him 'The Father of Railways'. George Stephenson was a quite astounding individual, a genuinely heroic figure who achieved eminence against all the odds, through extraordinary determination and will-power.

Stephenson was a great engineer and inventor. He did not invent locomotives, and nor was he the first engineer to use metal rails. Even so, the railway revolution and the immense changes it brought would have been much delayed had it not been for his inventive genius, and his gritty capacity to persevere in the face of ridicule and hostility. Stephenson's efforts were opposed by many influential people who were certain that his aims were impossible, and also by powerful landowners who suspected that railways would harm their own interests. George Stephenson was the butt of many insults from well-bred individuals who were convinced that nothing of merit could be created by an ignorant working man from the remote north-east of England.

Despite his lack of formal education, George Stephenson was a practical visionary as well as being a remarkable inventor. As early as 1814, when a locomotive engine that was efficient and reliable had yet to be invented, and there were no obvious reasons for thinking that locomotives could ever be other than cumbrous and dangerous machines, Stephenson had already become convinced that railway travel was a practical possibility. He was also sure that he personally would play a part in making that happen. 'I will' he said, 'do something in coming time which will astonish all England'.[1] His foresight would have been remarkable even in someone who had not grown up poor and unschooled in a region that most educated people regarded as a backwater. A bare decade later, Stephenson's own success had made it realistic for him to prophesy with some confidence to a young assistant that 'before you are a very old man you will see railways as the highways of the world'.[2]

George Stephenson demonstrated his commitment to turning his vision into reality by showing a willingness to put personal gain aside if doing that would bring closer the goal of practical steam locomotion. For much of his life he had to struggle financially, but by the age of forty, at the time when the Stockton and Darlington Railway was being constructed in the early 1820s, he was at last starting to prosper. He had taken out a

---

[1] Quoted by Rolt (1960), p. 54 (apparently said to Robert Summerside at Killingworth).
[2] Quoted in Summerside (1878), p. 8.

patent for cast-iron rails. It had been agreed that Stephenson's rails would be used for the new railway, bringing him a profit worth more than his yearly salary. So when he was asked to comment on the idea of introducing a different kind of rail, made of wrought iron and costing over twice the price of his own, an unenthusiastic response could have been anticipated. But Stephenson insisted on using the new 'malleable' wrought-iron rails, despite the financial loss to himself. He stressed their advantage of being unbreakable, unlike rails made of cast-iron, and he persuaded his employers that the reduction in repairs and delays would justify the extra expense.

George Stephenson was born 9 June 1781 in Wylam, a mining village on the Tyne, eight miles west of Newcastle. The coal that was mined in the area was valued because it could be taken along the river to the sea and thence to London, avoiding the prohibitive costs of haulage by road. A couple of generations earlier, another young working-class man from the north-east of England, James Cook, who was to become famous as the great British navigator and explorer who charted much of Australia and discovered Antarctica, had gained his navigating skills on the sturdy boats, known as 'cats', which carried the coal to London. Both men were unusually tall, and they were both strong and vigorous individuals who at an early age showed themselves to be resourceful as well as dependable. Stephenson's father, Robert, who had been born in Scotland and moved south when working as a servant, married the daughter of a dyer, and they had six children, George being the second. Robert Stephenson worked as a mine fireman, keeping one of the engines at the Wylam colliery in fuel. Stephenson's first biographer, Samuel Smiles, was told by local people who had known Robert that he never lacked company as he tended his engine fire, because the local children would gather around him to listen to stories. Unfortunately, his wage of twelve shillings per week was barely sufficient to keep his family in food. To put Robert Stephenson's yearly earnings into perspective, they were little more than a day's income for a moderately wealthy individual such as Charles Darwin's father. Unlike the Darwins, the Stephenson family were extremely poor. There was no money to send any of the Stephenson children to school.

The earliest years of George Stephenson's life were unremarkable. He played around the village and looked for birds' nests. The region was still largely rural: it was grubby from the mining works but had not yet become the blackened area of industrial activity that Samuel Smiles was to encounter when he visited the area soon after Stephenson's death. There were a few vague intimations of future achievements surpassing those of most boys from beginnings like his, and some anecdotes recorded in Samuel Smiles' biography give the impression that the Stephenson children were given more encouragement by their parents than would have been usual in the household of a poor mine labourer. George listened to his father's stories. He remembered the first time his father took him to see a blackbird's nest, full of the new offspring. As a middle-aged man he recalled his father's love of the robins that hopped around his feet to pick up crumbs from the dinner that young George had carried out to the workplace.

It is significant that the future railway engineer happened to grow up with railways in his front yard. They were wooden rails, along which coal wagons were pulled by horses – running just in front of Stephenson's home, a single room of a small cottage inhabited by four separate families. One of his first responsibilities was to care for his younger brothers and sisters and keep them out of the way of the wagons. That apart, however, nothing that is known about George Stephenson's early years provides any genuine reason for anticipating that he would become the great engineer and inventor who brought the railways to Britain, and whose confident face still looks out from every English £5 note. Stephenson was not a child prodigy, and was given no special early training and had no unusual opportunities. His family had no influential relatives or friends. There was never any hint of a wealthy patron to lend him a helping hand. Stephenson as a child had little in common with those individuals, like Mozart, whose earliest years have provided a special preparation for the person's subsequent career by providing unusual opportunities that would encourage the acquisition of skills and knowledge that the child could build upon. There was nothing like that in Stephenson's early life. His was the kind of childhood that would nowadays be described as educationally disadvantaged as well as impoverished.

So how was it possible for George Stephenson to become a genius and a great engineer, despite all these handicaps, and with no obvious advantages? How did he do it? The kinds of obstacles that Stephenson faced have stunted many a young person's progress, condemning large numbers of individuals to the restricted lives of illiterate and unskilled men and women. How did George Stephenson manage to escape that fate?

On the face of things, accounting for Stephenson's accomplishments seems quite impossible. Virtually all the elements that can encourage young learners to forge ahead seem to have been absent. His success in the face of all his disadvantages appears totally mysterious. Yet a careful examination of the young Stephenson's actual circumstances does reveal a few clues, providing the beginnings of an explanation. When we carefully trace the route taken by his early life it becomes clear that although

George Stephenson's early experiences were far from being ones that would normally be associated with the acquisition of exceptional expertise, they did nevertheless give him some uncommon chances to gain some of the special capabilities that would have helped a young person to become an engineer. And Stephenson's everyday experiences also presented him with special opportunities to know about recent technological advances that were beginning to make it possible for steam power, in combination with metal rails, to be exploited for moving coal and other materials within collieries.

So perhaps the young George Stephenson's prospects were not so entirely bleak as at first glance they seem to have been. During the years when he was edging towards adulthood, a perceptive worker like Stephenson might have perceived that steam locomotion was starting to be a practical possibility. And as he added to his practical skills, he would have become aware that he already possessed some of the knowledge and some of the capabilities that could help to make that possibility into a reality.

Almost all we know about George Stephenson's early years and much of our knowledge of his later life comes from the *Life of George Stephenson* by Samuel Smiles, who began work on the biography soon after Stephenson's death in 1848. It was published in 1857, two years before Smiles' better known *Self Help* appeared, and was a widely admired bestseller. George Eliot was among those who praised it.

The *Life of George Stephenson* provides a vivid and colourful picture of Stephenson's life. Samuel Smiles was particularly well-equipped to write about Stephenson, being the secretary of a railway company as well as an experienced journalist. He had seen Stephenson and had heard him lecturing, and he was given aid and encouragement by George Stephenson's already distinguished engineer son, Robert. To collect information, Smiles repeatedly visited the region where Stephenson had grown up. He located a number of old people who had known the great engineer and were happy to provide recollections of his childhood. Smiles, whose job working for a railway company had led to him becoming closely involved with many aspects of railway construction, put his own experience to good use in writing about the problems that Stephenson had encountered.

Smiles was a fervent admirer of George Stephenson. The engineer's lack of interest in religion would have troubled his more pious biographer, but that aside, Stephenson epitomised most of the qualities that Smiles valued: courage, thrift, optimism, diligence, and above all perseverance. Fortunately, Smiles was a superb storyteller. The disarming warmth, colour, and sincerity of his writing brings George Stephenson back to life. It is a most un-Victorian biography. But good as it is, Smiles' biography is not always reliable. At times it takes on a 'Life of The Saint' quality, in which successive scenes present our hero being kind to animals, exhibiting generosity to the needy, showing courage in adversity, and so on. Smiles was sharply aware of how very hard it had been for Stephenson to make his way, and in the early part of the biography he almost seems to be cheering his hero on, willing him to overcome the obstacles he kept encountering. Of course, we would not expect a biography published in 1857 to dwell on the faults of its subject. Paradoxically, however, the very one-sidedness of Smiles' account helps the reader to discern them, because the frankly partisan Smiles is so eager to leap to Stephenson's defence against his detractors that he only just stops short of revealing the substance of their attacks. After being urged to perceive that,

For the first fifty years of his life, he had everything against him. He owed nothing to luck, to patronage, to the advantages of education. . . . He had to conquer every inch of the ground on which he stood.

His conquests were not easy: for arrayed against him were, first, his own ignorance . . . and second, the opposition of men of knowledge and science, who stood united to oppose him and could only be silenced by success.

There is something tragic in witnessing the determined hostility which obstructed his efforts. The whole prejudice of the scientific world opposed him . . . He was not 'one of us;' he had never received an engineer's education. They would not admit his facts. They would not even enquire into his experiments.[3]

a reader of the *Life* will suspect that George Stephenson could not have always been the genial and even-tempered individual who is introduced by Smiles, with little pretence at impartiality.

Stephenson undoubtedly felt bitter and resentful about the vicious attacks that were made on him by people who in his eyes were pampered as well as ignorant, and incapable of understanding how hard he had struggled or appreciating how much he had achieved. He could not have survived without being forceful and aggressive. And yet when recent biographers point out that Stephenson could be irascible or overbearing, and inclined to bear grudges,[4] our admiration is only slightly diminished. He could be proud and jealous, and he sometimes failed to give credit to those who had helped him. Squabbles with rival engineers occasionally

---

[3] Smiles (1881), p. v-vi. (This and subsequent quotations from Samuel Smiles' *The Life of George Stephenson* are taken from the 1881 Centenary Edition of this biography, which was originally published in 1857).

[4] See, for example, Davies (1975), p. 167; Rolt (1960), p. 10.

festered into bitter disputes. But warts and all, George Stephenson was a most remarkable individual, a true hero from the working class, and a self-made titan.

Having established that George Stephenson's distinctly unpromising beginnings did contain a few elements that an energetic and resourceful young man just might have succeeded in turning into opportunities, we can now edge further towards providing an explanation of Stephenson's accomplishments. The starting point will be the conviction that if it is possible to trace the course of Stephenson's journey through his childhood in a manner that lays bare the route taken by him as he gradually moved ahead, it ought to be possible to begin to account for his capabilities. Extraordinary as these were, once his actual progress has been examined we can see that there is no compelling reason to believe that their origins were either mysterious or miraculous.

Fortunately, thanks largely to the biography that Samuel Smiles completed so soon after Stephenson's death, information that can help us to discern the route followed in Stephenson's early life is reasonably abundant. Unlike certain biographers who devote no more than half a dozen pages to their subjects' childhoods, Smiles did appreciate that events in a child's early years profoundly affect a person's development. He also knew that the progress of an individual depended upon the day-to-day accumulation of those experiences and activities that made up a person's life. In contrast with some authors, such as the biographer who attributes Alfred Hitchcock's lifelong fear of being alone or in darkness to a single frightening childhood incident,[5] Smiles never succumbed to the 'eventism' tendency, in which it is assumed that long-lasting dispositions are typically caused by particularly intense or traumatic single incidents. He was acutely aware that acquired attributes are rarely the outcome of one particular event, and far more likely to result from numerous repetitive and undramatic daily experiences that take place over a lengthy period. Exceptional capabilities are not created from occasional dramatic happenings. In reality they build up gradually, largely as a consequence of the steady repetition of unexciting daily routines and activities.

Psychological research into expertise has underlined the wisdom of Smiles' insights, confirming that individuals' capabilities are largely gained through lengthy exposure to the ordinary and routine background events, repeated day after day, that make up the bulk of a person's life, rather than by occasional foreground incidents that seize attention because of their dramatic or sensational nature. Gaining unusual degrees

---

[5] Spoto (1983).

of competence invariably depends on a person having frequent and regular exposure to experiences that provide practice and training, repeated hour after hour, over long periods of time. In a number of Samuel Smiles's books he also stresses the importance of personal qualities such as perseverance and determination, again drawing attention to the importance of qualities that have more recently been highlighted in research studies investigating the acquisition of expertise.

The account of Stephenson's life provided in Smiles' biography provides valuable glimpses of the activities that enabled the would-be engineer to gain the skills he needed. From the time when George was eight, when the mine where his father worked ran out of coal and was closed down, forcing him to find another job and the family to move to a one-room cottage near the new pit, the accounts that emerge from the recollections that Smiles collected from people who knew George as a child begin to suggest that the boy was unusually resourceful for his age. For example, there is a story of him spending a whole day looking after horses at the local market to earn a shilling so that his sister could buy a new bonnet, and another report of him getting a job minding cows at tuppence per day.

The charming simplicity of tales like these is of course no guarantee of their accuracy, and it is hard to decide how much credence to give to them. On the one hand it is apparent that Smiles did talk to a substantial number of individuals, and the content and tone of the different reports are persuasively consistent. On the other hand, however, experimental research has confirmed that people's recollections of events that happened a long time ago are often unreliable. Old memories *can* be accurate, but it is also the case that hindsight can affect people's recall of distant events, especially when the person whose deeds are being remembered has since become well known. Research findings have established that even the most confidently voiced recollections are suspect, the degree of confidence people have in the truth of their memories being no guide to their actual veracity. As Mark Twain remarked, what is particularly astonishing is not what people remember but the number of remembered events that did not actually happen.

We are probably on firmer ground with recollections that describe specific childhood activities, especially ones that are uncommon. There is a detailed account, which seems unlikely to be a pure invention, of Stephenson as a child making models of engines and mine machinery out of clay, supplemented by corks and twine and pieces of waste wood. Stephenson was not the only innovator to have been an enthusiastic model builder in his childhood: the young Isaac Newton was constantly building mechanical models. The descriptions of Stephenson's models make it clear that some of them were highly ingenious. By this time he was undoubtedly giving plenty of close attention to machines and carefully observing their workings. 'Much to the marvel of the pitmen',[6] Smiles reported, George and a friend constructed an elaborate apparatus in the form of a miniature winding machine, linked to a model engine made from clay from a local bog and hemlock branches that served as imaginary steam pipes. The apparatus simulated the activity of sending tubs of coal, which the boys modelled with hollowed-out corks linked by twine, up and down a mine, using a structure constructed from pieces of waste wood found in the nearby carpenters' shop.

Stephenson's activities as he approached adulthood provide firm evidence of a willingness to work hard and throw himself into the kinds of pursuits that would have extended his capabilities enough for him to have aimed at becoming more than an unskilled pit workman. As a child he worked at a variety of jobs, leading plough-horses, hoeing turnips, working as a colliery 'corf-bitter' employed to clear stones and dross from the coal, and looking after the horse-powered 'gin' or winding-wheel which lifted coal out of the mine. At the age of thirteen he was, in the recollection of one of Smiles' elderly informants, 'a grit growing lad, with bare legs an' feet' who was 'very quick-witted and full of fun and tricks: indeed, there was nothing under the sun but he tried to imitate'.[7]

Stephenson's earliest ambition was to become an engineman, responsible for the daily operation of a steam engine, and he made his first big step in that direction at the age of fourteen, when he was appointed as an assistant fireman, to be paid one shilling (a twentieth of a pound) per day. That job did not last long, because the pit closed down – as often happened at the time – but by fifteen he was a full fireman, although it was another two years before his income reached twelve shillings a week and he was making a man's wage. After a further move he became the 'plugman', or engineman, that he had aspired to be, employed to keep a pump engine working and remedy minor defects. This was a relatively skilled job, especially for someone of his age. It needed more knowledge than was required for his father's post as a fireman, and was also better paid.

By this time George Stephenson was not only displaying an intense interest in engines, but also gaining a degree of expertise. This is the point in Stephenson's life when we see the first glimmer of a possibility that the young man might eventually become a proper engineer, and perhaps an innovative one, despite his lack of formal education. As well as closely observing the engines he worked on, he extended, in more sophisticated

[6] Smiles (1881), p. 7.   [7] Smiles (1881), p. 7.

ways, his childhood pastime of building models of engines. Despite being unable to read, George Stephenson would sometimes conduct small experiments of his own to test ideas that came to him when he was told about scientific findings that had been reported in the newspapers. Smiles notes that when an engine suffered a serious breakdown the usual response of an engineman would be to send for the chief engineer. But Stephenson, who was still not eighteen,

applied himself so assiduously and successfully to the study of the engine and its gearing – taking the machine to pieces in his leisure hours for the purpose of cleaning it and understanding its various parts – that he soon acquired a thorough practical knowledge of its construction and mode of working, and very rarely needed to call the engineer of the colliery to his aid. His engine became a sort of pet with him, and he was never wearied of watching it and inspecting it with admiration.[8]

These activities, the sharp interest in the detailed working of machines, and the delight in persistently giving close attention to their operation and never tiring of observing how the parts of a machine act together, are almost defining marks of mechanical inventors.[9] The importance of actions of this kind has been repeatedly demonstrated in modern research examining the factors that contribute to the acquisition of expertise.[10] For an early nineteenth-century engineer, practical activities like that would have been as crucial to the acquisition of high levels of expertise as are activities such as the formal scales and other kinds of exercises that performing musicians have to practise at, and the various kinds of training and preparation that are necessary in order to move ahead in other spheres of attainment. Smiles was well aware of this, noting that,

The daily contemplation of the steam-engine, and the sight of its steady action, is an education of itself to an ingenious and thoughtful man. And it is a remarkable fact, that nearly all of that has been done for the improvement of this machine has been accomplished, not by philosophers and scientific men, but by labourers, mechanics, and enginemen. Indeed, it would appear as if this were one of the departments of practical science in which the higher powers of the human mind must bend to mechanical insight.[11]

But there was still a very long way to go before George Stephenson could acquire all the knowledge and skills that would eventually make him an effective engineer. Getting to that point took him another dozen difficult years. There were numerous setbacks and hardships on the way, and plenty of barriers to be overcome. For a start, at eighteen Stephenson was still illiterate, and although he had heard about the important new

---

[8] Smiles (1881), p. 9.
[9] See, for example, Colangelo, Assouline, Kerr, Huesman, & Johnson (1993).
[10] Ericsson & Charness (1994).   [11] Smiles (1881), p. 10.

developments to steam engines that had been made by the Scottish engineer James Watt and others, his inability to read made the information that he was so anxious to acquire practically inaccessible to him. Having never been to school, even basic arithmetic was beyond him, and he would have been unable to decipher the diagrams and plans that are essential to the work of an engineer. Another obstacle was his lack of any theoretical knowledge of the physical sciences.

It is hard to imagine how his life and prospects must have seemed to the young George Stephenson at that time, but the possibilities he would have been able to envisage for himself would inevitably have been restricted by the circumstances of his life as a poorly-paid illiterate workman living in an isolated part of England. He would have encountered only a few individuals who had been as far as London. He would have possessed limited knowledge of the possible consequences of being educated or of the means by which self-education might be acquired. Far from being in a position to envisage the possibility of becoming a qualified engineer himself, he would have had little access to the kind of information that he would have needed in order to know what being an engineer actually involved. A person who does not have opportunities to even become aware of what can be achieved is condemned to a restricted existence. For an illiterate young worker living at the end of the eighteenth century to be capable of seeing beyond the limits of his daily environment would have required a rare combination of curiosity and imagination, in addition to the energy and resourcefulness George Stephenson possessed in abundance.

In one respect Stephenson was fortunate. He was lucky enough to gain his engineering skills at a time when the practical knowledge that he could acquire in the course of his everyday life as a colliery worker was crucial, and his lack of the formal and theoretical kinds of knowledge that are only accessible to literate people was a less crippling handicap than it would have been only a few years later. Even so, illiteracy was a serious obstacle. Stephenson's growing interest in engines was making him increasingly aware of how much he needed the knowledge that his lack of education had denied him. So, at an age when many young people today would already be at university, Stephenson set out to give himself the beginnings of an elementary education.

He learned to read and write by attending lessons, travelling three nights each week to a neighbouring village after his long working day had ended. Soon afterwards he started to learn arithmetic as well. Stephenson was immensely determined, as well as being strongly motivated to gain these skills. A contemporary who began at the same time recalled to

Smiles that George Stephenson quickly moved ahead of him and 'took to figures so wonderful', probably because he attacked his studies with such enthusiasm. Smiles' informant recalled that,

George's secret was his perseverance. He worked out the sums in his by-hours, improving every minute of his spare time by the engine-fire, there studying the arithmetical problems set him upon his slate by the master. In the evenings he took to Robertson the sums which he had 'worked', and the new ones were 'set' for him to study out the following day. Thus his progress was rapid . . .[12]

At around this time Stephenson also extended his practical qualifications, learning the difficult skill of 'braking' the engines that transported miners and coal wagons to and from the surface. That job required a combination of steadiness, alertness and precision. Any error could easily damage the wagons being drawn out of the pit or even endanger the pitmen's lives. Stephenson worked as a brakesman for several years. During this period he added to his wage of around one pound per week with small sums earned by another skill he had managed by then to acquire, mending (and subsequently making) shoes for the local people. He worked late into the night at improving his reading, writing and arithmetic. His very first efforts at inventing date from this period, when he tried but failed to produce a brake that would automatically reverse an engine. With the long working hours that were customary at the time it would have been a struggle for him to squeeze all his activities into the time available to him. But somehow he did, and he even found time to get married, in November 1802. By then George Stephenson was twenty-one.

He continued studying hard in his spare moments, 'paving the way to being something more than a manual labourer',[13] and he 'set himself to study the principles of mechanics, and to master the laws by which his engine worked'.[14] Smiles depicts Stephenson at this period of his life spending his winter evenings sitting by the side of his young wife and occupied in studying mechanical subjects or modelling experimental machines, when not mending or making shoes, or constructing shoe-lasts, yet another activity which earned a few extra pence. As well as that, he started mending clocks, and found that people in his village were equally happy to trust him with their timepieces and their footwear. Like many mechanically-minded individuals before him and since, he set out to make a perpetual motion machine. Like all the others, he did not succeed.

Smiles exaggerates at times, and Stephenson cannot have been always quite so disciplined and determined as the figure Smiles portrays. But the account of Stephenson's everyday life in his early twenties must be largely

[12] Smiles (1881), p. 11.   [13] Smiles (1881), p. 15.   [14] Smiles (1881), p. 15.

correct, because only someone who could make an enormous and sustained effort to learn would have been capable of making the steady progress Stephenson had to achieve in order to transform himself from an illiterate labourer into an engineer. The French novelist Balzac wrote, perhaps ironically, of making himself into a genius: George Stephenson literally did just that.

In 1803 George's only child was born, Robert Stephenson. Tragically, Robert's mother died before he was two. The record of George Stephenson's life around this unhappy time is incomplete, but between 1802 and 1805 he changed jobs at least three times, moving to Montrose in Scotland, where he was employed to superintend the operation of an engine made by the innovative firm of Boulton and Watt. He impressed his employers with his ingenuity, on one occasion saving them a good deal of money by finding an effective way to prevent sand getting into the water that was drawn into the engine, clogging it up. But his troubles were not over. Returning home from Scotland, he discovered that his father had been blinded in a serious pit accident, and had no income to live on. George's sparse savings went in paying his father's debts. Shortly afterwards, at a time when taxes were rising and poverty was increasing as unemployment rose and incomes fell, large numbers of young men were being called into the military services to quell the unrest, and Stephenson was among those ordered to join up. The only way a man could avoid this was by paying for a substitute to serve in his place: Stephenson was able to do this, but he had to borrow the money. At this time he was understandably pessimistic about the future, and seriously considered joining his sister Ann and her husband who were emigrating to America. Only the fact that he could not afford the transatlantic fare stopped him doing so.

That grim period of Stephenson's life came to an end by about 1808. He was now twenty-seven, and once again working in the Newcastle region as a brakesman. It was a job with less responsibility than the post he had held in Scotland, and less pay, but the George Stephenson of this period was a confident and forceful young man, well aware of his abilities and not shy of displaying his knowledge. He was continuing his education, still conscientiously working on exercises in arithmetic during spare moments, and sending his slate to be marked when he was too busy to get to the teacher himself. Sometimes he used the side of a coal wagon as a blackboard to work on.

Stephenson learned much from the man who taught him during this period, John Wigham, a keen reader and a lively talker who enjoyed discussing ideas with his pupils. Wigham helped Stephenson to learn how to draw plans and sections, and together they worked their way through a book of lectures on mechanics. Stephenson constructed the apparatus required for practical experiments and demonstrations: Wigham supplied the theoretical knowledge needed to make the book comprehensible. George Stephenson was still maintaining the keen interest in machines he had first displayed as a child, and by now he was giving close attention to the education of his son Robert. Despite all the other demands upon his time he managed to be a conscientious parent, taking great pains to ensure that Robert was given the educational opportunities in childhood that he himself had missed. Later, when at the age of eleven Robert started attending a good school in Newcastle, the child's reading and writing skills quickly surpassed his father's, and he learned much that was beyond George's knowledge. The elder Stephenson's own intellectual development benefited from his continuing to be keenly interested in the education of his son.

As soon as Stephenson started work on the new brakesman's job he looked for ways to make economies. He noticed that the ropes which pulled coal out of the pit had been wearing out after only one month, rather than the usual three months or so. After establishing that the reason lay in excessive friction caused by the ropes rubbing together, he quickly remedied the problem by repositioning the pulley wheels. Another intervention during this period involved improving a winding engine by inserting a valve between the air pump and condenser.

Soon afterwards, in 1810, he drew attention to his out-of-the-ordinary capabilities by remedying a serious situation in a nearby pit at Killingworth, where the primitive and inefficient 'atmospheric' engine, of a type invented by Thomas Newcomen at the beginning of the eighteenth century, was failing to pump sufficient water out of the mine shaft for the pit to be workable. The problem had persisted for a year, keeping men out of work and losing money for the mine owners. According to Smiles' account, based on Stephenson's own often-repeated recollection, when George first announced that he could find a solution, no-one was willing to believe that someone who was only a brakesman would possibly be able to succeed where experienced engineers had failed. But after a number of unsuccessful attempts, the increasingly desperate owners finally agreed to let him try. '[Ralph Dodds, a senior engineer] being now quite in despair and hopeless of succeeding with the engine, determined to give George's skill a trial. George had already acquired the character of a very clever and ingenious workman, and, at the worst, he could only fail as the rest had done.'[15]

Dodds located Stephenson that evening ('dressed in his Sunday's suit,

[15] Smiles (1881), p. 20.

on his way to "the preaching" in the Methodist chapel') and asked for his help.

'Well, George,' said Dodds, 'they tell me that you think you can put the engine at the High Pit to rights.' 'Yes, sir,' said George, 'I think I could.' 'If that's the case, I'll give you a fair trial, and you must set to work immediately. We are clean drowned out, and cannot get a step further. The engineers hereabouts are all bet (sic); and if you really succeed in accomplishing what they cannot do, you may depend upon it I will make you a man for life'[16]

And of course Stephenson succeeded. Insisting on employing only men picked by himself, and aware of the ill-feeling of the workers regularly employed on the engine towards a young pit brakesman who was claiming to know more than they did about their own engine and to be able to remedy defects 'which the most skilled men of their craft including the engineer of the colliery, had failed to do', he proceeded to take the engine to pieces. He raised the water cistern that serviced the engine, enlarged one of the inlets, modified various valves, and increased the pressure. This was all done in about three days. By this time heads were shaking, with even Dodds declaring 'Why, she was better as she was; now, she will knock the house down' (that is, self-destruct from excessive vibration). But the engine was started up, and by the same night the water in the pit was lower than it had ever been. Two days later all the surplus water had been removed. The pit workers could finally be 'sent to the bottom' (of the mine) after a year of profitless inactivity.

    This was the big break for which Stephenson had prepared himself, and Dodds made good his promise to make him 'a man for life'. Stephenson's immediate reward was a gift of ten pounds, about £500 or 750 US dollars in the currency of the 1990s and hardly a generous sum in relation to the huge savings his intervention had produced. But more importantly, Dodds gave him a job and promised to keep him in mind for promotion when something better turned up. On the accidental death of the engine-wright at Killingworth in 1810, Stephenson was appointed to the post, at a salary of one hundred pounds per year. That was by no means a huge salary, but Stephenson was able to add to it by taking on extra assignments with the blessing of his employers, a substantial mine-owning company known as the 'Grand Allies'. He was given a horse to ride between the different mines. The pit workman had finally become the engineer.

    In his post as engine-wright at Killingworth, many of Stephenson's responsibilities involved finding improved ways to transport coal and other commodities. From around this time he started to work on tasks

[16] Smiles (1881), p. 20.

that equipped him with the capabilities that would enable him to explore
the possibility of developing engines that propelled themselves. One of his
first duties at Killingworth was to erect a (stationary) winding engine to
remove coal from a mine. It pulled wagons via a rope that was wound
around a revolving drum. At around this time he also designed a 'self-
acting' transport system for coal, in which empty wagons moved up to the
railhead by the power created by full ones moving down an incline. He
also found ways of using the surplus power from the underground
engines that pumped water to the surface, for hauling coal from deeper
parts of the mine. By introducing economies of this kind, as well as using
stationary engines to move coal trucks, Stephenson was able to reduce the
number of horses required in one pit from 100 to only 15 or 16. The mine
owners were quick to see the advantages of doing this, and they put him in
control of the colliery machinery in their other pits.

By now Stephenson was starting to think seriously about the possibility
of introducing locomotive engines. He would have heard rumours of
various attempts to produce engines that reliably moved themselves along
metal rails, rather than merely pulling vehicles from a stationary point.
Steam locomotives of a kind had already been invented. As early as 1804
one was being operated by an engineer from Cornwall in the south-west
of England, Robert Trevithick, but it was not economical. Soon after that
a locomotive to Trevithick's design was constructed at Gateshead, near to
Stephenson's home in the north-east. It was intended to be used at
Wylam, Stephenson's birthplace, but it never worked properly. By 1811 a
number of inventors were trying to develop practical locomotives,
although many problems still needed to be overcome. A reasonably reliable locomotive had been made in Leeds by John Blenkinsop, with
toothed wheels that moved along a racked line. In the long run this did
not prove to be an economical arrangement for moving goods or passengers along flat surfaces, but Blenkinsop's engine was a commercial
success and went on working for several years.

The colliery owner at Wylam, John Blackett, was sufficiently encouraged by the success of Blenkinsop's engine to have a second locomotive
made, despite the failure of the Trevithick engine he had ordered. The
new one, which was built at Gateshead, was designed in a way that combined elements of the Trevithick and Blenkinsop locomotives. This
engine weighed six tons and had a single cylinder and a fly-wheel. It was
described to Samuel Smiles by the engineer who supervised its construction (Jonathon Foster) as 'a strange machine, with lots of pumps, cog-
wheels, and plugs, requiring constant attention while at work'.[17] On

[17] Smiles (1881), p. 33.

completion it was transported to Wylam and attached to a tender containing a barrel of water, but at first it could not be induced to work at all. Eventually, the machinery did start moving. Soon however, Foster told Smiles, 'she flew all to pieces, and it was the biggest wonder i' the world that we were not all blown up.'[18] The engine never worked properly, and shortly afterwards it was dismantled.

Despite his two disastrous setbacks John Blackett did not give up. He ordered Jonathon Foster to make a third locomotive, this time in the workshops at the Wylam colliery. This one, which like Blenkinsop's had a cogged wheel that moved along a rack, was more effective than the others, but although it could pull eight or nine loaded coal wagons it moved at only one mile per hour, sometimes taking six hours to complete its five-mile journey, and was constantly needing repairs. However, a fourth locomotive, which did not use cogs and racks, worked better. Its success demonstrated that as long as sufficiently strong rails were used, locomotives could travel on smooth rail surfaces, contradicting the widespread view at that time that smooth steel wheels running on smooth iron rails would constantly slip.

Stephenson was taking the keenest interest in these developments at Wylam. He had already made considerable economies in the Killingworth pits, but he wanted to reduce even further the need for horse power, the cost of which was constantly increasingly as a result of rising prices. The price of wheat, which was needed in large quantities in order to feed the horses, had almost trebled between 1795 and 1800. As well as keeping in touch with progress at Wylam, in 1813 Stephenson took advantage of an opportunity to see a demonstration of a new Blenkinsop locomotive at Leeds. That engine was impressive: it pulled a 70–ton load at three miles per hour. But it was expensive to run, and unsteady, and regularly pulled its rails to pieces because too much strain was placed on the rack rail at one side. When the boiler blew up shortly after Stephenson's visit the locomotive was not replaced.

So in spite of the progress that had been made by 1813, a locomotive engine that was efficient, economical and reliable had still not been invented. Doing just that was the task George Stephenson set himself. By 1814 George Stephenson was displaying the impressive single-mindedness and the strong sense of direction that observers have remarked upon in Newton and Einstein and other great innovators. In Samuel Smiles' words,

Profiting by what his predecessors had done, warned by their failures and encouraged by their partial successes, he commenced his labours. There was

[18] Smiles (1881), p. 33.

still wanting the man who should accomplish for the locomotive what James Watt had done for the steam-engine, and combine in a complete form the best points in the separate plans of others, embodying with them such original inventions and adaptations of his own as to entitle him to the merit of inventing the working locomotive . . . This was the great work upon which George Stephenson now entered.[19]

By this time in his life Stephenson had finally succeeded in becoming prepared to make a real contribution to the improvement of steam locomotion. Someone knowing only what Stephenson had already achieved by then, and also knowing about the nature of his duties and the facilities that were available to him, might easily have guessed that he would subsequently have earned himself at least a footnote in the history of steam locomotion.

It had taken Stephenson a long time to reach the point of being ready to make a major impact as an inventor. His progress had been slow and effortful. By the summer of 1813 he was already thirty-two. Before reaching the equivalent age Schubert had died, leaving behind him a remarkable body of great music, Charles Darwin had pieced together (but not made public) the theory of evolution by natural selection, and Charles Dickens had already become the celebrated author, having written *Pickwick Papers* when he was twenty-four. By and large, the preparatory years of individuals who produce major accomplishments correspond with the years of childhood and adolescence, but that is not true in the case of George Stephenson. Even the most basic skills of literacy and numeracy were only acquired by him when he was already an adult. And yet even that handicap did not stop him eventually becoming an engineering genius.

Looking back at George Stephenson's life prior to 1813, and asking how and why he had managed to reach the point at which he was finally in a position to begin to establish a reputation as an innovative engineer, we can now be sure that there were no miracles involved: there is nothing totally inexplicable about George Stephenson's progress. Undoubtedly, the journey through life that had eventually led him to that stage was an unusually arduous one: he had to overcome obstacles that were more numerous and more serious than most would-be inventors have encountered. But our reasonably detailed examination of the route by he which eventually arrived at the stage of being ready to make a big contribution has shown that there were no sudden or incomprehensible advances in his capacities.

---

[19] Smiles (1881), p. 36.

Moreover, although Stephenson was a man with an impressive ability to profit from his experiences, and unusually dogged and determined, there are no signs that he learned more quickly or more easily than another similarly prepared and equally motivated and committed person would have done, or that he was able to dispense with the lengthy periods of preparation, practice, and training that others have had to undergo in order to achieve their goals. From afar, it does seem astonishing that someone whose lack of formal education and limited childhood experiences had left him so entirely unprepared for a career as an innovator could ever have come so far, and the fact that such an achievement is so rare adds to our amazement. But from closer up, whilst our admiration is undiminished, his progress no longer seems quite so hard to explain. It does now seem possible to understand how Stephenson gradually became capable of the advances he made.

Even his mechanical skills, extraordinary as they were, give us no reason for believing that Stephenson must have been born with any special gift or talent for learning. It seems more likely that his exceptional competence was the outcome of uncommon learning experiences and unusual determination, combined with remarkable energy. His lack of formal education in childhood certainly deprived him of opportunities for gaining the skills that a person requires in order to be literate and numerate, and yet he did have plenty of opportunities to learn about the practical mechanics of an engine. As we have seen, he was intensely interested in machines, spending a great deal of time closely watching engines in action and repeatedly taking them to pieces and reassembling them. These are precisely the activities that, when engaged in regularly and repetitively, lead to a deep knowledge of the practical working of steam engines.

This account of George Stephenson's gradual but steady progress has provided no reasons for believing that he possessed a special innate aptitude for learning. What marked him out from others was his sustained determination and the sheer intensity of his efforts, rather than the speed at which he gained knowledge and learned new skills. That does not rule out the possibility that some kind of special genetic endowment could have contributed to his success. Although what is known about Stephenson's forbears and his early life makes it seem unlikely that he had an inherent aptitude for engineering, it is conceivable that he did possess qualities that were not gained solely through his experiences. Take, for instance, his unusual determination and willingness to persevere. How did they originate? Do Stephenson's experiences provide an adequate explanation for those qualities as they do for the specific skills he gained, or were the self-confident determination and doggedness that he exhibited as he pursued his goals rooted in innate attributes that he inherited? Research has shown that there are developmental continuities in individuals' temperaments, enabling predictions about adult temperament to be made with better-than-chance accuracy on the basis of measures obtained in infancy.[20] The idea of a relatively complex psychological attribute such as perseverance or determination being directly inherited is scientifically implausible, but it is entirely conceivable that early differences between people in certain aspects of mental state, such as activity level or attentiveness, may indirectly contribute to later differences in more complex traits.

There is no way to know for certain whether Stephenson's early experiences alone created his unusually determined and single-minded personality, or whether innate causes were also involved. But it is possible to speculate on the kinds of childhood experiences that might have contributed to his distinctive personal qualities. The records of Stephenson's early days show that he had plenty of opportunities to learn that hard efforts bring success. He was five feet and ten inches tall, at a time when the average height was six inches less than it is now, and also strong and well-built, despite the fact that his father was unusually thin and his mother is said to have been slight and delicate. Stephenson was always willing to have a go at wrestling or athletic competitions, and in spite of the presence of coal mines in the region where he lived, his childhood was essentially a rural, outdoor one. From an early age he seems to have been well rewarded for being curious and showing initiative. Having to look after younger brothers and sisters would have encouraged him to form habits of accepting responsibility and acting independently.

The likelihood that Stephenson gradually got into the habit of doing things in the ways that led to a person being described using adjectives such as 'forceful' and 'determined' may help to explain his habitual diligence: someone who has *always* worked hard may find labour less daunting than others, and consequently achieve more. All the same, there was nothing easy or inevitable about his progress. He was constantly under pressure. It took plenty of self-discipline to maintain his onerous regime of work and study. We know little about his state of mind, but occasional anecdotes hint at a rigid self-control. Smiles mentions, for instance, that Stephenson had sometimes been persuaded by Ralph Dodds, his superior at Killingworth, to enjoy a lunchtime glass of ale. But on a later occasion, 'on his [Mr Dodds'] invitation to "come in and take a glass o' yel," Stephenson made a dead stop, and said, firmly, "No, I have made a resolution to drink no more at this time of day." And he went back.'[21]

[20] See, for example, Kagan (1989).   [21] Smiles (1881), p. 24.

This response is attributed by Smiles to Stephenson's awareness of 'men about him who had made shipwreck of their character through intemperance'. Smiles was probably wrong about that. Had he had more experience of lunching in pubs or bars he would have noticed that Stephenson was reacting like anyone who has much to achieve and knows what a couple of pints of beer can do to one's firmest resolutions. Stephenson probably felt, with good reason, that he could rarely afford to relax his efforts to get on.

The mature George Stephenson was sure of his own abilities as a practical engineer, but there were situations in which he was troubled by a profound lack of confidence. Until he was into his forties the prospect of having to speak in public put him in agony. He was often uncomfortable about mixing with people whom he perceived as highly educated or privileged. Fortunately, he could always rely on the help of his son Robert, whose education in Newcastle gave him some of the polish that George was so aware of lacking. When books had to be consulted or borrowed, Robert could be counted upon to know his way around the institutions that his father would have found dauntingly unfamiliar.

If George Stephenson's transformation from an illiterate workman at the age of eighteen to a thirty-two-year-old engineer capable of contributing to the practical development of steam locomotion no longer seems mysterious or inexplicable, his phenomenal progress in the next twenty years may still appear to resist explanation. By around 1812 there was considerable interest in the possibility of steam-powered railway travel, and Stephenson was by no means the only inventive engineer who was trying to overcome the remaining barriers. Why was it that this particular individual became the man whom we now regard as a famous engineering genius, rather than any of the hundreds of other engineers who were just as well qualified as he was?

The answer to that question may be easier to find than it first appears to be. We can make useful progress here by raising two additional queries. First, in the period beginning around 1812–14 what further problems needed to be solved in order for steam-based passenger transportation to become a practical possibility? Second, amongst the engineers who were working on steam locomotion at that time, which of them would have been best placed to help resolve a substantial proportion of those problems? When that line of enquiry is followed, the name of George Stephenson is one of the first to surface.

What were the problems that still remained, before passenger travel by railway could be a realistic possibility? There were many, but the following were especially crucial.

First, the accuracy with which it was possible to manufacture the moving parts needed to transfer the power of an engine to its wheels was limited by the primitive technology of the time. As a result, early locomotives shook, vibrated, and juddered to an extent that caused unacceptable wear and tear, as well as being noisy and inefficient. Sometimes engines literally shook themselves to pieces. To resolve these problems it was essential to start producing engine parts that were more accurately and precisely engineered.

Second, no-one was sure how to design effective combinations of locomotive wheels and railway lines. It was still widely (but incorrectly) believed that iron wheels would slip on iron rails. Also, the cast-iron lines then in use were easily dislodged or broken by the weight of the unsprung and often ill-balanced locomotives being made. Some people thought smooth or flanged lines would be more effective if they were covered with grit. Others, who were convinced that the wheels of steam locomotives would travel more efficiently over soft ground, tried (largely in vain) to develop steam locomotives that moved along roads rather than on rails. One of the less successful early locomotives was even propelled by a kind of walking movement instead of power to the wheels.

Third, the practicalities of constructing railway lines in difficult and hilly terrain had barely been considered. No-one knew what inclines were feasible for steam-powered trains. Many people thought that for moving trains over hilly country, stationary engines that pulled wagons along a chain would be more economical than locomotives. Others were not convinced that the uncertain advantages of engine power over horse power would outweigh the manufacturing and development costs.

Finally, so far as practical *passenger* transport was concerned, a huge leap forward was still needed from the stage that had been reached by around 1813. For some time locomotion would continue to be noisy and unreliable, with too much vibration and too little comfort to be acceptable for human travellers. In order for it to be possible to develop railways that were safe, reliable and comfortable, it was helpful to have a period in which gradual improvements could be made to existing steam locomotives, and in which the mistakes that would inevitably arise could be gradually rectified, in circumstances where there was no added pressure from the demand to meet the special needs of passengers.

George Stephenson had the advantage of being well-positioned to respond to all these challenges. His habitual close observation of the action of engines made him acutely aware of the consequences of imprecision in their parts. At first, all that could be done about that was to insist on employing the most skilled craftsmen and to set high standards. Later, in conjunction with his son Robert he established a factory that was dedicated to the manufacture of precisely engineered machine components. He was equally conscious of the need to design and manufacture rails that were strong enough to stand up to heavy trains as well as minimising the power required to pull heavy loads. His experiences as a pit engineer had showed him how important it was to improve the efficiency of rail traction. The unschooled Stephenson was virtually unique among the inventive engineers of his time in having undertaken experiments to discover the actual effectiveness of different combinations of wheels and rails.

During the second decade of the century Stephenson worked hard at achieving both of these objectives. And because he was working in collieries, where the purpose of his locomotives was to transport coal rather than people, he did not have to be immediately concerned about creating travelling arrangements that were sufficiently safe and comfortable to meet the needs of passengers. That was something that Stephenson could worry about later, when he had already succeeded in making locomotives that worked well enough for goods traffic.

The enormous difficulties of constructing railway lines over hilly routes also engaged his attention. He was probably the only engineer alive who had known a railway – albeit a wooden one – running past the house where he grew up. Stephenson's practical and largely intuitive approach to solving engineering problems, in which trial and error had priority over elaborate planning in advance, suited the particular tasks he faced. In the late 1820s he was to become involved in acrimonious exchanges, and was harshly criticised by the commissioners who examined his plans for the railway route that was to link Liverpool and Manchester. They wanted details: Precisely how did he intend to proceed? Exactly how much would each section cost? They accused him of being incompetent because he could not give precise answers to their questions. In many instances he truly did not know, but unlike his inquisitors he knew that in pioneering a new and untried enterprise like building the world's first large-scale railway it is sometimes best to get on with the job without having decided on all the details in advance, and without waiting until success is absolutely certain. Where others insisted on having precise plans and procedures before construction began, he realised that a trial-and-error approach sometimes works better. No-one knew if it was possible to build a railway line over boggy ground: the only way to make progress was to keep trying different approaches until one succeeded.

George Stephenson lived until 1848, but his reputation as a great railway engineer was established by the time the Liverpool and Manchester Railway was opened in 1831. The outline of his career after 1813 was roughly as follows. Between then and about 1819 much of his time went into developing a succession of increasingly efficient and reliable steam locomotives for transporting coal. Compared with the earliest of Stephenson's engines, the *Blucher*, which was completed in July 1814 (and first driven by Stephenson's older brother James) the later ones were better balanced, had more efficient systems for transmitting power to the wheels, and as a result of innovations such as blast pipes and multitubular boilers, were much more powerful in relation to their weight. During this period Stephenson also made other inventions, including a safety lamp that was as effective as the better known one that Humphry Davy designed (with considerable help from his young assistant Michael Faraday[22]) and probably predated it. He also made major improvements in the design of rails and the pedestals or 'chairs' connecting them to the ground and to each other. The rails developed by Stephenson and a partner, William Losh, overlapped, resulting in a considerable reduction in the number of derailments and rail breakages that occurred when rails became misaligned because of the jerks and shocks they received from heavy primitive locomotives running over them.

Although by 1819 Stephenson's engines at Killingworth had been in regular use for some time and were known to be considerably more powerful than the horses they had replaced, they attracted relatively little attention. However, Stephenson was asked to build two other railways, one in Ayrshire and the other in the Sunderland region, starting at a colliery known as Hetton. In 1821 he began work on a more ambitious project, after meeting Edward Pease, a wealthy Quaker who headed a group of industrialists interested in building a railway to transport coal and other merchandise between the Darlington region, which was rich in coal mines, and Stockton, whence materials could be sent by sea to London. The line opened in 1825, and for the first time ever, substantial numbers of passengers were carried by rail.

The success of the Stockton and Darlington railway stimulated interest in a much more ambitious project, a railway to connect the growing industrial centre of Manchester over hilly and sometimes boggy terrain with Liverpool and the sea. In 1831 that railway was finally completed, after a long, stormy and enormously difficult period of planning and construction in which Stephenson was heavily engaged at all stages. For Stephenson this was a time of constant pressure, which even Smiles confesses made him 'occasionally impatient and irritable'.[23] Eventually, however, the line was completed and Stephenson's locomotive *Rocket* demonstrated its superiority over a number of rival locomotives.

The construction of the Liverpool and Manchester Railway was a

---

[22] See, for example, Knight (1985), p. 42.   [23] Smiles (1881), p. 130.

magnificent engineering achievement. The success of that line produced an explosion of interest in railways. This was a key event in the railway revolution. In the 1820s very few people would have seen any sense at all in Stephenson's prediction that England would soon be covered by a network of passenger lines. And yet by the end of 1831 that outcome had suddenly become inevitable. Within a few years rail travel was becoming a commonplace element of everyday life, and George Stephenson's reputation was secure. After 1831 everyone knew about the engineering genius who had begun life as an unschooled child from the family of a poor pit labourer.

Although George Stephenson's lack of formal education did not prevent him from becoming a great engineer, when the word 'genius' is linked to his name it is sometimes preceded by an adjective such as 'practical' or 'mechanical', the intent being to indicate that his capabilities were restricted. Indeed they were, but nobody is an expert at everything. Doubtless Mozart would have made an indifferent engineer and Newton a poor musician. And yet with Mozart the adjective 'musical' is never appended to the term 'genius' with quite the patronising intent that is sometimes evident when writers refer to George Stephenson as a 'practical genius'. It is true, however, that even at the height of his powers Stephenson did have limitations that we might not expect to find in someone widely regarded as being a genius. The biographer who stated that Stephenson's brain 'totally lacked the capacity to store theoretical knowledge, even of the simplest kind'[24] was going too far, but nobody would have claimed that George Stephenson was good at handling abstract ideas, and his mastery of written English was limited.

It is also true that Stephenson was fortunate in being well placed to do what was needed at a particular time. But to varying extents that is the case with all geniuses. Had Einstein been born twenty years later than he was, the likelihood of him making a major scientific contribution would have been much reduced, because he was not equipped to excel at the more mathematically-based approaches on which physics was increasingly relying. The same could have been said about Michael Faraday. With some creative individuals, however, like Mozart or Dickens, it is less likely that a twenty-year alteration in their birth date would have diminished their accomplishments. In Stephenson's case, his reputation does seem to have depended to an unusually large extent on his good fortune in having happened to become equipped with a rare combination of the skills and qualities that were needed in order for essential advances to be made at a particular moment in history.

[24] Rolt (1960), p. 14.

Identifying limitations in George Stephenson's capabilities does not mean denigrating his achievements or denying his greatness, but it does raise a question about the broader implications of what we have learned about his early progress. The evidence of Stephenson's life and achievements proves that it was possible for someone to become a genius despite not having enjoyed a childhood rich in educational opportunities. A question that still remains is whether it is broadly correct to say that early stimulation and encouragement are inessential for the development of any genius, or whether they are only unnecessary for those people whose exceptionality is restricted to certain particular areas of accomplishment, such as engineering.

Despite what we know to be true of George Stephenson, it remains possible that for someone to become capable of many of the kinds of achievements that lead to people becoming known as geniuses, it is necessary for that individual to have enjoyed a rich blend of educational experiences and learning opportunities in childhood. The facts of George Stephenson's life show that someone from a poor and disadvantaged background like his could become a great engineer. But could a person whose early life was similar to his have been a distinguished scientist or mathematician, or a major novelist? We can be certain that success in certain fields would have been ruled out for someone from Stephenson's background. For example, without opportunities to gain basic musical skills during childhood, a successful career as a classical musician is almost ruled out, if only because unless there has been a good early start it is subsequently very hard for someone to find the 10,000 or more hours practising time needed to reach high levels of expertise.

So would it or would it not have been possible for someone whose early life was as circumscribed as Stephenson's to have become capable of high achievements in an area of expertise other than one that his surroundings specifically nurtured? Perhaps not. Some light is shed on the issue in the chapter that follows, which examines the early life of Michael Faraday, the scientist. Faraday had a vast impact on nineteenth-century chemistry and physics despite having left school at thirteen and being the child of a family almost as poor as Stephenson's. But as we shall see, Michael Faraday's scientific achievements were only possible because he was given some opportunities that were never made available to the young George Stephenson.

At the funeral of Charles Darwin in 1882 it was noticed that the dark clothes of the mourners in Westminster Abbey were brightened by coloured beams of light from a window-panel commemorating George Stephenson and his son Robert. Shine on!

4 Michael Faraday

Michael Faraday's scientific discoveries in the first half of the nineteenth century created a huge advance in the understanding of electricity. His many achievements made it possible for others to begin harnessing electricity's power, a leap forward that has transformed all our lives. As I write, electricity runs my computer and lights the room: it also powers the printer on my desk. None of that could have been imagined at the time Faraday was born.

How and why did Faraday become capable of his remarkable accomplishments? The challenge of explaining that seems an especially daunting one because, like George Stephenson (and unlike Charles Darwin), Michael Faraday came from a very poor family. Born in 1791, he grew up in London. He had to leave school at thirteen, and then spent seven years as an apprentice bookbinder. That is hardly a promising start for a great scientist.

Even Stephenson's compensations eluded Faraday. George Stephenson had benefited from the fact that his working environment kept him supplied with opportunities for practising the skills that made him a capable engineer. The circumstances of his everyday working environment helped him to gain many of the skills an engineer needed at the beginning of the nineteenth century, a time when engineering was still largely a matter of combining practical know-how and commonsense knowledge. But becoming a scientist has always been a very different matter. Knowledge of the everyday world cannot grow into scientific understanding, which is sharply distinct from practical common sense and often opposed to it.[1] A scientist has to take a mental stance that is reflective and detached, and scientific thought has to be grounded as much upon abstract information from books as on direct observation and experience.

The poverty of Faraday's early years could very easily have held him back. People today find it hard to imagine how someone whose life as a child so conspicuously lacked the kinds of opportunities we associate with

[1] Wolpert (1992).

a scientific education could ever become a major scientist. Understanding how he became a scientist at all seems difficult enough. Yet the young Michael Faraday did overcome these handicaps. How was he able to do that?

Finding an explanation becomes a little easier if we avoid viewing Faraday's progress from a narrowly twentieth-century perspective. Things look different when his early experience is seen in the context of a child's life at the beginning of the nineteenth century. Take, for instance, the fact that Faraday left school at thirteen. In today's world that would make it virtually impossible for a young person to get a solid grounding in science. People who learn about Faraday's childhood naturally assume that being able to stay on at school would have made a big difference for Faraday, as it would nowadays. But in Faraday's time, even if he had remained at school for several more years, the chances were that he would have received no scientific education at all. Even good schools taught little or no science then. As we have already seen, at Shrewsbury School, regarded as among the finest in England, Charles Darwin (born seventeen years after Faraday) and the school's other pupils were taught absolutely nothing about science. So it would be wrong to think that leaving school early deprived Faraday of a scientific education.

Faraday's long period of apprenticeship to a bookbinder is another fact of his early life that might appear to have ruled out his becoming a scientist. Once again, however, the real circumstances justify closer scrutiny. Certain aspects of Faraday's situation as an apprentice, when seen in the context of the period, were actually not at all unfavourable. One particular advantage was that throughout these years he was fortunate in having a good employer. George Riebau, whose business happened to be located round the corner from Faraday's home, was a bookseller as well as a bookbinder. Before starting his apprenticeship at the age of fourteen, Faraday had already been employed for a year by Riebau and his wife, delivering newspapers. They were kind and generous to him. The business provided an agreeable working environment in which there was always time for lively conversations. Riebau deserves credit for the fact that Faraday was not the only of his apprentices to do well: one eventually became a professional singer and another was a well-known comedian. Towards the end of Faraday's apprenticeship, when he was twenty-one, it was Riebau who arranged for him to be given some much-sought-after tickets to Humphry Davy's hugely popular lectures on chemistry at London's Royal Institution, initiating the all-important connection with a leading scientific figure that was to make Faraday's own career in science a real possibility. Michael Faraday made no secret of his debt to Riebau. Many years later he dedicated some volumes of scientific notes to him, remarking that, '. . . you kindly interested yourself in the progress I made in the knowledge of facts relating to the different theories in existence readily permitting me to examine those books in your possession that were any way related to the subjects occupying my attention.'[2]

Another big advantage of Faraday's workplace during his adolescent years was that it was filled with books. This was hugely important at that time. Books then were not only beyond the means of the poor, but pricey even for those who were comfortably off. The new books which Faraday could inspect as soon as they arrived at Riebau's shop included ones that would have seemed expensive luxuries even to a reader whose family was as wealthy as Darwin's. No school library at the time would have held a comparable collection of recent books on scientific topics. So in that respect Faraday was privileged, far from being disadvantaged.

Also, with the sciences being less fragmented then than now, and not so specialised, grappling with a new volume would not have been quite such an arduous undertaking as it would be today. A twentieth-century reader needs to have gained a solid grounding in the appropriate field in order to stand any chance of mastering an advanced monograph in a scientific specialisation. In Faraday's time most new books on science would have been accessible to a determined amateur. For a keen autodidact like him, Riebau's shop was a virtual treasure trove.

Yet another benefit Faraday enjoyed was that his work as an apprentice gave him the practical expertise demanded by his research. His skill at making apparatus and measuring instruments was often remarked upon. In the course of a lifetime in which he conducted thousands of experiments using apparatus made by himself, his competence at constructing equipment definitely added to his productivity. It was especially helpful that Faraday's employer allowed his workshop to be used for making electrical devices. Mr Riebau permitted his apprentice to create a small laboratory at the back of the shop, and if he felt any alarm at seeing the craft of bookbinding taking second place to the science of electricity, he never protested. The science of electricity owes much to Riebau's forbearance.

So the young Faraday's actual circumstances were nothing like so bleak as the bald statement that he left school at thirteen to be an apprentice bookbinder appears to imply. Even so, Faraday's early life was far from being an ideal preparation for a scientist. Although the premature ending of Faraday's schooling may have done him no damage so far as scientific knowledge was concerned, it definitely penalised him in other ways,

[2] Quoted in Williams (1965), p. 10.

leaving gaps that could only be filled by a strenuous programme of self-education. The kind of formal education that Faraday missed gives a child resources that someone who leaves school early is bound to lack, and poverty creates problems for any young person. So even if the circumstances of Michael Faraday's apprentice years were not quite so grim as they intially appear to have been, and would not have entirely prevented him from becoming a scientist, they were hardly calculated to make him into one. (Incidentally, Michael Faraday was not the only towering figure of his century to have gained from being employed by a kindly bookbinder. The great Mexican reformer Benito Juarez (1806–1872) was similarly favoured. Juarez, a Zapotec Indian who arrived in the city of Oaxaca speaking little Spanish, was enabled by his employer's generosity to train as a lawyer, and he eventually became president of Mexico.)

To discover why and how Faraday's life took the remarkable course it did, we need to take a closer look at the young apprentice's activities during his formative years. That is not easy, partly because for someone who was as celebrated during his lifetime as Faraday was, the biographical record of his childhood is regrettably sparse. His family were very poor (so much so that at the age of nine Michael had to survive for a whole week on one loaf of bread), partly because Faraday's father, a blacksmith, was often prevented from working by illness. His mother, the daughter of a farmer, had been a chambermaid before she married. She was a warm-hearted parent and immensely proud of Michael, but according to his biographers her own education was minimal.[3] His father could at least read and write. Faraday claimed that all he learned at school was reading, writing and simple arithmetic, and in his view that amounted to very little. Yet limited as his schooling was, it gave him more than he may have realised. Merely being able to read would have made it easier for Faraday, compared with an illiterate youth like George Stephenson, to add to his own knowledge and begin educating himself.

We know almost as little about the first years of Michael Faraday's apprenticeship as we do about his early childhood, but four years after the apprenticeship began his father recorded that although Michael had found things difficult at first, he soon 'as the old saying goes, got the head above the water'[4] and was very happy in his post. Most of Faraday's time as an apprentice went into his everyday work. Riebau's benignly observant eye noticed that the boy's mind was always busy. He saw that for young Faraday even a daily walk would turn into an expedition. Like the youthful Charles Dickens, Faraday as a child was a constantly alert observer of life, but while Dickens' attention was captured by people and

[3] Jones (1870), p. 8.   [4] Jones (1870), p. 11.

the ways in which they treated one another, Faraday – as Riebau noticed – concentrated on the physical world: 'he went an early walk in the Morning Visiting always some Works of Art or searching for some Mineral or Vegitable curiosity – Holloway water Works Highgate Archway, Middlesex Water Works – Strand Bridge – Junction Water Works etc. etc. . . his mind ever engaged.'[5]

As we have seen, the adult Michael Faraday was deeply grateful to Riebau for the opportunities he had been given to read books. In the earliest years of his apprenticeship Faraday's reading was wide rather than deep, the choice of material often being decided by whatever happened to come to his attention in his work as a binder of books. He read the *Arabian Nights*. He devoured novels, probably including Fanny Burney's *Evelina*:[6] there exists a copy of that bound by Faraday himself. Following Riebau's advice, Faraday copied down observations that struck him as insightful and reproduced illustrations that impressed him. He was always curious about new and interesting things.

Little is known about the way in which Michael Faraday began to gain an elementary knowledge of science. All that is certain is that between the ages of fourteen and eighteen he had plenty of opportunities to read and learn, that he took advantage of them, and that by eighteen his interests were largely directed towards the sciences. Perhaps the growth of his enthusiasm about science was fairly gradual: until he was sixteen or so he may simply have been excited by the unfamiliar and exotic world of knowledge which books opened up for him. But by the time he was eighteen his thirst for knowledge had become decidedly strong, and at around this period, probably in 1810, he was attracted by a number of items he encountered in *Encyclopaedia Britannica*. He told a friend that his mind had been turned towards science by an article on electricity written by James Tytler, which he came across when binding that encyclopaedia.

By then Faraday had changed from being a boy who was curious and energetic like many young people, to something rarer: an intense, exceptionally diligent and keenly committed would-be scholar. Somehow or other, Faraday had made himself into a reasonably well-informed young man with a serious interest in the sciences. He had already mastered a number of books on chemistry. It is possible that he had begun to form some vague career ambitions in which learning and scholarship played a part. By the end of 1810 he was a decidedly studious and disciplined individual, and already possessed a remarkable capacity – reminiscent of the young Isaac Newton – to keep persevering until difficult learning challenges were mastered.

---

[5] Quoted in Williams (1965), p. 11.   [6] Williams (1965), p. 11.

How did that change take place? In order to begin to understand Michael Faraday's genius and its origins it is important to know how it was possible for the young man to transform himself into a scientist, despite the obstacles created by the fact that he had left school so early. How was he able, notwithstanding his lack of formal education, to make himself into such a studious and well-informed young adult?

Riebau's observations apart, disappointingly few insights into Faraday's state of mind at that time have been made available, either by Faraday himself or by his contemporaries. But the fact that his workplace was a stimulating one certainly helped. A real advantage of Faraday's working environment was that it gave him some of the learning opportunities normally associated with schooling, but without any of the dull uniformity imposed by school routines and compulsory classes. His studying science was his own decision, not his teachers'. Science had no negative associations for him. He may also have been attracted by the comfortable or even glamorous lifestyles of the educated people he came across in Riebau's shop. But that is unlikely to have been a major influence, since Faraday was always a somewhat unworldly individual.

Yet these advantages would hardly have compensated him for all that he was missing. Faraday's limited schooling would have left him ill-equipped with the mental skills and study habits a serious student needs in order to succeed at the arduous and time-consuming struggle to become a scientist. At first, lacking any basis for making well-informed decisions about what to read, Faraday must have looked at any books on science that happened to attract his attention. But during the years of his apprenticeship Faraday's choice of reading had to become less random. He would have needed to introduce a degree of planning into his learning activities, since without it an unschooled person's haphazard reading can easily lead nowhere.

Perhaps Riebau helped by drawing his young apprentice's attention to those books that he thought would be most helpful to him. However, it is just as likely that the self-discipline of a serious student was acquired by Faraday's own efforts, even though that would not have been at all easy. Being attracted by books is one thing, but persevering at the prolonged study of them that is necessary in order to master their contents is much more difficult, and especially so for a young person who has had little encouragement to acquire the habit of regular studying. The advantages of Faraday's workplace and the excellence of Mr Riebau certainly provided benign influences, but even their combined effects cannot have been enough to account for the unschooled boy's remarkable transition into a serious young scholar of science. Plenty of young people are given more advantages than Faraday had without ever managing to create anything special or distinctive. So Faraday's self-made transformation still remains largely unexplained. But until it is accounted for, we cannot be sure that there was no magic or mystery about the causes of Faraday's genius, or improve on those 'magic ingredient' pseudo-explanations that I criticised in Chapter 1, which blithely attribute genius to the effects of ill-defined inborn gifts and talents.

Fortunately, some further information comes to our aid here, powerfully assisting our efforts to explain. Faraday was greatly helped at this time by two other unusual circumstances. These, in combination, made all-important contributions to his progress, giving him the extra help he required. First, he benefited from his family background. This was unusual in the extent to which it supplied just those qualities that help a young person to become capable and productive. Second, he had the luck to discover a remarkably useful 'self-help' volume for would-be scholars. There has never been a shortage of books designed to assist people who wish to educate themselves. One that Faraday encountered turned out to be exceptionally helpful and perceptive: it was the ideal guide for someone like him.

Consider Faraday's background in the light of Mihalyi Csikszentmihalyi's research findings (described in Chapter 2), who pointed towards some of the benefits that young people gain from receiving a combination of stimulation and support at home. Taking the former component first, stimulation, ostensibly Faraday's early life was far from being advantaged in this respect. In such a poor family as his there would have been neither the money nor the time to permit much attention being given to a child's education. However, Faraday's case is unusual, because there was a strong compensating influence arising from the fact that during his crucial adolescent years his working environment as an apprentice was a strikingly stimulating one. Riebau's shop would have provided in large measure any learning opportunities that the young Faraday may have lacked at home. As a result, in spite of his family's poverty, Faraday's daily life would have been more than adequately provided with the first of the two essential components identified by Csikszentmihalyi, stimulation to learn.

Just as importantly, Faraday was also blessed with a home background in which Csikszentmihalyi's second component, structure and support, was provided in abundance. At first glance it may appear not at all likely that these qualities could have been prominent in the family of a poor blacksmith who was often unwell. Nevertheless, they were. The reasons why become clear from a brief description of Michael Faraday's very unusual family circumstances.

Faraday and his relatives belonged to a close-knit religious sect that was distinctive in a number of respects, one of them being the extent to which its members provided mutual support for one another. Throughout his life, Faraday was an active member of this dissenting Christian group, known alternatively as the 'Glasites' and the 'Sandemanians'. The sect had originated in the late 1720s, when a Scottish Presbyterian minister named John Glas became convinced that since the alliance between church and state is not sanctioned in the Bible, it could not be justified. Glas's ideas brought him into conflict with the church authorities, leading to his deposition in 1730, but sufficient members of his congregation had been converted to his views for him to create a new church, at Dundee. By the middle of the eighteenth century the movement had grown and was well established. It had a simple creed, based on fairly literal observance of the words and spirit of the New Testament. There was a pronounced ascetic element, and firm injunctions to help the poor and avoid accumulating material wealth. Within the sect there was much emphasis on giving mutual support and acting with kindliness.

Being Sandemanians affected the lives of Michael Faraday and his family in a number of ways that would have influenced his temperament and personality. At least in principle, the Sandemanian faith did not weigh down its adherents with either the sense of guilt or the feelings of fear that were encouraged by other Christian sects. Members of the congregation could feel calm and serene, thankful for Christ's sacrifice, happy to be denied worldly goods, and cheerful about the absence of worldly pleasures in their lives, knowing that this was pleasing in the eyes of the Lord. Members of the sect supported each other and depended upon one another, working to maintain consensus within the group and avoid strife. Michael Faraday's own air of serenity was often remarked on, and it was an obvious source of strength for him.

The Sandemanian church was a central element of the home background in which Michael Faraday grew up. As well as being mutually supportive and governed by clear rules and obligations, its members placed emphasis on stability. Adherents were serene and calm, kindly but somewhat controlling, and relatively untroubled by guilt and anxieties. For Faraday the Sandemanian church was a safe haven which he could always fall back on and rely upon. The sect would have given him precisely those elements of support and structure that Csikszentmihalyi's research has identified as being instrumental in helping young people to cope with the demands of independent studying. Crucially, it provided precisely the kind of background that makes it possible for a young person to get into the habit of engaging at those activities that demand sustained concentration.

In short, despite his family's poverty and his lack of formal education,

Faraday as a teenager was not by any means starved of those resources that nourish a young person's mental development: the essential elements were firmly in place. Daily life in Riebau's business provided intellectual stimulation, and his family's membership of the Sandemanians helped to ensure that he could rely on the firm advantages provided by having a stable and supportive home background.

The second unusual advantage that Faraday enjoyed arose from his good fortune in encountering a book which told him how to become a serious student. The title of the book was *The Improvement of the Mind*. The author, Isaac Watts, who died in 1748, is remembered today as a writer of hymns. These include some of the most beautiful in the English language, such as 'When I survey the wondrous cross . . .' and 'Joy to the World . . .'.

Faraday himself regarded Watts' book as having been enormously influential in his development into a competent scholar and scientist. It probably became available to him in 1809, when Michael Faraday was eighteen. One biographer[7] notes that an edition of this book was published in that year, and suggests that Riebau would have stocked it for sale in his shop, where Faraday may have discovered it. However, there were earlier versions, including one printed in 1801, and if that was the one Faraday came across, he could have read it earlier than 1809. In any case, Faraday made very considerable use of the book, and in a letter written in 1812 he described Watts as being 'great in all the methods respecting the attainment of learning'.[8]

Isaac Watts' *The Improvement of the Mind* is one of the very best in a long tradition of self-improvement books addressed to readers who are keen to extend their knowledge and mental skills. It was not written just for unschooled people who needed to educate themselves, but a self-educated person like Michael Faraday would have been especially likely to profit from it. The author had thought at length about the learning activities that result in a person gaining the intellectual powers that furnish an educated mind, and as a practical guide, *The Improvement of the Mind* is not at all inferior to most of the 'How to Learn' books that are to be found in bookshops today. As a source of insight into the experience of becoming educated it is considerably better. Watts' book would have helped Faraday to decide on effective daily study activities. It would also have extended his understanding of the ways in which a student can add to his abilities by building on what is already known.

The book has twenty chapters on a wide range of topics, including reading, lectures, acquiring new languages, 'fixing the attention',

---

[7] Williams (1965), p. 12.   [8] Quoted in Jones (1870), p. 16.

memory, reasoning, observation, and learning from conversations. Throughout it Watts emphasises the necessity for a student to make sure that the process of learning is as active and as meaningful as it can be. Watts warns readers against assuming that a clever individual can become a wise person without having to bother with learning and studying. As he puts it, 'it is no idle thing to be a scholar indeed'. But on the other hand, 'neither must you imagine that large and laborious reading and strong memory can denominate you truly wise',[9] because:

It is meditation and studious thought, it is the exercise of your own reason and judgement upon all you read, that gives good sense even to the best genius, and affords your understanding the truest improvement. . . . but if all your learning be nothing else but a mere amassment of what others have written, without a due penetration into the meaning, and without a judicious choice and determination of your own sentiments, I do not see what title your head has to true learning.[10]

Throughout *The Improvement of the Mind* there is repeated insistence on the need for the student to be more than a passive recipient of other people's knowledge. Watts advises learners against having too much reverence for the books they read. He tells them not to hesitate to use a book in any way that serves the learner's needs, for instance by marking contents, underlining words, clarifying, and supplementing or reorganising passages which are unclear. Following some pages of down-to-earth advice about learning from a book (for example, Watts advises learners not to get too anxious if not everything is clear at the first reading, and to 'mark what is unknown to you, and review whole chapters, pages or paragraphs'), Watts encourages taking a robustly critical and even sceptical approach to a book's contents. Advice like that would have been especially reassuring for someone like Faraday, because self-educated learners are especially prone to think that the printed page has more authority than it actually has. The injunction against too reverential a stance towards the contents of books provides a needed balance. Watts urges, for example,

if [the writer] does not explain his ideas or prove the positions well, mark the faults or defects, and endeavour to do it better . . .

If the method of a book be irregular, reduce it in to form by a little analysis of your own, or by hints in the margin: if those things are heaped together, which should be separated, you may wisely distinguish and divide them:[11]

---

[9] Isaac Watts, *The Improvement of The Mind: or a Supplement to the Art of Logic:* (containing a variety of remarks and rules for the attainment and communication of useful knowledge in religion, in the sciences, and in common life. To which is added, *Discourse on the Education of Children and Youth*: two parts, complete in one volume). Printed by J. Abraham, Clement's Lane, Lombard Street, 1801.   [10] Watts (1801), pp. 6–7.
[11] Watts (1801), pp. 34–5.

Reading *The Improvement of the Mind* would also have made Faraday more aware of the necessity to undertake a number of different activities that all contribute to learning. Reading is essential, Watts agrees, but reading on its own is insufficient, and the student must think about the material he has read. Study is vital, but it is not enough to simply remember the material. Careful thought is important, but it is only effective in conjunction with information that is accurate and reasonably detailed. Attendance at lectures is valuable, but in order to get the most from them the student needs to take notes during the lecture and go over them and revise them afterwards. The acquisition of new information is also vital, but it is equally necessary to be able to distinguish between words and things. A student should never be contented with learning lists of words and phrases, without properly understanding them, 'less your laboured improvements only amass a heap of unintelligible phrases, and you feed upon husks instead of kernels'.[12]

Watts' writing manages to be erudite and practical at the same time, and Faraday's confidence in himself as a scholar would almost certainly have increased as a consequence of his having access to it. The book offers convincingly down-to-earth advice about the procedures and activities that result in effective learning. That would have helped Faraday to gain a broad view of the possible route by which he could achieve his aim of educating himself. Prior to encountering *The Improvement of the Mind* he had probably formed some idea of what he wanted to achieve as a learner, but without a proper knowledge of how to do that he would not have been at all certain that his rather vague goals were realistic. Watts' book showed Faraday how he could move ahead. It gave him a clear picture of what was possible. Armed with it, Michael Faraday would have gained some idea of what had to be done in order to make further progress. His initially vague aspirations would have started to seem like practical possibilities, ones that could be achieved by making sensible plans and diligently following them.

Fortified by what he had learned about the process of becoming a scholar from Watts' guide, and helped by the calm and supportive background of his own home life and the stimulating environment of his apprenticeship, Michael Faraday now threw himself into the pursuit of a scientific education. By around the time he became eighteen in 1809 Faraday had already made himself into a reasonably well-informed young man who had a serious interest in the sciences and had already mastered a number of books on chemistry. By the end of the following year he was a studious and disciplined individual, capable of persevering until difficult learning challenges were mastered.

[12] Watts (1801), p. 107.

From about that time Faraday's progress as a scientist can be plotted in greater detail. We know about the lectures and meetings he attended, the books and scientific papers he read, and the friends and instructors who taught and encouraged him, and with whom he discussed his ideas. Numerous examples of Faraday's own notes and illustrations still survive. There is substantial documentation of his activities, in the form of papers, reports and letters. These make it clear that his efforts to learn were well planned and thorough, involving a larger range of enterprises than before. He was taking Watts' advice seriously. At around this time there may have been a marked acceleration in the intensity of his efforts. He was extremely conscientious about his studies, and very diligent, going to great lengths to follow to the letter the advice he received from *The Improvement of the Mind*.

For instance, Faraday reported that when he started attending lectures in 1810 he would habitually take a number of steps, all as recommended by Watts, to ensure that he gained the maximum profit from them. First, during the lecture (where he usually made sure he had a seat in the front row) he would be careful to write down on a sheet of paper 'the most prominent words, short but important sentences, titles of the experiments, names of what substances came under consideration and many other hints that would tend to bring what had passed to my mind'.[13] Next, as soon as he arrived home after the lecture he would start on a second set of notes prepared from the original ones but 'more copious, more connected and more legible than the first'. Using these notes he then proceeded to write out the whole lecture. The notes he had taken made this possible, because they served to remind him of the detailed topics that had been mentioned and to indicate the order in which the different parts of the lecture had presented and in which the various experiments had been described. With the assistance the notes provided, Faraday was confident that he could then supply the rest of the information from memory. In this manner he was able to reconstitute the whole of a lecture. He found that he could do that with a fair degree of accuracy.

Proceeding through all these steps must have involved much time and effort, even a degree of obsessiveness. But there is no denying the effectiveness of this meticulous procedure: by the time Faraday reached the end of it he would have internalised a firm and detailed version of the lecture. Faraday was a model student, a young man who regularly carried out the study activities that 'How to Learn' books sensibly advise but which few of their readers are sufficiently painstaking to practise. These

[13] Quoted in Williams (1965), p. 16.

learning procedures adopted by the young Michael Faraday – making good notes, writing information out in one's own words, attempting to reconstitute a lecture on the basis of the notes one has taken – are all ones that do indeed help students to retain information in a readily accessible and usable form. Since Faraday's time, the effectiveness of the study activities he engaged in, following Watts' recommendations, has repeatedly been confirmed in empirical investigations.[14]

Csikszentmihalyi's findings undoubtedly help us to understand why the activity of studying may have been less burdensome for Michael Faraday than for other boys of his age. Even so, it is still not entirely clear what, in those late teenage years, impelled Michael Faraday to work so intensely as he did at his studies. What drove him on? Reconstructing the motives of a long-dead individual is tantalisingly difficult, and it has to be based partly on speculation. Doubtless a number of different factors had a role in spurring his efforts. As we have seen, the manner in which people spend their time partly depends upon habit, and Faraday's circumstances would have favoured a studious and diligent outlook on life. In addition, his increasing scientific knowledge, and the sense of accomplishment that he gained from it, would have pleased him and sharpened his curiosity. Today we are not entirely comfortable with the notion of 'thirst for knowledge' as a driving power, but science for Faraday was unquestionably new and must have seemed genuinely exciting. For him science would not have evoked any of the boredom that can be induced by overfamiliarity or too much time spent in the company of the bunsen burner. Another motivating force may have been a broadly-based desire for self-improvement. Samuel Smiles admired Faraday as a great scientist and saw him as a marvellous exemplar of 'self-help', despite the fact that his knowledge of Faraday's early life happened to be somewhat hazy. And with Faraday having a strong religious faith, it is also possible that a wish to reveal the works of God may have been a major spur to his efforts.

There were conflicting elements in his personality, which have never been satisfactorily explained. Michael Faraday's contemporaries claimed to see a fiery and passionate temperament behind his calm outward manner. That tension could account for the observation that his behaviour sometimes appeared obsessive and over-controlled. However, when we are trying to come to grips with the causes of genius it is important not to assume that the unusual is necessarily synonymous with the pathological. Instances of that fallacy are not uncommon, an example being a recent Darwin biographer's taking that scientist's casual remark that his work was sometimes a solace to him as evidence of a neurotic personality.

---

[14] See for example, Howe and Godfrey (1977).

It is true that geniuses are often far from ordinary in a number of ways. The sheer force of their enthusiasms is often extraordinary, as is their single-minded devotion to particular interests. Some geniuses, like Newton, might conceivably be regarded as having been egocentric to an extent that justifies calling their actions 'pathological'. Simply because geniuses are exceptional, it is perhaps inevitable that some of the descriptive terms others apply to them are ones that are often associated with abnormalities that take pathological forms, creating in people's minds a link that may be illusory. In the particular case of Faraday we can note that although it is certainly possible to describe his efforts as being obsessive, that word could just as fittingly be applied to the majority of exceptionally creative individuals. Furthermore, the act of labelling a person as obsessive does little to help reveal the actual causes or motives underlying his or her activities.

The rate of Faraday's progress towards changing himself into a well-informed amateur scientist was undeniably impressive, but perhaps no more so than might have been expected in an unusually well motivated young learner who was capable of persevering at the intense regime of learning and study activities that Faraday set himself. In that respect Faraday was not unlike Stephenson. The immense enthusiasm for learning that is seen in both these men, amounting almost to a hunger for it, is to some extent characteristic of intellectually curious individuals who are conscious of having missed out on schooling and anxious to catch up.

As with Charles Darwin and George Stephenson, when Michael Faraday's steady advance towards becoming an exceptionally capable individual is carefully charted, we conspicuously fail to encounter any obvious gaps or sudden leaps: each new capability or fresh understanding can be seen to build upon ones that have already been gained. There is no point at which Faraday inexplicably magnified his capabilities or suddenly expanded them. In making that observation I do not claim that any person sharing Faraday's intense motivation and devotion towards learning would necessarily have made equivalent gains. Yet there is clearly no need to assume that Faraday could not have made the progress he did unless he possessed some inherently special powers of learning. Nor are there any convincing reasons for believing that Michael Faraday was innately more clever than most other people. Outside his particular areas of interest he was not noticeably well-informed: he never seemed to know much about the crucial political events of his lifetime, for example. And far from regarding himself as being unusually intelligent, he was always conscious of what he perceived to be limitations, particularly in regard to remembering. He seems to have been convinced that his memory was defective. He may have been right about that, although it is possible that the lapses which distressed him were no more than the absent-mindedness of someone whose deep preoccupation with his own particular interests restricted the amount of attention that could be directed to the external practicalities of everyday life.

As in the case of George Stephenson, what is most impressive of all about Faraday's achievements as a student is not the size of the learning gains he made relative to his efforts, but the sheer magnitude of the efforts. So if we are to look for qualities in Michael Faraday that resist an explanation based on his unusual experiences and mental activities, it is more likely that they will involve his exceptional determination and capacity for sustained concentration on problems than his learning or thinking capacities as such. But as we have seen, there is every reason to believe that no special explanation is required. His remarkable powers of determination and concentration were nurtured by his experiences, and fuelled by an understandably acute desire to learn.

At least up to the stage of his life when he reached the age of twenty-one in 1812, there is no evidence at all to suggest that the contributing causes of Faraday's capabilities were fundamentally different to the various influences that help determine ordinary people's abilities. Faraday was remarkable and extraordinary, of course, but the influences that resulted in him gaining exceptional capabilities do not appear to have been fundamentally different from the ones that have enabled other people to acquire more ordinary levels of competence. Nothing that has been observed in the course of Faraday's life up to this point provides any grounds for believing that his progress was assisted by exceptional mental processes, or by special inherent qualities that are exclusive to geniuses. No firm indications exist of innate gifts or talents playing a role. Nor is there any evidence that Faraday possessed fundamentally enhanced learning powers or especially speedy cognitive processing capacity, or totally inexplicable powers of creativity.

Aided by the advice he encountered in *The Improvement of the Mind*, Faraday's efforts to educate himself from 1810 until the completion of his apprenticeship in 1812 took the form of an organised campaign. The regime he followed would have ensured that someone as strongly motivated as him, and as able to tolerate long periods of hard effort, could hardly have failed to acquire a sound grounding in what was known about chemistry and physics at the beginning of the nineteenth century. He was always very aware of his lack of formal education, and during those years he almost certainly overestimated the benefits that other young people gained from the schooling he had missed. At that time he believed that only by Herculean efforts on his part could the lost ground be made up. Only later in life did he start to appreciate that an education which is largely directed by the learner's own choices and voluntary decisions has advantages as well as limitations, and in certain respects can be the best kind of education there is.

The range of Faraday's learning activities broadened. Attending and writing-up lectures were not the only ways in which he pursued his aims for self-improvement. In 1809 he had begun to keep a journal in which he collected items of scientific information that came to his attention. He organised a discussion group. From his tiny income he saved money to purchase primitive equipment that enabled him to replicate some of the experiments he had read about, in particular ones exploring the powers of electricity. He started writing letters on scientific and philosophical matters to a friend, Benjamin Abbott, a clerk who worked in the City and had similar interests to his own. This correspondence continued for years, on a frequent and regular basis. He also took serious steps to improve his command of written language, arranging weekly lessons which he persisted at for seven years. He even had instruction in drawing, benefiting from the presence of a talented emigrant from France who may have been lodging in Riebau's house at the time. All these educational activities are recommended in *The Improvement of the Mind*.

By the summer of 1810, as well as going to scientific lectures, Faraday had started to give occasional lectures himself. The ones he was regularly attending at that time took place at meetings of a group known as the City Philosophical Society, which had been established in 1808 by a Mr John Tatum. The meetings took place in Tatum's house, and on alternate Wednesdays Tatum himself would lecture there on some aspect of science. At a time when societies played a major role in the dissemination of scientific knowledge, Faraday would have found the meetings – with the opportunities they provided to discuss ideas with like-minded individuals – congenial and stimulating. On those weeks when Tatum was not lecturing the other members took turns to contribute. It was at one of these occasions, probably in April 1810, within a few months of his beginning to listen to Tatum's lectures, that Faraday's own first lecture was delivered. It was on electricity. By then he had already read fairly widely on that subject and knew about a variety of rival views that had been put forward. Even at the time he gave his first lecture he was sufficiently confident to advocate an approach to his topic that sharply diverged from the one favoured by Tatum.

Faraday has often been described as having been self-educated, but so far as the actual content of his education was concerned, that designation is slightly misleading in his case. His independent efforts were conspicuous in the initiating, arranging, controlling and directing of his educational arrangements, but not in the process of instruction. He learned much from various people, making excellent use of the help he was given by a number of individuals who served him as teachers and lecturers. Taken together, all the various learning and studying activities that Faraday undertook during these years gave him a scientific education that was superior to anything that could have been obtained from most schools at this time, especially in the sciences.

Yet despite all the progress he had made, when his apprenticeship came to an end in 1812, Faraday, now almost twenty-one, found himself with no prospect of a job that would permit him to pursue his scientific interests, let alone one in which he would be paid to practise the skills and knowledge that he had so painstakingly acquired. It is hard to believe that Faraday had not given some thought to the question of how he might find a position that did not involve him spending his days binding books, a prospect that could not have seemed attractive to a young man who in most respects had become highly educated. But perhaps his religious faith as a member of the Sandemanian sect had encouraged him to take an attitude of 'take no thought for the future'. In any case, by October 1812 Faraday was fully aware of his predicament, and was in despair. He was still working as a bookbinder, but reluctantly. He ached to leave his job and find a better alternative, and yet he could see no prospect at all of finding a satisfactory situation. Even forty years later, Thomas Huxley, Darwin's vigorous disciple and the founder of a scientific dynasty, was complaining that anyone who chooses a scientific life 'chooses not a life of poverty, but so far as I can see, a life of *nothing*, and the art of living upon nothing at all has yet to be discovered'.[15] Paid positions for scientists were very rare. For a young scientist with no university qualification and no good connections they were almost non-existent. As Faraday wrote to a friend, 'indeed, as long as I stop in my present situation (and I see no chance of getting out of it just yet), I must resign philosophy entirely to those who are more fortunate in the possession of time and means.'[16]

Then, quite suddenly, his fortunes improved, and Michael Faraday found himself with an excellent position and a powerful mentor. That word is perhaps too narrow to cover the range of roles through which mature, well-educated or wealthy individuals have provided assistance to ambitious young people in want of resources that are necessary in order to get ahead. A minority of geniuses, including Stephenson, Newton and Einstein, have depended only to a limited extent upon this kind of assistance. Sometimes parents have served as a young person's most important mentors, as did James Mill (who himself benefited as a young man

---

[15] Quoted in Newsome (1997), p. 71.   [16] Quoted in Williams (1965), p. 28.

from having a wealthy sponsor) for John Stuart Mill. Some geniuses have received help from a number of different individuals. Charles Darwin, for instance, was given considerable assistance by his sisters (who taught him as a child), his father, his brother, and by a variety of university scientists, notably Robert Grant at Edinburgh and John Henslow at Cambridge.

Faraday's powerful mentor was Humphry Davy, the celebrated chemist. Davy was not the first person to be helpful to Faraday, of course. Riebau had done much to encourage him in the early years, and others, such as Tatum, aided him at a later stage. But Davy's patronage was especially significant, because he commanded a position right at the apex of British science.

There was a large element of luck in Faraday's gaining a post with Davy, although it was not a matter of luck alone. Faraday had already been fortunate in his choice of employer when he began his apprenticeship. Perhaps even at that time Faraday or his father might have perceived that Riebau would prove unusually kind and encouraging, although it is more likely that nobody had anticipated just how favourable the circumstances of his apprenticeship would turn out to be. With Faraday's second major stroke of luck, he was taken on by Humphry Davy as an assistant at the Royal Institution. Davy's highly original research in chemistry and his reputation as a popular lecturer had made him one of the most fashionable British scientists of the time, and undoubtedly the most glamorous.

Faraday knew just how valuable a chance he had been given. He had done all he could to bring that about, having brought himself to Davy's attention earlier. He had also approached Sir Joseph Banks, the wealthy and powerful naturalist who in his twenties had travelled around the world with Captain James Cook in the *Endeavour*. But Banks was now almost seventy, and not prepared to exert himself on behalf of a young man he had never heard of. However, largely by chance, Faraday's efforts to gain Davy's help did succeed. At a moment that might have been precisely calculated to cater for Faraday's aspirations, the irresponsible behaviour of Davy's laboratory assistant prompted his employer to look for a replacement. It quickly became obvious that the eager young Michael Faraday was the ideal candidate.

Faraday had known about Davy's work well before 1812. Two years earlier he had read a book entitled *Conversations on Chemistry* by Mrs Jane Marcet, in which she gave a clear account of the views that Davy was propounding in the highly acclaimed series of lectures he delivered at the recently founded Royal Institution. Their original purpose had been to disseminate knowledge to the artisan class, but the audience soon came to be dominated by young ladies who flocked to see this brilliant and attractive young scientist, and tickets were hard to obtain. Faraday was given some tickets early in 1812, and he was enormously impressed by hearing and seeing Davy, whose research was beginning to reveal the immense importance of electricity in chemistry. In October of that year, Davy suffered an eye injury, and needing a helper for a few days he temporarily employed Michael Faraday. But once this very brief period of work ended, Davy had no further need for assistance, and when Faraday wrote to Davy in the following December, enclosing some examples of his writing and asking about the possibility of a job, Davy was unable to help.

Quite suddenly however, Faraday's situation changed dramatically, when the Royal Institution's laboratory assistant was discharged after getting involved in a brawl. Faraday, startled by a footman's thundering knock on the door of his home as he was undressing for bed one evening, saw a carriage in the street and discovered that he had been summoned to talk to Davy at the Royal Institution the next morning. He was quickly appointed to the post of laboratory assistant at one guinea (just over a pound) a week, roughly what Stephenson had been earning at the same age, but with the added benefit of rooms in the Institution as well as fuel, candles and aprons, and – most important of all – the privilege of using the Institution's apparatus for his own research.

Michael Faraday's appointment as Davy's assistant was a momentous event in his life. It brought him into touch with prominent scientists and their activities. His efforts in earlier years had made him well prepared for the post, and he rapidly made a reputation as an able assistant whose efficiency and reliability would have been especially noticeable because of their absence in his predecessor. Even the physical dexterity that augmented his experimental expertise gained him favourable attention. As well as performing his duties he immediately plunged into research of his own, and he was often asked to assist with lectures at the Institution. He did not neglect his own general education and his plans for self-improvement, and with a group of friends he arranged weekly mutual-improvement meetings, in which members read to one another and helped each other by criticising and correcting their essays and other writings.

An interesting feature of the Davy–Faraday relationship is that in some respects it anticipates arrangements that are more characteristic of today than of the early nineteenth century. In the present century mentoring functions in science have tended to become diffused and institutionalised. Among Nobel prizewinners, for instance, the status and prestige of the institution a young scientist attends, and the extent to which it attracts active scholars and keeps in touch with current developments, may be at least as crucial as the personal assistance provided by individual mentors.[17]

[17] Zuckerman (1977).

As Harriet Zuckerman has shown in her research into the careers of Nobel prizewinning scientists, a typical prizewinner will have attended one of a small number of prestigious universities and gained advantages from working with high-ranking scientists, will have had access to good facilities, and will also have become known to other active scientists as a person who is associated with a highly regarded institution.[18] At the Royal Institution Faraday would have enjoyed similar advantages, even though his relationship with Davy was always formal and not particularly close, and strictly confined to scientific activities. Like Faraday, Davy, who was only thirteen years older than him, had known poverty in his early life, but the two men could not have been more different. Where Faraday was modest and unworldly, Davy was ambitious and urbane, with an eye for worldly success.

Someone as vain and egocentric as Davy was might appear to have been a less than ideal candidate for the role of mentor. Unsurprisingly, the relationship between the two men was clouded at times. A biographer who had known Faraday for the last thirty years of his life perceived that, 'Davy was hurt by his own success. He had very little self-control, and but little method and order'.[19] Faraday himself, his first biographer reported, 'has been known to say that the greatest of all his advantages was that he had a model to teach him what he should avoid'.[20] Yet Davy's sheer enthusiasm for science was infectious, and Faraday would have been inspired as well as intrigued by the great chemist's eagerness to talk about his current interests to anyone who would listen, and think aloud about the problems he was engaged on, as is evident from the reports of Davy's thoughts and speculations that pepper the journal made by Faraday in the eighteen-month period he spent accompanying his employer on the European mainland. In that respect at least, Davy, for all his faults, would have been a better mentor for a young scientist than Faraday ever could have been, despite his being an excellent lecturer and a more generous and less selfish individual than Davy. Unlike the extroverted Davy, Faraday found it impossible to think aloud and would rarely discuss his own ideas with other people until they were fully formed. He was a very private man. Faraday was not unfriendly and did not lack a sense of humour, but there were firm limits on his everyday sociability. There was a spirit of exclusivity in the Sandemanian sect which had such an important place in his life, and this made Sandemanians seem antisocial to outsiders. Even within the sect socialising was largely restricted to Sundays.

These constraints do not seem to have impeded Faraday's development as a scientist. Sundays apart, his scientific interests filled most of his

---

[18] Zuckerman (1977).   [19] Jones (1870), p. 190.   [20] Jones (1870), p. 190.

available hours. In many of his day-to-day relationships with other people his predominant role was that of either learner or teacher. He tended to avoid social events if he could, especially after his marriage in 1821, and that freed him from distractions that would otherwise have interfered with his scientific work. On Sundays his scientific activities were temporarily forgotten: during the weekly period of respite from his work Faraday's mind was occupied with his fellow Sandemanians and their mutual faith. He played a leading role in the sect and was a frequent preacher. That pattern of life persisted until his death.

Newton's response to the question of how he was able to achieve his prodigious accomplishments, 'by working on it continually' is valid for virtually all great innovators in the arts or sciences. As I have already remarked, every creative individual has to find a way to form some kind of protective shell that cuts out mundane disturbances and makes lengthy contemplation possible. In Faraday's case, that was achieved by his adopting a persona that kept him partly detached from other people and their concerns. He was totally uninterested in political issues, his 400 surviving letters barely mentioning the turmoils and crises that for many people were burning issues. Modest and genial, he was rarely unkind, but he put sharp limits on his involvement with others. For all his serenity and goodness, the sense of a sharply defined personality who is forceful and effective in his dealings with the outside world is less evident in accounts of Faraday than it is in contemporary reports of other great innovators. Although his humility and benevolence were often remarked upon and he was conscientious in meeting his obligations – making young relatives and other visitors welcome in his laboratory and enthusiastically entering into their games, going to enormous lengths to produce lectures that were as clear and effective as he could make them, putting special efforts into the science lectures for children which he introduced at the Royal Institution – he was in many respects a solitary scholar. He was happy to know that his lectures were enjoyed by the many people who attended them, and his audiences included literary figures like Dickens as well as scientists such as Darwin. But he usually avoided having students working under his supervision. He admitted that when he and an assistant were working in his laboratory, many hours might pass without a word passing between them. So far as was possible, he worked unaided, and as he undertook the routine work on an experiment, his mind would be totally engaged in his thoughts. As one of his biographers put it, Faraday's dialogue was with nature.[21]

---

[21] Williams (1965), p. 99.

Faraday's horizons expanded when Davy, having recently married a wealthy widow, embarked in October 1813 on a long tour of Europe, taking Faraday with him. With characteristic recklessness Davy chose to begin the visit at a politically sensitive moment, with France and Britain seemingly on the verge of hostilities. Until then Faraday had hardly travelled at all, and even the Devon scenery which he passed through on the journey to Plymouth came as a surprise, rapidly altering his ideas about the nature of the earth's surface. The tour lasted almost eighteen months, and it involved visits to the major European cities and the laboratories of a number of prominent scientists, including Vauquelin and Ampère. The journal Faraday kept at the time, and his letters to friends, demonstrate that, predictably enough, he continued to learn from the sights and experiences he encountered. Less predictably, during this period there occurred one of the few emotional crises that disturbed Faraday's habitual serenity and threatened to destroy his self-control. During the first year of the tour neither Faraday's letters nor his journal gave any hint that things were going anything but well, but quite suddenly, in a letter written in November 1814, Faraday poured out his heart to a friend, saying that he had been unhappy for some time and wished he had never left home. The ostensible reason was the behaviour of Davy's wife. He found her haughty, proud, and snobbish, and said that she never stopped talking. She seemed to enjoy taunting and humiliating those within her power. The naive and unworldly Faraday, 'believed at that time that she hated me and her evil disposition made her endeavour to thwart me in all my view and to debase me in my occupations'.[22]

He eventually did learn to cope with her, but one cannot help wondering whether Lady Davy really was the sole cause of Faraday's unhappiness. Perhaps he was simply very homesick, and he might have attributed to her a larger role in forming his mood than her actions really justified. At the beginning of the tour, Davy, whose own servant had refused to accompany him on the tour, had asked Faraday to take on some of the duties of a valet, a request which Faraday was in no position to refuse. Humphry Davy may not always have been considerate to his part-time valet, and if that was the case Faraday would have found it hard to admit to himself at the time that the great scientist and admired mentor on whom his livelihood depended was far from perfect. The tour of Europe would have given Faraday endless opportunities to observe his patron's less attractive sides, and being always at the beck and call of an employer who had fallen from grace in his eyes would have been unpleasant for the young Sandemanian.

---

[22] Quoted in Williams (1965), p. 40.

Davy was certainly haughty on occasions. Around 1816 he happened to be in dispute with George Stephenson, then an unknown engineer, concerning the question of who was the true inventor of a safety lamp for miners. Each of them had independently developed a lamp at roughly the same time. Davy was petulant, arrogant, and thoroughly disagreeable, snobbishly refusing to accept that an uneducated man who was claiming to have forestalled him could be anything but an imposter.[23]

Despite the difficulties, Faraday survived his period on the European mainland and returned to England maturer, more knowledgeable about science, a little more worldly-wise, and better prepared to embark on independent research of his own. A month after his return to England in 1815, not yet twenty-four, he was promoted at the Royal Institution to the important-sounding post of Assistant and Superintendent of the Apparatus of the Laboratory and Mineralogical Collection, at an increased salary. He continued to work with and for Davy, who encouraged him and acknowledged the assistance Faraday gave him, although there were soon to be serious disputes between them. These culminated in 1824 in Davy's making himself appear ridiculous as well as vindictive in a vain attempt to bar Faraday's admission to the Royal Society. But Faraday was now less dependent upon Davy than he had been when he first began to work at the Royal Institution, and he had more contact with other prominent chemists, such as William Brande. Michael Faraday was now giving numerous lectures himself, and he soon found himself being frequently called upon to use his expertise as an analytical chemist in order to advise industrialists on practical questions. Within a year of his promotion at the Royal Institution his first scientific paper had been published, quickly to be followed by others.

The twenty-five-year-old Michael Faraday was now on the road to becoming a major scientist, having prepared himself superbly for a productive life in science. Of course, it was still not inevitable that he would be exceptionally successful, and for that to happen his subsequent creative efforts had to be extraordinary. But that further progress did not need to be either magical or mysterious. Although Michael Faraday's years of careful preparation may not have made his later achievements certain or even probable, they did much to help make them possible. And however impressive and even dazzling the creative feats of Faraday's mature years as a scientist were, they present no features that are qualitatively harder to account for than are those advances that generated his earlier progress. The feat of climbing Mount Everest may have once seemed a complete mystery, but as soon as we learn how climbers could reach the point of establishing a base camp close to the summit we can perceive that the whole ascent is possible after all. Similarly, the discovery that Faraday's earlier development into an accomplished scientist required no miracles, makes it seem likely that his later achievements too, for all their extraordinariness, can be accounted for along broadly similar lines. Once again, the facts do not point to a need for inherently special powers that are unique to geniuses. The challenge of explaining Faraday's genius confronts us with problems rather than mysteries.

Even in comparison with the very few other highly promising young scientists who were engaged in research at the time and might have been regarded as Faraday's potential competitors, Michael Faraday at twenty-five had some distinct advantages. His position at the Royal Institution made him as well placed as anyone to conduct experiments and to learn about new discoveries and developments. It has also been suggested that even the fact that – partly as a consequence of his being self-educated – his mathematical competence was restricted may have worked to his advantage. That is indeed possible, because the more mathematical approach that he might otherwise have favoured could have imposed unhelpful constraints at that particular stage of scientific discovery.[24] Michael Faraday's extreme diligence was a further strong asset, and so too were the practical skills, acquired in his apprenticeship, that made him such an expert at building scientific apparatus. Finally, Faraday's religious beliefs, which inclined him to perceive his work as part of an enterprise that helped to reveal the secrets of a divinely created universe, may have been especially congruent to the conceptualisation of physical phenomena (in terms of fields and forces) that was central to the scientific progress he made.

Michael Faraday conducted thousands of experiments and made many important discoveries. His reputation as a major scientist was sealed when he discovered electromagnetic induction, just a year after George Stephenson's place among the great inventors had been secured by the opening of the Liverpool and Manchester Railway. Coincidentally, in the month of Faraday's most earth-shaking discovery Charles Darwin was making the decision that led to him embarking on the voyage of HMS Beagle, setting in train the series of creative thoughts that eventually resulted in yet another momentous achievement.

[24] Williams (1965).

Every so often my daily newspaper has an item on a child prodigy. Some of these reports are followed up over periods of years. That happened in Britain with the chess-playing Polgar sisters and with a few young mathematicians, such as Ruth Lawrence. Other prodigies are quickly forgotten by the media. In most of the cases it is obvious that one or both of the child's parents has gone to some length to stimulate the young person to make better than average progress. To differing extents, instances like these of precocious development accompanied by close parental involvement in the child's progress are manifestations of a deliberate plan to transform children into extraordinary men or women. Often there has been an intention to equip the young person with exceptional capabilities. In a few instances the parent has consciously set out to create a genius.

The belief that genius can be manufactured has had some influence on the upbringings of a number of outstanding individuals. Naturally, the forms of the parents' plans for their children have varied. Certain fathers have made a firm decision to produce a superior individual, and have actively pursued that intention, more often than not with a certain flair and a degree of success. James Mill, the father of the great nineteenth-century thinker John Stuart Mill, firmly belonged in this category. So too did the father of the eminent American mathematician Norbert Wiener, who founded the science of cybernetics, as did the parents of an unhappy contemporary of his, William Sidis. The actions of many other parents have betrayed a similar striving to make a child exceptional, although many of them would never have admitted to having that intention. A number of parents, often people whose own educational opportunities had been restricted, have begun investing large chunks of time and attention in their child's early education after becoming intrigued about the possibility of accelerating a young person's progress, perhaps from reading a newspaper or magazine article. And there is a further category of parents who became convinced, in some instances even before their child was born, that fate had decreed that the child was destined for greatness. Some of these people – who include parents of Yehudi Menuhin, the architect Frank Lloyd Wright, and the economist Maynard Keynes (whose mother worried about him working his brain too hard even before he reached the age of two[1]) – have gone to immense lengths to give their child special opportunities. Despite that, some of these parents have been inclined to see their own actions as being ones that merely nurtured an existing natural talent, rather than active interventions designed to create special abilities.

Certain other parents who have become heavily involved in activities designed to help a child to gain exceptional abilities have been members of cultural groups in which it has been customary for the parents to decide upon a child's vocation. Family traditions have played a part here. These parents have often made a start at a very early stage in their child's life, and there may have been little or no provision for the child's own desires to influence the training activities. The early musical experiences of the famous Chinese cellist Yo Yo Ma reflect a modern form of this kind of background. The childhoods of Wolfgang Mozart and his sister, Nannerl, exemplify earlier versions of these practices.

All these parents have been alike in going to lengths that many would think extreme in order to invest in their children's futures. The motives have varied, although in many cases the parents have been men or women who believed themselves to have been prevented from making the best of their own careers. Some were immigrants who could not fulfil their ambitions because they were unable to restart their professional career in a new country. Others have been disadvantaged men or women determined to give their children opportunities that were denied to themselves. Often these people have had time on their hands, or they have possessed more surplus energy than would be present in individuals with demanding careers of their own. A notable exception is James Mill, the father of John Stuart Mill. As we shall discover, James Mill put enormous efforts into giving his son a remarkable early education at the same time as being engaged in a massive intellectual project of his own.

How successful have these efforts to produce superior children been? To assess the effectiveness of the parents' activities it is necessary to pose two distinct questions. First, to what extent has the intention to equip a child with special knowledge or skills been achieved? Second, how effective have the parents been at ensuring that their child also gained the broader kinds of competence that a person needs to have in order to enjoy a productive and fulfilling life? These wider capacities include various practical attainments and social capabilities that make a young person

---

[1] Skidelsky (1983).

independent and self-sufficient, and mature enough to be able to get on with other people.

Compared with the challenge of instilling a young person with extraordinary special abilities, succeeding at these broader aims appears to be a goal that can be more easily achieved. After all, most ordinary mothers and fathers do manage to make their children independent and socially competent, while only a small minority of parents have children who become extraordinarily accomplished. And yet, amongst those parents who have deliberately set out to make their child superior in some or other respect, an appreciable number have succeeded at that seemingly difficult aim while failing at the apparently less daunting one of making sure that their child gains the qualities that make a person independent and socially mature.

That pattern of success and failure may seem paradoxical, but there is a reason for it. The very same influences that lead to certain men and women deciding to make an especially heavy emotional investment in their child's progress can also blind people to important practical realities. This is especially liable to happen with those parents who most closely identify with their children, and who have a tendency to experience successes vicariously, through their child's triumphs. In some cases, families can become too inward looking, with parents and children being overly dependent upon one another. The adults may fail to appreciate that children have to be encouraged to strike out on their own and lead their separate lives, even when that involves moving in directions other than the ones the parents would have chosen for them. It may be difficult for the parents to accept that in order to develop into self-sufficient adults, with their own sense of direction, children need to be given opportunities and experiences that help make that possible. Unless they are encouraged to make their own decisions (and their own mistakes) they may never become capable of making sensible plans and choices. Similarly, young people who have had no opportunity to share experiences and play activities with other youngsters are likely to lack some of the social skills that are required for getting on with others.

Just how badly things can go adrift is illustrated by the tragic case of William (Billy) Sidis (1898–1944). As a child, Sidis was described as 'the most remarkable boy in the United States'.[2] He was an indisputably brilliant child prodigy. He taught himself Latin at the age of four, and by the time he was six he could speak and read eight languages. Between the ages of six and eight he wrote four books and invented a new language. He passed the Harvard Medical School anatomy exam and also the entrance

---

[2] Wallace (1986), p. 47.

examination for the Massachusetts Institute of Technology. It was confidently predicted that he would become a great mathematician. He was admitted to Harvard at eleven, and at the same age he delivered a brilliant two-hour lecture on four-dimensional space to the Harvard Mathematical Club. Yet Billy Sidis never fulfilled his promise. After graduating from Harvard he suffered a mental breakdown and became increasingly eccentric, refusing to engage in any work that made proper use of his intellectual abilities. In spite of his early brilliance, as an adult he failed to produce a single creative achievement. Sidis died young, at forty-six: poor, unhappy, unemployed and unfulfilled.

What went wrong in his case? The answer is not immediately obvious. The education his father provided for him was unusual, but it was neither narrow nor unenlightened. The elder Sidis claimed to be strongly opposed to the use of any pressure or compulsion in education. He was critical of the educational practices of the day, arguing that teachers and parents should pay more attention to children's own interests. Billy Sidis's father was never deliberately cruel, and his teaching methods were less harsh than those of certain other parents whose children, unlike Billy Sidis, did go on to enjoy creative and successful adult careers.

And yet it is not difficult to find reasons for Billy Sidis's failure. Although his parents were highly effective at accelerating his mental development, they let him down badly in other ways. They failed to teach their son to be independent and capable of looking after himself, with the result that until he was well into adolescence he was unable to get dressed properly or even keep himself clean. His father did not seem to understand that a growing child needs physical as well as mental exercise, and healthy outdoor activities. Also, both parents were too inclined to show their son off, partly in order to demonstrate the soundness of their own educational theories. In particular, they seem to have been too self-obsessed to appreciate that a young prodigy may need to be protected from the sometimes intrusive interest of the press. One consequence was that Billy Sidis, whose all-too-evident social immaturity contrasted sharply with his mental excellence, was often ridiculed in newspaper articles.

Most crucially of all, Billy Sidis suffered from a painfully unhappy home life. The family was dominated by the destructive struggles of the parents. Both of them were selfish and overbearing people, preoccupied with fighting their own battles against each other and the outside world. Neither parent was at all sensitive to the emotional needs of their growing son. Consequently, the home background conspicuously lacked the supportive structure that is one of the two essential elements highlighted in the findings of the research by Csikszentmihalyi into family background influences on young people's progress. Although Sidis was given lashings of intellectual stimulation he could never rely on the equally vital benefits of having a supportive and structured home environment.

Happily for others, the case of Billy Sidis was unusual in the extent to which its disastrous aspects outweighed the positive consequences of the parents' efforts. In other instances in which a child's upbringing has been broadly similar to that of Sidis, the resulting triumphs and failures have been more closely balanced. One especially valuable source of insights into the likely consequences of a situation in which parents have formed the deliberate intention of making their child into something approaching a genius is the autobiography of the distinguished American mathematician Norbert Wiener. In contrast with Sidis, Wiener did have a successful and highly creative adult career, although in other respects the two men's upbringings were remarkably similar. Both were brought up in the Boston area and were students at Harvard University. Although Wiener was three years older than Sidis, the two knew each other moderately well. Like Sidis, Wiener was a remarkable child prodigy: in his childhood and early adult life he experienced many of the same advantages and a number of the same difficulties that Sidis encountered.

Norbert Wiener's childhood was almost as unusual as that of William Sidis. He was born in 1894. When he was a young child his family moved to Boston, where his father, Leo Wiener, a philologist who was fluent in a number of languages as well as being a good classical scholar and an amateur mathematician, found a position at Harvard University. The family background of Norbert Wiener was like that of Billy Sidis in a number of ways. Both sets of parents were recent Jewish immigrants to the United States. Both fathers had arrived in America in the 1880s from Russia, where they had been highly precocious in their own childhoods. Each father had a variety of intellectual interests and held strong (and similar) views on education, a topic which they both wrote about at length. Both of them were described by others as being noticeably intense and fiery men, ambitious and full of energy, and somewhat domineering and overbearing.

Leo Wiener's views about education had been influenced by a book – which he translated into English – written by an Austrian cleric named Karl Witte. In 1800, on the birth of his son (another Karl Witte), Witte had formed the intention of making the boy into 'a superior man'. He and his wife proceeded to do just that, with considerable success, and the son eventually became an influential literary authority on the Italian poet Dante. The Witte parents' approach was sound and down-to-earth. Although the father was determined that his son should be encouraged to become outstandingly able, his main priority was to make sure that the young man would also be healthy, strong, active and happy. As the proud parent reported to his readers 'in this, as everybody knows, I have succeeded'.[3]

Karl Witte was impressed by young children's curiosity and enthusiasm to learn, and he was acutely conscious that opportunities to teach them are often wasted. If only a parent would seize these chances, Witte observed, 'What an immeasurable amount a child will learn in six, eight or ten years, that is, in 3,650 days, in 36,500 hours, reckoning the day at ten hours, if every conversation with him or in his presence teaches him something!'[4]

The perspicacity of that observation has been amply confirmed by twentieth-century research findings. In one recent investigation, for instance, it was observed that three-year-olds from different social classes differed considerably in the scope of their spoken vocabularies. Searching for an explanation, the researchers discovered enormous variations in the children's actual experiences of language. Even by the age of three, those children who came from professional families had already heard more than thirty million words directed specifically towards them. In sharp contrast, children from working-class families had heard around twenty million words, and children in families living on welfare had heard only ten million words, on average.[5] This demonstration of the huge variability in children's early experiences, and the likely consequences, underlines Karl Witte's good sense in drawing attention to the numerous opportunities for learning that are present in the early years of a child's life. It also illuminates the depressing extent to which such opportunities are commonly wasted, even today.

Pastor Witte was convinced that despite the prevailing view which held (then as now) that a person's achievements largely depend upon inborn aptitudes and talents, in reality the child's opportunities to learn during the early years formed a more crucial influence. Like conscientious parents today, Witte and his wife went to great pains to fill their boy's waking hours with as rich and as varied a range of experiences as they could provide for him. They were ahead of their time in having an intuitive understanding of the fact that acquiring a good grasp of language greatly amplifies a child's mental powers. They saw that language 'makes the child intelligent at an early time, for it puts his attention and his several mental powers continuously in action. He is obliged always to search, distinguish, compare, prefer, report, choose, and in short he must work, that is, think.'[6] Knowing that, they made sure that their boy

---

[3] Howe (1990), p. 230.   [4] Witte (1975), p. 86.   [5] Hart & Risley (1995).
[6] Witte (1975), p. 75.

learned many things in the arms of his mother and in my own, such as one rarely thinks of imparting to children. He learned to know and name all the objects in ten different rooms, the rooms themselves, the staircase, the yard, the garden, the stable, the well, the barn, – everything from the greatest to the smallest, was frequently shown and clearly and plainly names to him, and he was encourage to name the objects as plainly as possible.[7]

For a growing child, the Witte parents were formidably careful guides. They took care to make sure that their son was exposed to all kinds of objects and events, and they drew his attention to the most informative and interesting aspects of the things they showed him. They let him see watermills and windmills, owls and bats, as well as concerts and operas, and even lions and elephants. Always they took pains to explain things carefully, in ways that a young child could understand. They made sure that he noticed whatever was important, and encouraged him to respond. Consequently the child 'became accustomed to what he had seen and heard, and he himself addressed us, enquired, reported, retorted, etc.'[8] And he was stimulated to understand the objects and events he witnessed not 'by merely staring at them, as children generally know them, but thoroughly'.[9]

When he was translating Witte's book, Leo Wiener must have been struck by the Wittes' unusual sensitivity to their child's feelings and wishes. He could not have failed to notice the importance they placed on making sure that the child was always motivated to engage in the learning activities they provided for him. With reading, for example, the parents went to some lengths to be sure that, before any kind of instruction was given, the child definitely *wanted* to read. Pastor Witte also drew attention to the necessity to keep things informal when encouraging a young child to learn. On one occasion he discovered that the child had been put off learning to read because his mother had been teaching in too formal and heavy-handed a manner. Afterwards, the father was especially careful to delay teaching new reading skills until the boy had clearly demonstrated that he was eager to acquire them.

From Norbert Wiener's account of his early years it is clear that although his father had been greatly influenced by Witte's book, Leo Wiener's somewhat domineering personality made it impossible for him to match either the Wittes' relaxed informality or their genuine sensitivity to the feelings and wishes of their son. Leo Wiener was not perceived by his son as an ideal teacher, and in some respects his faults exceeded those of Billy Sidis's father. He was often insensitive and overbearing. As the adult Norbert Wiener recalled, 'He tended to impose his amusements

[7] Witte (1975), p. 71.   [8] Witte (1975), p. 81.   [9] Witte (1975), p. 81.

and preferences on those about him without fully realizing that many of them might have come to a fuller participation in a life together with him if this participation had not been so obviously enforced.'[10]

That tendency to impose on others seems to have been a hallmark of Leo Wiener's personality. It was especially evident in his teaching methods. According to his son, Leo Wiener's lessons were neither gentle nor relaxed. Norbert Wiener recalled how, 'He would begin the discussion in an easy, conversational tone. This lasted exactly until I made the first mathematical mistake. Then the gentle and loving father was replaced by an avenger of the blood. The first warning he gave me of my unconscious delinquency was a very sharp and aspirated "What!"'[11]

Yet his father's excesses did not stop Norbert Wiener from making a success of his life. Unlike Billy Sidis, Norbert Wiener did survive his childhood and adolescence more or less intact, even if the process of growing up was not all easy for him. But he found it painfully difficult to break away from his parents in early adulthood and become an independent person with a life of his own.

There was more than one reason for the fact that Norbert Wiener eventually managed to break away from his family and get started on a creative career, whereas Billy Sidis stayed defeated by the miseries of his childhood and adolescent years. Examining the crucial differences between the two is helpful here, shedding light on a number of the positive and negative influences that are likely to emerge when parents allow their child's upbringing to be influenced by the idea of trying to manufacture a genius. One important difference was that Wiener, unlike Sidis, could readily see his parents' positive sides. These compensated for and perhaps outweighed the negative ones. Norbert Wiener perceived that for all his faults his father was something of a hero, always admirable, sometimes warm and loving, constantly enthusiastic. As he put it, 'my father was a romanticist . . . His righteousness partook of the elemant of élan, of triumph, of glorious and effective effort, of drinking deep of life and the emotions thereof. For me, a boy just starting life, this made him in many ways a noble and uplifting figure, a poet at heart . . . my taskmaster was at the same time my hero . . .'[12]

Also, Leo Wiener's help and support could always be relied upon. That was still true even when Norbert had reached the advanced stage of preparing for his doctoral exams at Harvard. Norbert Wiener particularly dreaded the oral component of the examinations, but he could still count on his father's assistance, and 'Every morning he went for a walk with me to keep up my physical condition and to reinforce my courage . . . He

---

[10] Wiener (1953), p. 18.   [11] Wiener (1953), p. 67.   [12] Wiener (1953), p. 74.

would ask me questions concerning the examinations that were ahead and would see to it that I had a fair idea as to how to answer them.'[13]

Throughout Norbert Wiener's childhood there were enjoyable experiences as well as frustrating ones. His childish curiosity was never discouraged. His mother read to him often, and living in a house that was populated by a large collection of books which he could see being regularly used and enjoyed, he quickly came to see the value of being able to read by himself. There was plenty of encouragement for his efforts to learn reading. Predictably in these circumstances, Norbert Wiener quickly became a voracious reader. His parents responded by feeding his curiosity in a number of ways. They kept him supplied with the kinds of books that nourish a child's imagination, such as *Treasure Island* and *The Arabian Nights*, as well as factual books that answered his questions and added to his knowledge.

So Wiener's early life at home was one of incessant intellectual stimulation. Scholarly activities surrounded him. 'Ever since I can remember', he recalled, 'the sound of the typewriter and the smell of the paste pot have been familiar to me'.[14] The social and intellectual milieu of his parents' lives brought solid practical advantages. For example, Norbert's father could seek out suitable books for him from the library at Harvard, and also the Boston Public Library, where he was friendly with several of the librarians. One of them (who was married to a writer of children's books) had a daughter who Norbert played with. Better still, a number of neighbours and family friends were active scholars. Next door but one lived an eminent mathematician, and Norbert and his sister were friendly with his children. A little further along the road there was a close friend of Norbert's mother who was married to a distinguished physiological chemist, and Norbert was encouraged to make use of his library. Other family friends whose lives and interests were intellectually exciting included Walter Cannon, the famous physiologist (whose own early life as the son of a railway worker had been one of real poverty, like Michael Faraday's and George Stephenson's), and a brilliant Assyriologist, Muss-Arnoldt. Both of these men talked to the child about their interests. Cannon showed him the recently-developed X-ray machine he was working with and explained how X-rays were beginning to contribute to the study of the human body. Norbert's father had serious interests of his own, of course, and he was always keen to tell his son about them. He taught him botany as well as mathematics, introduced him to the study of farming methods – another enthusiasm – and took Norbert with him on fungi-collecting expeditions. Unlike Billy Sidis's father, Leo Wiener was

[13] Wiener (1953), p. 172.   [14] Quoted in Howe (1990), p. 134.

healthily aware of the benefits of vigorous outdoor pursuits and physical activities.

In short, Norbert Wiener benefited from having a childhood that was extraordinarily richly supplied with the intellectual nourishments that stimulate the growing mind of a child who is eager to learn. By the standards of most people his home environment was an intellectual hothouse, but to him it seemed entirely natural. He thrived in it. He learned to perceive intellectual pursuits as routine elements of everyday life, and had regular opportunities to see how people went about their scholarly activities. As a learner he was given every opportunity to become capable and self-confident. He discovered that mental effort definitely paid off. His own experiences taught him that the enterprise of adding to his mental skills and his knowledge was often useful, sometimes exciting, and usually within his grasp.

He was certainly an unusual child, as is apparent from Wiener's own description of his attitude to knowledge at the age of six or seven. Even by then, he says, 'in zoology and botany, it was the diagrams of complicated structure and the problems of growth and organization which excited my interest fully as much as the tales of adventure and discovery.'[15]

At the age of eleven Norbert Wiener became an undergraduate student at Tufts College. He graduated at fourteen and then enrolled as a graduate student at Harvard. He gained his doctoral degree at eighteen. After spending some time abroad, including a spell working under Bertrand Russell, he returned to the United States. In 1919, now twenty-five, and well on the way to establishing a reputation as a leading mathematician, he gained a position at the Massachusetts Institute of Technology. He was to remain there for thirty-three active years.

That brief sketch of Wiener's early life may give the impression that even if his father was not the easiest of parents, the young man's progress was smooth and untroubled. But this was far from being true. Life can be difficult enough for an exceptional child even when parents and teachers make considerable efforts to be sensitive and understanding. Other problems apart, it is hard for adults to be constantly aware of the contrasting needs of a young person who may simultaneously be a sophisticated thinker and a socially backward and emotionally vulnerable child. A brief anecdote of Wiener's nicely illustrates that baffling contrast. He relates that for all his brilliance as a child it was not until he was seven that he discovered that Santa Claus does not exist. And yet, 'at that time I was already reading books of more than slight difficulty, and it seemed to my parents that a child who was doing this should have no difficulty in

---

[15] Wiener (1953), p. 64.

discarding what to them was obviously a sentimental fiction. What they did not realize was the fragmentariness of the child's world.'[16]

The years of Norbert Wiener's adolescence and early adulthood were difficult for him in a number of ways, not all of which sprang from strained relationships within the family. He was frustrated because he was clumsy and short-sighted. It was never easy for him to mix with class-mates at school and college, most of whom were some years older than him and far more socially developed. Their interests and passions would have been very different from his.

But the dominant source of his frustrations was the near-impossibility of getting on with his parents. Although both of them expected a great deal of their son, neither was prepared to give him the freedom of action needed – in his eyes, at least – by a growing young man. For several years he perceived himself as being intellectually equal to his parents but treated by them as a child. He was totally dependent upon them financially, and with numerous responsibilities but no authority to make decisions for himself. For example, he was expected to devote a large amount of time to teaching his younger brother, but never allowed to decide how the child should be taught. He was required to help around the home and the garden, but his parents made all the decisions.

Wiener may not have appreciated just how common it is for young people to experience frustrations like these, but in his case they were espe-cially prolonged as well as acute. Well past the time when it would have been sensible for him to have been living on his own, he was obliged to go on residing at home, in a family 'living too close together and driven in upon itself'.[17] He became angrily aware of the fact that his Jewish parents not only ignored their own cultural roots and the Jewish religion, but had a negative and prejudiced attitude towards other Jews. (That was not uncommon at the time among recent immigrants anxious to become assimilated in their new country, and as Wiener later recognised, it was to some extent understandable.) But Norbert's awareness of his parents' hypocrisy undermined his respect for them, and yet he remained tied to the family home. His moving away would have eased the tensions which his growing awareness of his parents' faults exacerbated, but the very idea of his leaving home infuriated his mother. She insisted that such an action 'would be held against me for all eternity, as a sign of my ultimate failure, and would mean the complete and final collapse of family relations'.[18] Eventually, of course, Norbert Wiener did make the break from the family home, married, and embarked on a life of his own, but getting to that point involved him in a long and exhausting battle.

[16] Wiener (1953), p. 81.   [17] Wiener (1953), p. 157.   [18] Wiener (1953), p. 162.

Norbert Wiener's experiences as a young person left him acutely aware of the problems that can make life difficult for a child raised by parents who have set out to create a superior person. Compressing his feelings into one eloquent admonitory sentence, he advised, 'Let those who choose to carve a human soul to their own measure be sure that they have a worthy image after which to carve it, and let them know that the power of molding an emerging intellect is a power of death as well as a power of life.'[19]

It is a warning worth heeding.

In his autobiography, Norbert Wiener comments on the sad life of Billy Sidis and also mentions a number of other child prodigies he was acquainted with. Not surprisingly, those whose parents had played a highly active role in their early education, as his own parents had done, particularly interested him. Wiener was especially intrigued by John Stuart Mill's famous account of his upbringing at the hands of his father, James Mill. On reading Mill's detailed description of his father's teaching methods, Wiener discovered that his own experiences with a domineering parent helped him read between the lines of Mill's relatively constrained description of his father's approach. He recognised there the signs of a somewhat tyrannous regime. The guarded tone of Mill's account could be taken to indicate a completely virtuous relationship on both sides, Wiener noted, but 'I know better, and when I read his few words about his father's irascibility I know just how to interpret these statements. I am certain that even if that irascibility had been more decorous than that of my father, it had probably been no less unremitting.'[20]

John Stuart Mill's *Autobiography* is a candid and immensely valuable source of insights into the circumstances in which one parent's plan to manufacture a genius was actively pursued. Mill wrote it, he said, unconsciously echoing the elder Karl Witte's views and anticipating those of Leo Wiener concerning the wastefulness of the usual methods of educating young people, so that 'there should be some record of an education which was unusual and remarkable, and which . . . has proved how much more than is commonly supposed may be taught, and well taught, in those early years which, in the common modes of what is called instruction are little better than wasted.'[21]

Three features in particular help make Mill's *Autobiography* a remarkable document. First, as an account it is both detailed and (on the whole) objective. It gives a careful and accurate description of Mill's early

---

[19] Quoted in Howe (1990), p. 126.   [20] Wiener (1953), p. 68.
[21] John Stuart Mill's, *Autobiograpy*, edited by Jack Stillinger (Mill, 1971), p.3. [Mill's *Autobiography* was originally published in 1873.]

education, describing in some detail how the father carried through his intentions. The task he set himself was, as the son recognised, a monumental one, to which James Mill directed 'an amount of labour, care, and perseverance rarely, if ever, employed for a similar purpose, in endeavouring to give, according to his own conception, the highest order of intellectual education'.[22] The achievement was made all the more impressive by the fact that James Mill was a major scholar and thinker in his own right, and at the same time as he was making his son into one of the dominant thinkers of his century he was also turning out some very substantial achievements of his own. But despite John Stuart Mill's vast admiration for his father, he was not so reticent about criticising him as Norbert Wiener implied, and the son's respect for the parent's immense strengths is balanced with a willingness to describe in considerable detail those of his father's actions that he found oppressive.

Second, the *Autobiography* is remarkable by virtue of being a description of an education that in important respects was brilliantly successful. As the father intended, his child did become a man who unquestionably belongs within the category of geniuses. John Stuart Mill was a great social reformer. Mill's insights on economics, politics and philosophy helped to create modern democracy and combat poverty and injustice. His ideas continue to influence modern thinking about social issues. The *Autobiography* is indisputably an account of the development of a great thinker.

Third, Mill himself was very conscious of the fact that the intellectual qualities he possessed had to a large extent been deliberately instilled in him by his father. 'Manufactured' was his own choice of word for this state of affairs. In this respect Mill was totally different from other geniuses of his era, such as Stephenson and Faraday, who were largely self-taught. He was equally unlike Darwin, who became a genius almost *despite* the efforts of his teachers, who would have thought his choice of natural history as a vocation quite absurd. There is no other genius for whom the term 'manufactured' is quite as fitting as it is for Mill.

The shock of discovering in his early twenties that acquaintances regarded him as being a manufactured man, capable only of reproducing opinions stamped on him by others, led John Stuart Mill to change some of his ideas rather abruptly. Even so, he could never forget that he was the son of a parent who had set out to manufacture a genius. He was only too aware that his successes and failures bore the marks of the effective if heavy-handed education his father had personally implemented in order to realise the intention of bringing up a child who would be, as James Mill

[22] Mill (1971), p. 5.

had said to his friend and patron Jeremy Bentham, 'a successor worthy of both of us'.[23]

The manner in which James Mill proceeded to implement that intention is described in John Stuart Mill's account, in his *Autobiography*, of his extraordinary upbringing. John Stuart Mill was a scrupulously honest man, and in most respects his narrative is as accurate and as fair as the limitations of human memory allow. It is occasionally misleading, however. The absence of information about his mother has encouraged readers to infer that she lacked significance in Mill's early life to a degree that is belied by family correspondence and visitors' observations. Also, the lack of references to his eight brothers and sisters leaves the reader with the impression that he was a more solitary child than could have been possible in a houseful of children who displayed 'a plentiful lack of manners, and as much impertinence, sometimes called impudence, as any children need to have'.[24] The depiction of a constrained family life is partly belied by a friend's observation that the Mill parents did not prevent John's younger brother James from trundling his hoop round the great hall of Ford Abbey, Jeremy Bentham's mansion, where the Mill family enjoyed a number of summers.[25]

John Stuart Mill was born in 1806, a year after the marriage of his parents and just under three years before Charles Darwin's birth. His father, James Mill, had been a prodigy himself. James Mill had been born in Scotland, the son of a shoemaker, and by the time he was seven he had drawn attention to himself as a clever child. His mother had high expectations for him, and made sure that unlike other children in humble rural families he was spared all household chores and encouraged to spend his time on his studies. On leaving school he came to the attention of a local landowning family, the Stuarts (after whom John Stuart Mill was given his middle name), who were looking for a suitable tutor for their daughter. The patronage of the Stuart family made it possible for James Mill to attend Edinburgh University. But he found it hard to make a living in Scotland, and in 1802 he moved to London, at the age of twenty-nine. He thrived there, and by the time of his marriage three years later he was

---

[23] Quoted in Mill (1971), p. xi.   [24] Packe (1954), pp. 33–4.

[25] The reasons for Mill's *Autobiography* giving the misleading impression that his father was the only member of the family to have influence upon him may have stemmed from his guiltily uncomfortable feelings, following a falling out at the time of his marriage to Harriet Taylor, with whom he had already spent some years of – sexless – intimacy, despite her already having a husband. Mill's way of keeping at bay the tensions this uncomfortable domestic situation aroused in him was to see Harriet as the perfect woman, against whom any hint of a slight was evidence of unjustified hostility. He behaved uncharacteristically badly towards his sisters and his mother, apparently because they did not quite succeed at solving the delicate problem of responding to the news of his marriage in a way that he found acceptable.

editing a newspaper and earning at least four or five times as much as the fathers of George Stephenson and Michael Faraday were ever paid. Soon after John Stuart Mill was born, James Mill decided to devote most of his time to writing a history of India. That enormous project necessitated financial sacrifices and was to drag on for almost twelve difficult years, which roughly coincided with the period in which James devoted a major portion of his considerable energies to the education of his eldest son. Eventually, ten substantial volumes were completed, establishing James Mill's reputation and bringing him a series of influential jobs and financial security.

We must be careful not to misinterpret James Mill's reasons for shouldering the onerous task of making his son into one the most powerful thinkers of his century. He did not see himself as taking on some kind of challenge or test. Nor did he regard the task as an experiment to discover if it was actually possible for a parent to create a son who was capable of major intellectual achievements. He rarely betrayed doubts about the practicality of his intentions. James Mill's massive self-confidence left him no reason for questioning his belief that what he set out to do was achievable, so long as he put sufficient effort into it. As we have already seen, the immense amount of work he invested in the task of educating his eldest child was motivated by the desire to produce a son capable of carrying on his own labours. Undeniably, taking that stance demanded a degree of conceit or arrogance, in addition to a certain lack of sensitivity to the child's own needs. And yet it has to be said in James Mill's defence that building on his own enormously valuable intellectual work was a job worth doing.

The young John Stuart Mill was certainly a child prodigy, but unlike many prodigies he was never encouraged to see himself in that light. For better or worse, his father was meagre with praise and constantly reminded the boy of his imperfections. James Mill deliberately avoided giving his son the impression that he was more able than other children of his age. Consequently, 'From his intercourse with me I could derive none but a very humble opinion of myself . . . if I thought anything about myself, it was that I was rather backward in my studies, since I always found myself so, in comparison with what my father expected from me.'[26]

As we shall see, there were negative as well as positive outcomes of the approach taken by James Mill. Constant criticism is never beneficial for a young person. But at least John Stuart Mill was spared the intrusive press attention that can damage an immature child.

Since James Mill knew that he could hardly prevent the boy becoming

[26] Mill (1971), p. 21.

aware for himself that others of his age did not possess knowledge and mental skills matching his, he was careful to persuade his son that he should take no credit for any superiority he noticed in himself. He told the boy that any advantages that he came to possess were solely the result of the superior education he had received. Whether or not James Mill was entirely correct about that is open to question, of course – a matter that will be discussed in Chapter 9. But it is interesting to observe that this very same view was emphatically held by all the other parents – those of Witte, Wiener and Sidis – who have featured most prominently in the present chapter.

In the *Autobiography*, John Stuart Mill reports that he had no recollection of his life before starting to learn Greek, but that he had been told that instruction began when he was three years old. He remembered having to memorise lists of common Greek words written on cards prepared by his father: the Greek words were paired with the English equivalents. Grammar was introduced later. It was not until he was seven or eight that his father began teaching him Latin. His ignorance of that language added considerably to his father's burden in teaching him Greek, the reason being that there was no lexicon that enabled Greek words to be translated directly into English, or *vice versa*. It was therefore necessary to translate via Latin. Consequently, when John Stuart was set to making translations (starting with *Aesop's Fables* and Xenophon's *Anabasis*), he had to ask his father to provide him with the meaning of each and every Greek word that he did not already know. So James Mill would have been constantly interrupted. Nevertheless, 'This incessant interruption he, one of the most impatient of men, submitted to, and wrote under that interruption several volumes of his History and all else that he had to write during those years.'[27] One cannot help wondering how often it crossed James Mill's mind that life might have been easier had he decided to teach his son a little Latin before starting on Greek.

Until he was eight, the more formal aspects of John Stuart Mill's education were restricted to Greek and arithmetic. He disliked arithmetic intensely. He spent much of his time reading, and each morning, as he accompanied his father on a walk before breakfast, he gave an account of what he had read on the previous day, prompted by notes made on slips of paper while he read. Perhaps surprisingly, the young Mill seems to have quite enjoyed this activity of reporting back to his habitually impatient parent. He says in the *Autobiography* that he remembers it as having been a voluntary exercise rather than a prescribed one. Its pleasurableness doubtless reflected the fact that the books he read were mostly ones that

[27] Mill (1971), p. 6.

he greatly enjoyed. He had relatively few children's books, but although his father only allowed them sparingly, James Mill did manage to borrow for his son various books that a child could enjoy, such as the *Arabian Nights*, *Don Quixote*, and Miss Edgeworth's *Popular Tales*. The child also warmed to *Robinson Crusoe*, which he had been given as a present. And even when James Mill was directing his son towards books written for adults, he seems to have been good at finding ones that a boy would genuinely enjoy. John Stuart Mill got particular pleasure from descriptions of explorations, such as a collection of accounts of voyages around the world, and many of the other books that his father obtained for him in the early years were historical volumes with a strong narrative element.

Mill lists a large number of books on history that he read as a child, and he makes it clear that he enjoyed most of them even if he understood them imperfectly. Predictably, but not at all unwisely, James Mill 'was fond of putting into my hands books which exhibited men of energy in unusual circumstances, struggling against difficulties and overcoming them'.[28] But he also made his son read and report on books such as ecclesiastical histories and the biographies of religious leaders. Most children would have found these extremely dull, and even for a young person as remarkable as John Stuart Mill, they 'would not have interested me sufficiently to induce me to read them of myself'.[29]

Latin was introduced in the child's eighth year, and within a short time he had read numerous books in that language, as well as mastering the works of many Greek authors. At around that time John Stuart Mill was given the task of teaching his younger sister. In common with Norbert Wiener, he loathed that responsibility. Bitter experience soon convinced him that 'the plan of teaching children by means of one another . . . is very inefficient as teaching, and I well know that the relation between teacher and taught is not a good moral discipline to either'.[30] All the same, he had to admit that being obliged to teach others did have the advantage of ensuring that knowedge was acquired especially thoroughly.

Mill's education always involved more than merely reading the books his father obtained for him. James Mill made sure that his son was an active rather than a passive learner. The child was required to summarise arguments, transcribe works into his own words, translate from one language into another, and respond to an author's argument with an opposing point of view. After reading a treatise, he would be required to give a detailed account of what he had read and answer his father's searching questions. These activities were designed to ensure that John Stuart Mill really understood the knowledge he was acquiring, and were not at all

[28] Mill (1971), p. 7.   [29] Mill (1971), p. 7.   [30] Mill (1971), p. 6.

unlike the ones that Michael Faraday had been encouraged to engage in by the author of *The Improvement of the Mind*. As the years went by the training became more onerous and intensive until he reached the age of fourteen and went to live in France for a year. His education continued after that, of course, but subsequently he was not so closely supervised by his father.

By the time he came to start writing the *Autobiography* at the age of forty-seven, John Stuart Mill felt ready to look back on his extraordinary education and make a careful appraisal of its strengths and its weaknesses. There were, he perceived, many aspects of James Mill's teaching that deserved praise. He was particularly glad that his father had taken pains to make sure that he was familiar with logic, which benefited his thinking greatly. And he could see that the father's approach was not infrequently restrained and sensitive. For example, when John Stuart Mill as a young child took it into his head to engage in the activity of what he called 'writing histories' his father avoided criticising these doubtless naive efforts, being content to encourage his son 'in this useful amusement, though, as I think judiciously, he never asked to see what I wrote; so that I did not feel that in writing it I was accountable to any one, had the chilling sensation of being under a critical eye'.[31]

A particularly important positive aspect of James Mill's approach was that it avoided rote learning and drill. At all times, what was learned had to be genuinely meaningful to the child. In John Stuart Mill's own words,

Most boys or youths who have had much knowledge drilled into them have their mental capacities not strengthened, but overlaid by it. They are crammed with mere facts, and with the opinions or phrases of other people . . . so often grow up to be mere parroters of what they have learnt, incapable of using their minds except in the furrows traced for them. Mine, however, was not an education of cram. My father never permitted anything which I learnt, to degenerate into a mere exercise of memory. He strove to make the understanding not only go along with every step of the teaching, but if possible, precede it. Anything which could be found out by thinking, I never was told, until I had exhausted my efforts to find it out for myself.[32]

James Mill also had the good sense to make sure that his son did not become arrogant. He was very careful to protect him from situations in which people would comment on his exceptional abilities or compare him favourably with other boys of his age. In this the parent was almost too successful, and John Stuart Mill became convinced that he was in no respect inherently special, and even rather backward in his studies. He was also sure that he possessed no capabilities that could not have been

[31] Mill (1971), p. 10.   [32] Mill (1971), p. 20.

acquired by any ordinary child who was given the training he had received.[33]

So James Mill's teaching had a number of good features. But it had some glaringly negative aspects as well. For a start, the instruction Mill provided for his son was not invariably as careful or as thorough as it might have been, and even when it was not he tended to blame the child for his failures. With mathematics, for example, James Mill could not spare the time to teach his son properly, leaving him to learn almost entirely from books. Yet he made his son aware of incurring parental displeasure by his inability to solve difficult problems 'for which he did not see that I had not the necessary previous knowledge'.[34]

There were further manifestations of this inability or unwillingness to perceive that the boy's defects were the result of inadequate teaching rather than some basic fault. For instance, the child found it hard to read Greek aloud, and experienced particular difficulties in regard to arriving at correct voice inflexions, or modulations. This irritated the father, who sharply criticised each error. But according to his son, although James told his son what he should have done he never took the more sensible step of actually showing him how to do it. In these and other ways James Mill failed to provide help which was sufficiently practical and concrete to match the needs of a child. The defect here, according to the son, was of 'trusting too much to the intelligibleness of the abstract, when not embodied in the concrete'.[35]

James Mill also failed to teach his son to be tactful or diplomatic. John Stuart Mill observed in the *Autobiography* that despite the fact he was not an arrogant child, and never had an inflated opinion of his own powers, adults often found him 'greatly and disagreeably self-conceited'.[36] The reason for this perception, he suggested, was that he was disputatious, and did not hesitate to contradict people, a habit that he believed to have been acquired as a consequence of being encouraged to discuss matters beyond his age with adults, without having been taught to respect or defer to older people. He thought that the probable reason for his father failing to correct 'this ill breeding and impertinence' was that he was simply unaware of it, because in his father's presence the son 'was always too much in awe of him to be otherwise than extremely subdued and quiet in his presence'.[37]

The awe in which John Stuart Mill held his father was a sympton of the most crucial defect of all in the educational regime that James Mill devised. That defect is encapsulated in the brief statement, in a discarded draft of the autobiography, that 'mine was not an education of love but of

[33] Mill (1971), p. 20.   [34] Mill (1971), p. 9.   [35] Mill (1971), p. 17.
[36] Mill (1971), p. 21.   [37] Mill (1971), p. 21.

fear'.[38] Mill expanded on this in a passage in which he said that he grew up as a child who had nobody to whom he could express his feelings, because the only person he spoke to about important matters, namely his father, was someone he feared too much for it to have been possible to act spontaneously or naturally in his presence. The result was to make the young man reserved and inhibited, lacking strong impulses of his own. And because the father was so strong-willed and forceful, his child became accustomed to being told what to do. It became habitual for him to leave moral judgements and decisions to his father, rather than doing these things for himself. John Stuart Mill was convinced that living in the shadow of a dominating parent had badly stunted his personal growth. And there were further criticisms, too. Mill felt that there had been too much emphasis in his education on knowing at the expense of doing. He was never encouraged to gain practical skills. Also, because his father kept him away from other boys of his age, fearing 'the contagion of vulgar modes of thought and feeling',[39] he never learned any of the things that young people acquire from their contact with others.

Certain biographers in the psychobiographical tradition, notably Bruce Mazlish,[40] place enormous emphasis on the influence of unresolved and largely unconscious father–son conflicts on the younger Mill's development, but it is doubtful whether such psychoanalytically-based efforts to produce insights provide any real advance on what can be learned from John Stuart Mill's own accounts of life with his father. Unencumbered by Freudian theories, Mill was very much aware of how his father's domineering personality had affected him.

The outcomes of Mill's extraordinary education mirrored its strengths and defects. As we have noticed, so far as instilling intellectual capabilities was concerned, James Mill's regime was resoundingly successful. The intense grounding he provided helped to produce a young man who was an extraordinarily knowledgeable and rigorous thinker. But the defects of the regime created serious problems. John Stuart Mill blamed the deficiencies of his education for his lack of physical skills and manual dexterity, and for the difficulties he experienced in getting on with other people, and also for his lack of passion and inability to express those feelings he did possess.

Fortunately, Mill was able to endure the ill-effects of his education, and did not suffer the devastating consequences that were to blight the adult life of Billy Sidis. However, in common with Norbert Wiener, Mill did find it very difficult to establish himself as an independent adult, and he experienced problems that seriously threatened his mental equilibrium.

---

[38] Mill (1971), p. 33.   [39] Mill (1971), p. 22.   [40] Mazlish (1975).

In particular, he experienced a serious mental crisis which began at the age of twenty, when he fell into a deep depression. He found himself lacking any strong feelings, and despite possessing all the intellectual equipment that was necessary for making a real contribution, he had no clear sense of direction nor any enthusiasm for undertaking intellectual projects. He was, he said, 'left stranded at the commencement of my voyage, with a well equipped ship and a rudder, but no sail, without any real desire for the ends for which I had been so carefully fitted out to work'.[41]

Mill's own explanation for his depression put stress on the peculiar form and content of his education, although it is more than likely that the domination of his early life by a parent who was constantly critical and discouraged any expression of feelings or emotions made a larger contribution. Certainly, Mill was right to put his finger on the damaging influence of a regime in which intellectual qualities were forced at the expense of practical accomplishments and many other of the capabilities that young people normally acquire.

Of course, it is rarely possible to pinpoint with absolute certainty the most important influences in a particular individual's life. And as we have seen, particular foreground events, even dramatic ones, play a smaller role than the cumulative effects of the numerous everyday experiences that gradually carve the character and furnish the mind of a developing person. Yet it does seem very likely that had James Mill been a less harsh and joyless parent, or a less grimly demanding one, his brilliant son would have become a warmer and happier adult than he turned out to be, and might have been spared the serious depression that he experienced. It is surely significant that with all three of those 'manufactured' individuals whose problems in early adulthood have been discussed in the present chapter, there seem to have been clear and direct links between the kinds of defects and excesses that were evident in their upbringings and the form of the difficulties they experienced as adults. Norbert Wiener, for example, experienced a period of unhappiness not at all unlike Mill's, leaving him frustrated and in despair, and conscious of a profound lack of self-esteem. Like Mill, Wiener blamed his difficulties on the defects of a childhood in which the actions of dominating and over-critical parents ensured that intellectual qualities were forced at the expense of opportunities for feelings to develop and other qualities to flourish. Perhaps it is also significant that another leading intellectual of Mill's period, his near-contemporary John Ruskin, the eminent Victorian social commentator and writer on art, who had received an intensive and rather severe early

---

[41] Mill (1971), p. 84.

education not unlike Mill's, also experienced profound mental crises when he was an adult.

Whether or not the idea of setting out to manufacture a genius can ever be a sound one, the examples that have been given in the present chapter show that at least some of those parents who have deliberately attempted to equip their child with special mental capabilities have achieved that with considerable success. But, as these examples have also demonstrated, there is a price to be paid. For a young person who is the unwitting participant in such an enterprise the costs may well outweigh the benefits.

6   Einstein and the prodigies

According to a romanticised notion of the child prodigy that has been portrayed in a number of novels and films, the typical prodigy is brought up in unpromising circumstances until it is discovered that the child possesses some rare innate gift. Thereupon a wealthy or powerful sponsor arrives on the scene to rescue the *Wunderkind* from poverty and make available those opportunities that will enable the young person's special gift to be properly nourished. Thus armed, the child rapidly becomes a star at the activity at which he or she excels, and before long is hugely successful, rich and celebrated.

In Frank Conroy's enjoyable novel *Body and Soul*,[1] for example, the story begins with a description of the childhood of the illegitimate hero Claude, neglected by his overweight alcoholic mother who regularly locks him into their squalid basement apartment while she earns a meagre living driving taxis. Eventually Claude discovers an old nightclub piano. He is fascinated by the sounds he can produce on it and gradually learns to reproduce a few tunes heard on the radio. Some time later, he wanders into the nearest music store, where the kindly owner notices his interest in pianos, explains to him the basis of musical notation, gives Claude an elementary self-teaching lesson book, and invites him to return when he has worked his way through the exercises. When Claude rises to this challenge further opportunities open up, and he is encouraged to practise on a valuable Bechstein instrument. This is later bequeathed to Claude on the death of its owner, who turns out to have been a famous composer. One thing leads to another, and by the time the reader has turned a few hundred pages Claude has become a brilliant and envied musician.

In real life, stories of that kind are rare, although not entirely unknown. One actual person whose life that did have much in common with the above fictional account was George Bidder, an eminent nineteenth-century British engineer. Bidder's considerable achievements included the construction of a number of railways and some major docks, amongst

[1] Conroy (1995).

them the Victoria Docks in London. He also masterminded the construction of numerous ships, bridges, aqueducts, viaducts, sewage and purification works, and telegraph facilities.

George Bidder was born in 1806 in Moretonhampstead, a tiny market town in Devon, in the south-west of England, where his father worked as a stonemason. At the age of six the boy began to take a keen interest in mental arithmetic. People started noticing that whenever simple calculations involving small sums of money needed to be done, George always had the correct answer. This gained the child attention in his immediate neighbourhood. On a typical occasion in the local blacksmith's shop,

They then went on to ask me up to two places of figures . . . I gave the answer correctly, as was verified by the old gentleman's nephew, who began chalking it up to see if I was right . . . this increased my fame still more, and what was better, it eventually caused halfpence to flow into my pocket; which, I need not say, had the effect of attaching me still more to the science of arithmetic, and thus by degrees I got on . . . [2]

Soon after that, George's father, intent from avarice or need on getting some reward from his son's growing skill at calculating, started exhibiting the child at local fairs, and by the time George Bidder was nine his fame had spread and he had gained a national reputation. He gave numerous demonstrations of his mental calculating skills, which were advertised by handbills that touted his abilities with descriptions of recent feats. For instance, one advertisement for a forthcoming performance boasted about a previous one that had been attended by a number of prominent worthies, including King George III's wife Queen Charlotte, two dukes and an earl, the Lord Mayor of London, and Sir Joseph Banks, the now-elderly patron of the sciences who had financed Captain James Cook's travels (but had recently baulked at aiding the young Michael Faraday).

According to a handbill, Bidder had correctly solved a number of difficult problems. Asked to multiply 7,953 by 4,648 he had quickly told the audience that the answer was 36,965,544. When the Queen asked him how many days it would take for a snail, moving at the rate of eight feet per day, to creep the 838 miles from Land's End to the northernmost point in Scotland, he told her that the snail would need 553,080 days to make the journey. Bidder's mental calculating was fast as well as accurate. It took him just one minute to work out the distance between the Earth and the nearest fixed star, after he had been informed by the astronomer Sir William Herschel that light takes eight minutes to reach Earth from the Sun, 98 million miles away, and six years and four months from the

---

[2] Clark (1983), pp. 3–4.

star. But even Bidder needed all of thirteen minutes to do the enormous mental calculating task of multiplying 257,689,435 by 356,875,649.

At this time Bidder had received very little formal education. He had attended a small local school, but his biographer describes him as having played truant much of the time,[3] and according to one report he could still not read and write when he was eight.[4] It is significant that Bidder started to become interested in arithmetic before he had learned to read, because (although he would not have known it at the time) the most effective methods for doing quick mental calculations are very different from the pencil-and-paper calculating techniques that schools teach. Had he learned arithmetic at school before he became interested in mental calculating, George Bidder's school learning would have impeded his progress as a mental calculator rather than helping him. As Bidder himself explained, there is a fundamental difference between mental calculating and calculations based on pencil and paper. In the former, but not in the latter, it is vital to keep the amount of information that needs to be stored (in memory) while the calculating is proceeding, to an absolute minimum.

Bidder used the example of a multiplication problem to demonstrate how mental arithmetic works. Someone is asked to multiply 279 times 373. He begins by multiplying 200×300, which comes to 60,000. Next 200×70 ($= 14,000$) is added to that, making 74,000. Now the previous total (60,000) can be forgotten, and at any future moment as the calculation proceeds it is only necessary to keep in memory the most recent total. Next, to the current total of 74,000 the calculator adds, successively, 200×3 ($= 600$), then 70×300 ($= 21,000$), 70×70 ($= 4,900$), 70×3 ($= 210$), 9×300 ($= 2,700$), 9×70 ($= 630$), and, lastly 9×3 ($= 27$). Finally, after proceeding through each of these (relatively easy) steps, one at a time, the calculator arrives at the final total, 104,067.

This is a more cumbersome technique for multiplying large numbers than the ones taught in school. There would be no point in using it when it is possible to store (in writing) the separate results of the various stages of a calculation task. But the methods taught by schoolteachers would present insuperable problems for someone who had to rely on mental calculation alone. That is because of the sheer number of digits that the person would have to store in memory in order to retain the results of the intermediate steps in the calculation. Yet with the strategy described above, all that needs to be retained in memory whilst the computation is proceeding is a single running total.

A key implication of this fundamental difference between mental cal-

---

[3] Clark (1983), p. 3.   [4] Clark (1983), p. 5.

culating techniques and paper-and-pencil methods of calculating is that, other things being equal, someone who has not learned arithmetic at school may find it easier than a school-taught pupil would to learn to be a good mental calculator. Consequently, for an unschooled child like George Bidder, doing feats of mental calculation was an ideal way to demonstrate unusual capabilities. His capacity to master those particular kinds of intellectual task would not have been at all negatively affected by any of the handicaps usually associated with a lack of formal schooling.

Apart from the financial rewards, the most important consequence of Bidder's demonstrations of mental calculating was that his abilities came to the attention of potential patrons who were prepared to help further the formal education of such a promising young person. A group of scholars at Cambridge University arranged for him to be sent at their expense to Wilson's Grammar School, near London. He did not spend much time there, partly because his studies were constantly being interrupted by public tours and exhibitions, but when he was thirteen it was decided to give him tutoring that would prepare him for entry to Edinburgh University. He began at Edinburgh in 1820, when he was only fourteen (two years younger than Darwin), and stayed until 1824. He took courses in mathematics and other subjects and eventually qualified as an engineer. Among the friendships Bidder made at Edinburgh, the one that was most significant for his subsequent career was with Robert Stephenson, the son of George Stephenson. George Stephenson himself warmed to his son's friend, perceiving in him a young man whose early struggles had been not entirely unlike his own. In his later years George Stephenson invited Bidder and his wife to stay at Stephenson's house in Derbyshire.

Bidder's association with the Stephensons, which became closer in the 1830s when he entered into a kind of partnership with Robert Stephenson, contributed to the fact that from the time he left Edinburgh University there was always a demand for his engineering skills. Like the Stephensons and their great rival Isambard Kingdom Brunel, he was regarded by his contemporaries as an unusually vigorous and energetic individual. Bidder rapidly became one of the leading engineers of his time. Following Robert Stephenson's death in 1859, Bidder succeeded his friend as President of the Institution of Civil Engineers. He died in 1878. George Stephenson's biographer Samuel Smiles mentions that his eminent subject sometimes liked to forget his work and relax by challenging Bidder to an arm-wrestling contest. Smiles wrote to Bidder on a number of occasions, although he never seems to have been made aware of the remarkable story of Bidder's childhood.

Bidder's case apart, there have been few factual parallels to the romanticised view of child prodigies portrayed in novels like *Body and Soul*. Nevertheless, it is not hard to locate historical instances of attention being paid to young people from poor origins as a consequence of their unusual capabilities, leading to some kind of sponsorship that enabled the individual to have access to formal education. Michael Faraday's mentor Humphry Davy, the son of a woodcarver, benefited in this way. So did the great navigator James Cook, and also John Stuart Mill's father, James Mill. In the absence of some kind of sponsor or mentor, the chances of a child born into poverty getting ahead were much reduced. In the rare case of George Stephenson, the fact that he became a great engineer without enjoying any of these advantages makes his achievements all the more remarkable.

It is much more common for the identification of special abilities to follow rather than precede the making available of favourable opportunities and a fair amount of assistance. The majority of prodigies have grown up in relatively affluent families. Many have had parents who took a close interest in their child's early education. Even substantial libraries were at hand in the family homes of a number of those distinguished people who were prodigies as children, including the mathematician Leibniz, Jeremy Bentham the economic thinker, and the historian Thomas Macaulay. A few prodigies, including the illustrious German writer Goethe and the great mathematician Pascal, as well as John Stuart Mill, have had parents who were impressive scholars themselves.

A 'rags to riches' element is present in a number of autobiographical narratives written by child prodigies, and this has helped to spread the idea that poverty is a common feature of their early lives. The true picture is somewhat different, however, even if it is true that, as George Stephenson's case demonstrates, early poverty and a lack of formal education have not always prevented a young person from eventually achieving eminence. It is easy to be misled by the not-uncommon tendency of successful people, including a number of former prodigies, to magnify their achievements by exaggerating the poverty or misery of their origins. According to George Bernard Shaw's accounts of his childhood, for instance, his early life was dominated by penuriousness and the inconstancy of a rejecting mother. In reality, that playwright enjoyed the advantages of a stimulating and lively home, which provided all kinds of opportunities that were beyond the reach of most children. And even when an autobiographical portrayal of childhood deprivation is largely accurate, often that is not the whole story. For example, the author H. G.

Wells recalled that his parents were poor and unhappily married, and not well educated. He recollected spending his childhood years in a squalid house that was damp and bug-infested, and in which all the carpets were frayed and worn and the furniture old and discoloured. All that is entirely true, but Wells' account does less than full justice to a number of mitigating factors. His father, who played cricket for Kent, was something of a local celebrity, and also a keen reader and a thoughtful man who went to great lengths to broaden his knowledge. Wells' mother, too, was a not entirely ordinary woman. She kept a daily diary, and, unusually for a working class wife in the 1860s, she made a big effort to give her young son a good start in life. She taught him to count, and when he was five she pasted up large letters from the alphabet in the kitchen. Between them, Wells' parents made sure that he was always supplied with books, paper, and pencils. It was largely because of the encouragement they gave him that by the time H.G. Wells was seven he was already, like his father, an enthusiastic reader.

Another unfounded common belief is that the typical prodigy's special abilities suddenly appear without any assistance at all. This view has sometimes been promoted through the reports of parents who have wanted to convince others that their child's accomplishments were a sign that the child had been chosen to be the recipient of special God-given powers. Such parents have tended to portray themselves as having made no active contribution to their child's abilities, and simply looking on admiringly as they saw their child's marvellous capabilities magically unfolding.

It is conceivable that a few of these accounts may be reliable, but in a substantial proportion of them the professed passivity of the parents is clearly belied by the fact that their descriptions contain detailed information about the child's achievements, which could never have been obtained without a big investment of time and considerable planning. For instance, the parents of one child prodigy claimed to have resisted any temptation to help their child to learn, let alone actively teach her, and yet they nevertheless kept a meticulous record of her progress, noting, for instance, that her speaking vocabulary at sixteen months was 229 words, and that at five years of age she introduced 6,837 words over a six-month period, all of which had been listed and classified into the different parts of speech. With another set of parents, who insisted that their daughter learned to read entirely unaided and claimed that they only realised this when they discovered her reading *Heidi* at the age of four, it turned out that they too kept elaborate records of the child's accomplishments, such as the precise letters she had learned at various ages, the time at which she first mastered the alphabet, her counting skills, and the colours she recognised.[5] It is hard to believe that parents who have devoted as much time as these people did to making detailed records of their children's progress could possibly have avoided becoming actively involved in the children's early learning.

Accounts of the lives of prodigies are a rich source of information about the antecedents and possible causes of genius. In particular, they can tell us much about relationships between the events of someone's childhood and that person's adult achievements. But the links between being a child prodigy and being an adult genius are not always straightforward. There are no inevitable connections. Some prodigies become geniuses, but the majority do not. Conversely, although a number of geniuses were prodigies in childhood, others, such as Darwin, were not at all precocious.

The extent to which having been a prodigy conveys an advantage, if it does so at all, will depend to a considerable extent upon the nature of the creative activity at which a person excels. In some fields of accomplishment, such as music, being a child prodigy is especially advantageous, or even essential, if a person is to make the kind of early start that is needed in order to become exceptionally capable. In this and some other areas of achievement, because of the sheer amount of time that is needed in order for someone to become sufficiently trained and prepared to make a unique or original contribution, only a person who has already gained considerable expertise by the end of childhood will stand a good chance of being exceptional as an adult achiever. As the eighteenth-century artist Sir Joshua Reynolds observed of the skill of drawing, '. . . if this power is not acquired when you are young, there will not be time for it afterwards: at least the attempt will be attended with as much difficulty as those who learn to read and write after they have arrived at the age of maturity'.[6]

Cataloguing the links between being a child prodigy and becoming an adult genius is made difficult by the fact that deciding whether or not particular individuals can be placed within the prodigy category is just as difficult as deciding if a person ought to be regarded as a genius. There is no obvious or non-arbitrary way of knowing where to draw a line between children who definitely belong within the category of prodigies and those young people who, although especially able or precocious, are not quite exceptional enough to be called prodigies. Making decisions about that might not be too difficult if all prodigies excelled at the same skills. In that event it would be possible to agree on criteria that would indicate the standard of achievement a child would need to reach by a certain age in

---

[5] See Fowler (1981).   [6] Quoted in Hamilton (1997), p. 13.

order to be designated a musical prodigy, or a chess prodigy, for example. But in the real world children excel in different ways, and it is simply impossible to make valid comparisons between individuals who are extraordinarily successful in differing domains of skill or knowledge. So, for example, if we are confronted with an outstanding ten-year-old violinist and an exceptional twelve-year-old mathematician, there would be no satisfactory way to select the one who has the strongest claim to being described as a prodigy.

That complication contributes to a state of affairs in which the relationship between the degree to which a young person's attainments are exceptional and the likelihood of that person being described as a child prodigy is far from perfect. An added difficulty is that because capabilities differ in the extent to which they are likely to be on display, or apparent for other reasons, some exceptional skills are more likely than others to be given the kind of adult attention that results in their possessor being called a prodigy. For example, if a child is a young performing musician, or a chess player, or a tennis player who participates in competitions, it is more than likely that if the child's capabilities are genuinely exceptional a substantial number of adults will become aware of them. However, if the child's interests are directed towards an activity that is less obviously or less frequently on display, such as science or philosophy, or literature, it is entirely possible that other people will be unaware that the child possesses special abilities.

Differences in the visibility of various precocious capabilities help account for the fact that whilst a substantial number of great musicians were regarded as being prodigies when they were young – including Handel, J. S. Bach, Beethoven, Mendelssohn, Chopin, Liszt, Schumann, and Debussy, in addition to Mozart[7] – that has less often been the case among, say, scientists. This helps to explain why it is that by no means all scientific geniuses have been regarded as being prodigies at the time that they were children, despite the fact that the majority of geniuses have exhibited a precocious ability of some kind in their early years. Take the case of Albert Einstein, for instance. The young Einstein was not widely regarded as a child prodigy. Nonetheless, when we examine his early progress sufficiently closely to know about the books he was reading and the scientific problems he was grappling on during his childhood, it becomes evident that his intellectual capabilities were just as exceptional as those of some children who, unlike Einstein, *were* regarded as being child prodigies.

[7] Lehmann (1997).

An account of Einstein's early life can provide some helpful insights into possible relationships between being a prodigy in childhood and being an adult genius. Ostensibly, of course, Albert Einstein seems a distinctly odd choice for an example of a child prodigy. Nobody disputes his genius, but the accepted view is that he was far from being a prodigy. He was, we are told, a backward child who was born with an oddly shaped skull, making him a late speaker and a poor student. He is said to have been a trouble-maker at his high school (which he left prematurely) and a pupil who gained low grades, failed examinations, and was particularly weak at languages. Unable to get the kind of job he sought on completing his education, Einstein was obliged, we are told, to take a menial post in a patents office. Matters were not helped by his father being a bankrupt. The Einstein family, members of a persecuted Jewish minority, had to leave their home in Germany and take up residence in Italy, where they suffered from being alien immigrants who lacked even the basic security conferred by citizenship. Against this unpromising background, it seems hardly surprising that Einstein's sudden bursting into prominence as a scientist of unique brilliance and originality has been regarded as magical. Here is genius at its most mysterious. He must, it appears, have been born to be a genius. No alternative explanation appears possible.

None of the above statements about Einstein is totally unfounded. Nonetheless, and contrary to what is widely believed, the young Einstein undoubtedly was a child prodigy, albeit a largely unrecognised one. Numerous observations of the progress he made while still a child illustrate his prodigiousness. From very early days the young Albert Einstein, born in 1879, made a distinctly favourable impression on others. Just a few months after his second birthday his maternal grandmother was writing to a relative that Albert, whom she described as sweet as well as good, was already creating amusing ideas. Her letter is one of a number of items of evidence obtained at the time of Einstein's early childhood that firmly contradict the much repeated claim that his language development was retarded. Another is an anecdote that can be precisely dated to the time when he was aged two years and eight months. This describes him reacting to being told on the occasion of the birth of his baby sister that he now had a new playmate, by asking where were the wheels on this new toy. The child's confusion is unexceptional, but the language development of a two-year-old capable of articulating such a question cannot have been impeded.

Like many intelligent children, Albert Einstein was sometimes reluctant to talk, and a maidservant once called him stupid because she observed he had a way of repeating everything twice. The most likely real explanation for that behaviour was that he was determined to speak in complete sentences: when asked a question he would work out the answer in his head and try it out for himself, and then repeat the sentence aloud when he had assured himself that he had it right. What he was actually displaying here was not stupidity at all, but the strategic activity of a determined and self-critical child making a deliberate effort to do his best. Already, Einstein was keen to get things correct and unusually willing to persevere at tasks. Even at this age he was often engaged in play activities that involved solving puzzles and problems. He was already demonstrating a painstaking thoroughness, making elaborate structures from building blocks and, later, houses constructed from cards.

The adult Einstein's earliest memory of experiencing profound curiosity about a scientific mystery related to an occasion at the age of four or five when his father first showed him a magnetic compass. This, Einstein later recalled, made a lasting impression. He remembered his sense of wonder at observing the needle behaving in a manner that simply did not make sense in terms of his conceptual understanding of the world. He knew that there had to be some cause, but it was frustratingly hidden from him.

In early childhood he was unenthusiastic about playing with other children and was inclined to tantrums, but these disappeared at around the time Einstein started school. In his first years there he seemed to be a reserved and isolated child, and yet it was apparent that he was bright and capable. At the end of his first year of school (in August 1886) his mother was writing to her sister that Albert had brought home a brilliant report. She noted that he was at the top of his class, and not for the first time. Out of school he was equally impressive, his preferred spare time activities being mentally stimulating ones such as making fretwork articles, working with a metal construction set, and playing with a small model steam engine which a relative had given him.

There is a persisting although wildly inaccurate claim that Einstein was a bad pupil who failed to flourish at the Munich high school, or Gymnasium, which he attended from the age of nine and a half. In fact this assertion was firmly refuted as early as 1929, at which time the school's then principal searched the old records and was able to confirm that all the evidence demonstrated that Einstein had actually been a very good student. There had been no complaints about him and, no marks that were other than good. The written evidence of Einstein's performance also proved that the newspaper reports, in which Einstein was said to have been an especially poor student of languages, were totally unfounded.

Einstein did well at school despite the fact that neither the ambience nor the curriculum was particularly suitable for a Jewish child of his temperament and interests. There were eight hours of Latin every week, and four of Greek from the fourth year onwards. This left little time for other subjects, and so there were only three mathematics classes per week, and only two science and geography classes. Physics was not taught at all until the seventh year. Fortunately for Einstein, he had made considerable progress in those subjects by private study in his spare time, reaching levels of attainment well beyond the school's requirements.

By the age of eleven or so Albert Einstein was reading about science and philosophy in books that were beyond the understanding of most children. He was already contemplating the conflicting claims of science and religion, and had become convinced that much that he had read in the Bible could not be true. At the same age he became enchanted by mathematics. On encountering Pythagoras' theorem he determined to prove it. He succeeded, but only after three weeks of the kind of strenuous and unremitting contemplation that (although Einstein would not have known it at the time) was a characteristic mental activity of his great predecessor Isaac Newton. In common with Newton and a number of other outstanding thinkers (including Galileo and Bertrand Russell)[8] Einstein became particularly strongly attracted to the certainty and purity of Euclid's geometry. Before the age of twelve he had quickly worked his way through a geometry textbook and made a serious start on the study of advanced mathematics. Such was his progress that the family friend who had first encouraged his interest was soon finding it impossible to keep up with the child.

Science and mathematics were not the only difficult subjects Einstein began to master in his childhood. At the age of thirteen he studied – and appears to have enjoyed and comprehended – Kant's notoriously daunting *Critique of Pure Reason*. A classmate from this period later recalled how impressive a conversationalist the boy had already become. His main interests were intellectual ones, although he could be a mischievous practical joker at school. He was also acquiring a love of music. His mother, a capable pianist, had arranged for him to have lessons from the age of six. For years the child made very little progress, but at thirteen he suddenly acquired a passion for Mozart's sonatas, and leaped ahead, discovering that 'love is a better teacher than a sense of duty – at least for me'.[9] His much-admired expertise at playing the violin gave him enjoyment throughout his life.

Clearly, the young Albert Einstein was indeed a child prodigy. His accomplishments by the age of twelve were already far beyond the average, especially in science and mathematics. Yet as is true of the other

[8] Fölsing (1997), p. 23.   [9] Quoted in Fölsing (1997), p. 26.

geniuses we have encountered, there are no indications that Einstein was born unusually clever or that he learned more easily than other people: the qualities that did set him apart from other children seem to have been rooted more in his personality and temperament and his mental habits than in innate intelligence. As Einstein remarked on a number of occasions, he was passionately curious from an early age, and intrigued to discover how things work. Like virtually all great scientists he was immensely determined and dogged: he was always prepared to continue concentrating for very long periods on any challenge that gained his attention. At an early age he gained a capacity for unceasing reflection and contemplation. He insisted that he had not been born with any special gift.

The knowledge that Einstein was in fact an extraordinarily precocious child makes it clear that the monumental achievements of his mid-twenties were far from being the first and unanticipated signs that a new scientific genius was alive. However, although it is important to establish that Einstein was already intellectually remarkable when he was a child, doing that does not account for his prodigious powers. Knowing that he was a prodigy rather than the backward child he is often supposed to have been resolves some apparent mysteries, but leaves other questions unanswered. How and why did he become a prodigy in the first place? The unpromising early family circumstances that have already been outlined give no real clues here. They offer no reasons for anticipating that this particular child's early progress would be at all superior to the average.

Yet, as in the case of a number of other early lives we have encountered, and as the examination of Michael Faraday's adolescence revealed with particular clarity, brief accounts of the outward circumstances of a young person's life can be inaccurate and even misleading indicators of the true state of affairs. That is undoubtedly true of Einstein. As in Faraday's case, the actual experiences of Einstein's early years were enormously more advantageous than a cursory glance would suggest. Once we are able to gain a reasonably full picture of the actual everyday world the young Einstein inhabited, it is evident that his real circumstances were not remotely unfavourable. In reality, the events and the influences that made up Albert Einstein's early years were almost ideal ones for nurturing the development of an enthusiastic young future scientist.

Right from the beginning, the young Albert Einstein was given plenty of encouragement and intellectual stimulation. He came from a large and generally prosperous family, in which a number of relatives could be counted upon to provide help on those occasions when Einstein's own parents experienced difficulties. At one time an aunt in Italy helped to finance Albert's studies, and Einstein's maternal grandparents were comfortably placed for giving assistance when it was needed. It is true that

Albert Einstein's father got into difficulties at times, but for substantial periods he flourished and prospered.

At the time of Albert's birth, his parents lived in a comfortable apartment in the city of Ulm, in southern Germany. They moved to Munich a year later. It was a good marriage, and the child's home background was harmonious as well as being unusually supportive. Einstein's mother and father were educated people who took their parental responsibilities seriously, making sure, for instance, that their eldest child always finished his school homework. Both of them respected their Jewish origins but took little notice of Jewish religion or ritual. They did not attend a synagogue, and no specifically Jewish rites or customs were followed at home, and nor were Jewish cooking rituals obeyed. Their reading, in which the works of authors such as Schiller and Heine were prominent, mirrored that of other cultured Germans of the time.

In short, Einstein's early family background was one that provided large measures of mental stimulation for the growing child, and also gave him the support and structure that would have enabled a child to flourish. So both of those attributes of a home background that Csikszentmihalyi's investigations have shown to be especially crucial for promoting mental expertise and competence were present in abundance in the Einstein home. For a growing scientist, his was an exceptionally privileged childhood. The advantages he was given could never have guaranteed that his progress would be exceptional, let alone as prodigious as it turned out to be, but they undoubtedly did contribute to his intellectual development.

Albert's uncle Jakob, his father's younger brother, was a qualified engineer as well as an ambitious industrialist who at times enjoyed very considerable success. At the time of Albert's birth Jakob Einstein was running a firm that provided gas and water installations. In 1880 he was joined by Albert's father, and the business was substantially enlarged by the purchase of a company that made gas boilers. The brothers extended their activities to the new field of electrical engineering, and by 1882 they were participating in an international electro-technical exhibition that was held in Munich, where they exhibited dynamos, arc lamps, light bulbs, and a complete telephone system. As this side of the business expanded and developed, the gas and water installation operations were faded out and the boiler making works were abandoned. There was a further expansion in 1885, when the brothers opened a new factory specialising in electrical engineering. At its peak the firm employed two hundred workers.

Unfortunately, the brothers were to overreach themselves. Their business got into difficulties and eventually had to be liquidated. But the company's failure could not alter the fact that the young Einstein had enjoyed the extraordinary opportunities and advantages of living among close relatives whose daily activities revolved around the application of new science and technology. The industrial plans of the brothers were boldly innovative. As a recent biographer puts it, they were what we would now describe as high-tech venture entrepreneurs.[10] They exploited recent scientific advances and combined them with the most recent technological developments. Their activities placed them at the cutting-edge of the era's technology.

There are obvious advantages for a would-be scientist of growing up against a background of constant engagement in recent scientific discoveries and their applications. Those advantages might have been less marked had Albert not been encouraged to become interested in the scientific problems that were occupying his close relatives. However, the child did receive ample encouragement. His father took a close interest in Albert's scientific education. One of his uncles, Caesar Koch, stimulated his interest in electricity and magnetism. Uncle Jakob, too, did much to help provide the child with learning opportunities. It was Jakob who first drew his attention to Pythagoras' theorem. Competent mathematicians were rare, and Albert Einstein was lucky to have one as a close relative. He was doubly fortunate in being able to profit from the stimulating influence of an uncle who was keen to share his enthusiasm for mathematics with his young nephew.

The young Albert Einstein never lacked mentors. Uncle Jakob was the first of a number of scientists and intellectuals who gave him considerable help. At the age of ten Einstein was introduced to Max Talmud, another person who was to offer him substantial encouragement and assistance throughout his adolescence. Talmud was only twenty-one himself when he started to become a regular visitor to the Einstein family, but he was an extremely well-read, as well as free-thinking young man. He was soon engaging Einstein in vigorous intellectual conversations and he regularly brought books to the home. Those which Talmud introduced to Albert Einstein included volumes that many families would have thought too revolutionary or too tainted by atheism to be suitable reading for a young person. So Einstein never had to suffer from being 'protected' from ideas that were considered to be dangerous or shocking for him. Darwin's theory of evolution was among the more revolutionary scientific works that Einstein encountered at an early age.

Like Uncle Jakob, Max Talmud also contributed to the nurturing of Einstein's growing interest in mathematics. As we have seen, Talmud soon found himself unable to keep up with the young prodigy, who

[10] Fölsing (1997), p. 10.

amazed him with his remarkable progress and capacity to absorb scientific knowledge. Right from the beginning, advanced mathematics was for Einstein more than just another subject to study. He wondered at it and was enchanted by it, finding mathematical problems endlessly fascinating. His delight in solving them was emotional as well as intellectual, and he was attracted rather than repelled by the impersonal quality of mathematics, which many students have found off-putting.

By this time Einstein was already acquiring a taste for getting engaged for long periods in purely reflective activities. Doing that was beginning to become a habitual activity, and mathematical thinking perfectly suited his inclinations. And Kant's highly abstract philosophy provided further nourishment for his increasingly contemplative mind.

The later years of Einstein's late adolescence were unsettling ones. His father's financial problems, coupled with the fact that it was necessary for the immediate family to leave their home in Germany and settle in Italy when Einstein was fifteen, made it necessary for Albert to leave school prematurely. Nevertheless he continued to pursue his intellectual interests with impressive energy and determination. The cultural atmosphere of the Gymnasium he attended in Munich had never suited him, although he had usually found it possible to identify a few teachers whom he could admire and some friends who shared his interests.

Einstein's first application for admission to a university-level institution, the Zurich Polytechnic, was rejected. But while that much remarked upon fact is correct, the equally common inference that he was considered by the authorities to be simply not good enough, is not true at all. At the time he was a full two years younger than the normal minimum age for admission to the polytechnic, and admitting him then would have required a special exemption. The authorities decided that it would be better for the young scholar to delay entry until he was a year closer to the minimum age. But they also made it clear that they were extremely impressed by his exceptional qualities, and one professor warmly invited Einstein to attend his physics lectures.

In the event, Einstein spent the following year at a school situated thirty miles from Zurich. This school turned out to be a forward-looking institution, which encouraged its pupils to think for themselves. It allowed Einstein to fill some of the gaps in his previous education. The school was particularly unusual for its time in having an excellent scientific laboratory. Einstein lodged with the family of one of the teachers, Jost Winteler, a remarkable man who became another of Einstein's mentors. Winteler, who was particularly helpful to Einstein at the time when he was making the important step of renouncing German citizenship, had the rare foresight to prophesy the appalling turn of events that fermenting German nationalism would create in the early twentieth century.

In 1896 Einstein finally enrolled at the Zurich Polytechnic, although at seventeen he was still below the official minimum age for admission. By this time Einstein was making a vivid impression on people. His strong sense of humour and distinct self-assurance were being noticed, and he had become a lively and highly sceptical conversationalist. He was now sure of his ambition to be a scientist, and was already starting to have original ideas about the propagation of electromagnetic waves. The training that he was to gain in the next few years would enable him to become a serious scientific thinker and give him the mental skills and knowledge that made possible the massive creative achievements that he was to bestow on the world in 1905.

Einstein's creative work of that especially momentous year was, of course, immensely original. Yet as we have seen to be true of all the great achievements of geniuses, it was only possible because Einstein had made excellent use of a long and intense period of learning and preparation. In the course of that period he diligently directed his fierce energy and his intense curiosity, as well as his capacity for sustained reflection on problems, to the questions that captured his interest. Of course, what he finally accomplished took Einstein beyond what anyone else had achieved, but stupendous as his attainments were they should not blind us to the fact that Einstein, in common with Newton and Darwin and the other great scientists, was like other people, a member of the human species. The fact that his creative attainments took Albert Einstein further than anyone else had gone is not a reason for inferring that Einstein must have begun his life as inherently exceptional, with some rare innate gift or endowment that others have lacked. There are no genuine grounds for believing that Einstein was born to be a genius. There was nothing inevitable about the fact that he became one.

Einstein's course at Zurich lasted four years. By now the somewhat withdrawn child had become an outgoing and sociable young man who, like Charles Darwin, made friends easily with people who shared his enthusiasms. On the whole the Polytechnic was an excellent institution. It employed some outstanding professors, especially in mathematics. During the period he spent there Einstein became a self-assured and well-grounded young physicist. However, as he was the first to admit, he was far from being a model student. He was too sure of himself and too independent to conform to the expectations of all his teachers. He had his own goals and scientific priorities, which did not always coincide with theirs. Moreover, he soon discovered that there were important recent developments in physics that he would have to study independently, because they were not covered in any of the teaching provided at Zurich. For example, only through working on his own was he able to master certain advances that were crucial to his own special interests, in particular the theoretical discoveries of physicists such as Michael Faraday's successor James Clerk Maxwell, and Ludwig Boltzmann. But despite his independent streak, Einstein managed to do extremely well at some of his examinations, particularly in the initial years. His exam performance in the fourth year was less impressive, because by then his efforts to extend his mastery of mathematical physics were being largely directed by his own particular interests.

Nevertheless, on graduating Einstein was confident of getting a university position, and he was surprised and depressed when he failed to do so. A number of factors contributed to his lack of success. Sheer bad luck and poor timing were two. Anti-semitism may have been another reason, although there is no firm evidence of that. A more powerful cause of failure was that during his student years, whilst Einstein undoubtedly did make a strong impression on those professors who were subsequently in a position to offer him employment, a number of them had found his independent and non-subservient approach to his studies intensely annoying. He had ruined his chances of getting employed by one of the professors who was needing an assistant, by neglecting enough of the practical work he was obliged to undertake to earn himself a reproof for 'lack of application'.[11] Another professor who might have been able to find a job for him had been antagonised by Einstein's lack of respect and by the rather mediocre essay he had submitted. Yet another potential employer among the Zurich professors was probably put off by the unapologetic tone of Einstein's confession that he had failed to attend any of the man's seminars. The frustrated Einstein was forced into taking a temporary teaching position that provided an income for a few months. He became convinced, almost certainly wrongly, that one of his professors was working against him by giving him poor references.

Finally, however, in June 1902 Einstein did manage to find a job. It was not a university position but a post in the Swiss Patent Office in Bern. He had first heard about this opportunity early in 1901 from another student who was a close friend, and whose father recommended Einstein for the post.

A job in a patent office may appear to have represented a distinctly less attractive proposition for Einstein than the university position he had hoped for. In reality, however, as Einstein quickly appreciated, it was an excellent opportunity. For a start, the post was permanent, offering better pay and more security than a university assistantship, and good chances

---

[11] Quoted in Fölsing (1997), p. 57.

of promotion. It was a challenging position and the workload was heavy, but it was stimulating and interesting work. He was required to evaluate the work of inventors; doing that demanded clear thinking and a critical approach. Einstein enjoyed the job's practical aspects, and he found the task of having to investigate patents provided him with valuable training. He stayed in the post until 1908, well past the time when he began to produce major scientific achievements of his own, and he continued doing occasional work on patents long after that.

Einstein's period at the Swiss Patent Office was a time of enormous creativity. Until 1904 he produced few publications apart from some reviews of the work of others, but in 1905 the twenty-five-year-old Albert Einstein speedily assembled the four hugely important theoretical papers that were to make his reputation as the greatest physicist of the twentieth century.

Einstein's case illustrates, among other things, the importance of keeping in mind that whether or not a child has been labelled as being a prodigy is only loosely and somewhat arbitrarily related to the extent to which the young person really was exceptionally capable. This complication makes the fact that a child has been described as a prodigy a less than satisfactory indicator of the child's actual exceptionality. Like the term 'genius', 'prodigy' is as much a social construct as a natural category. And since neither of these words provides anything like an objective indicator of a person's actual capabilities, it is clear that we are on slippery ground when trying to tease out the relationships between someone's having been a child prodigy and the same person's becoming a genius.

Notwithstanding these problems, there is no doubt that links do exist between the state of being a child prodigy and that of being a genius. Descriptions of children who have been identified as prodigies provide useful insights into the connections between childhood abilities and the capabilities possessed by an adult, even though the form of the relationship may differ from one case to another.

The majority of child prodigies have not become geniuses, but most seem to have had relatively successful adult careers, and very few prodigies have had adult lives quite as unhappy as that of William Sidis, who we encountered in Chapter 5. One other exception was Erwin Nyiregyházi, a dazzling young Hungarian pianist born in 1903. Like William Sidis, Nyiregyházi was an immature and dependent young man, still unable to feed himself properly or tie his shoelaces at the age of eighteen, although by then he had already enjoyed successful debuts in Berlin and New York. After a disastrous marriage he abandoned his career as a concert pianist, except for a brief re-appearance in his seventies. But he did at least enjoy longevity. He died in 1987, survived by his tenth wife.[12]

For any child, there can be both positive and negative consequences of having precocious abilities. In certain spheres of ability the learning that is necessary in order to acquire essential basic skills may be less onerous for younger people than for older ones. Often, too, there are practical advantages to be gained by making an early start. The sheer amount of time needed to gain the expertise a person must have in order to be capable of creative or innovative achievements may be huge, sometimes as much as 10,000 to 20,000 hours. And simply because of that, unless considerable progress has been made in the years of childhood, finding the time and maintaining the degree of commitment needed to reach the highest levels of mastery may not be possible. The everyday demands of adult life may combine to prevent an adult beginner sustaining the single-minded dedication that would be needed in order to reach an exceptionally high level of expertise. So it is hardly surprising that amongst champion chess players, or outstanding musical performers, or exceptional mathematicians, it is unusual to find outstanding individuals who had not already achieved very high standards prior to their reaching adulthood.

There are other areas of expertise in which the capacity to make creative achievements is less dependent upon individuals possessing a particular body of acquired knowledge or skills. There are ones in which it is just as beneficial to have a wide range of different experiences. Here it is less likely that a person will be handicapped by not having been extraordinarily precocious in childhood. Amongst major novelists, for instance, although many were precociously well-read children, few were identified as being prodigies. And in some instances the particular benefits that are conveyed to a child as a consequence of being recognised as a prodigy may be outweighed by the disadvantages. While Mozart clearly did profit from the fact that he was seen as a prodigy, if only because people paid to watch his early performances, Billy Sidis's reputation as a prodigy brought him nothing but trouble. Without it, he would have had a far better chance of being able to make proper use of his impressive capabilities and enjoy a productive adult career.

Although the advantages of making a good early start often make it more than likely that a child who has been called a prodigy will do better as an adult than a child who lacks exceptional abilities, within a group of people who have all been prodigies in their childhoods there does not appear to be any clear relationship between the extent of individuals' precocity and their eventual degree of excellence. There are numerous well known instances of remarkable prodigies who have gone on to become remarkable adults, as Yehudi Menuhin did, for example, but there are also instances of striking child prodigies whose adult careers have not thrived at all. And in families where there has been more than one prodigy among the children, the sibling whose early feats are most spectacular does not always become the most illustrious. Of the two precocious sons of James Thomson, a professor at mathematics, it was the older brother who won all the prizes in his early career, but his eventual minor fame as an engineer was eclipsed by the reputation of his younger sibling, the great physicist Lord Kelvin.

Similarly, a recent study of the childhoods of twenty-five exceptionally successful American concert pianists in their early thirties revealed that few of them had shown distinct early signs of their future excellence. Even after the young people had been playing the instrument for seven or eight years, these individuals' levels of expertise, although admittedly high, were matched by hundreds of other enthusiastic and ambitious young musicians. Had the individuals who participated in the study been examined at this time, when they were around the age of fourteen or fifteen, with the majority of them there would have been no reason for predicting that those particular instrumentalists, among the many other young players who also aspired to become concert pianists, would find places among the extremely few who would eventually do exceptionally well.[13]

There has been much debate about the extent to which child prodigies are formed by genetics or experience. Their parents have often taken extreme positions on this question. Some, as we have seen, have been happy to portray themselves, somewhat unconvincingly, as essentially passive bystanders doing nothing apart from observing their child's amazing development and recording it for posterity. In contrast, as was illustrated in the previous chapter, those parents who have admitted taking a more active part in their child's early education have often taken the opposite stance. These people have insisted that their child was in no respect inherently exceptional, and that had it not been for the parents' special efforts to manufacture a superior individual there would have been no reason to expect the young person to be at all exceptional. Pastor Witte strongly held to this viewpoint, and so did James Mill and Leo Wiener. A few parents seem to have held both of these extreme (and incompatible) opposing views simultaneously. Leopold Mozart, for instance, promoted his son as both an amazing natural phenomenon and also the product of the father's superb teaching.

It is extremely difficult to arrive at firm conclusions concerning the

[13] Sosniak (1985).

extent to which genetic causes of variability between people affect the chances of any individual becoming exceptionally capable. That is certainly true of child prodigies. Inherited influences definitely contribute to the fact that people are different, but we cannot with any confidence be much more specific than that, as we shall discover in Chapter 9. It would of course be helpful to possess detailed descriptions of those attempts by parents to make their child into an exceptionally capable person that have totally failed. But understandably enough, only in the more successful instances have either the parents or their children been inclined to produce written accounts.

There must have been numerous unrecorded failures. It is known, for example, that Leo Wiener was almost as keen to accelerate his daughter's education as he was to promote his eldest son's (although he had run out of steam by the time Norbert's younger brother arrived). Why did her accomplishments not match Norbert's? Was she a child prodigy who in later life did not live up to her early promise, perhaps because of the restrictions imposed on a girl? Or did her abilities fail to match Norbert's even in childhood?

Even if information about failed attempts by parents to make their children into geniuses was less scarce than it actually is, important questions would remain unanswered. It would be hard to be sure to what extent these failures reflected children's limitations and to what degree parental inadequacies were responsible. Many a parent has strived to encourage their child to learn more, but has been too heavy-handed, or too poor a teacher, or insufficiently sensitive, or unable for other reasons to motivate their child. But it is hardly conceivable that all failures by mothers or fathers who have set out to make a child exceptional can be attributed to the parent's inadequacy as a teacher. Any two children are different from one another. Even if a pair of siblings are brought up in environments that their parents try to make identical, and are treated in exactly the same manner, so far as is humanly possible, the chances are that they will end up with differing personalities and distinct patterns of abilities. One reason for that is that even when adults largely succeed in creating identical environments for different children, they do not succeed in making the children's *experiences* identical. Psychologists sometimes make the mistake of assuming that environment and experience are the same. But they are not, and imposing identical environments on two children by no means guarantees that they will have identical experiences. That is not to deny that children's learning environments are important, but it is equally necessary to appreciate that the influence of anyone's environment is restricted by the fact that it is always indirect. The most direct influences on a person, and consequently the strongest, are the individual's unique experiences.

However hard parents try, they can never have complete control over their children's experiences. That is partly because a person's experiences are always partly determined by the individual's own biological endowment. Consequently, with the possible exception of those rare instances in which the children are identical twins whose parents strive to treat them in precisely the same manner, there are always going to be substantial differences between children in the way in which they actually experience those everyday events and activities that help determine their interests and abilities.

Imagine, for example, being the elder or younger daughter of parents who try hard to be entirely fair and even-handed in their approach to their offspring. These parents conscientiously act towards one child in exactly the same manner as they did towards their other child at the same age.[14] There comes a time, however, when the older sister notices that the younger sister is being treated differently from her. Perhaps the parents are less strict towards the younger sister, or expect less of her. Conversely, the younger sister begins to notice that her sibling is being given more responsibility, or is allowed to stay up later. In short, the older sister is experiencing the life of an older sister, and the younger sister is experiencing family life very differently. Over a period of time there will be many situations that the two children experience in contrasting ways, with consequences that will ensure that however similar the two girls' environments are they will eventually become women who differ from one another in a variety of ways.

Many of the questions people raise concerning possible links between being a child prodigy and becoming an adult genius have to do with the antecedents and consequences of being a prodigy. For example: In order to become a highly creative adult, is it necessary to have been a child prodigy? If not, is it usually helpful, or can it be a positive disadvantage? To become a child prodigy in the first place, is it essential to have experienced a stimulating and supportive early background? Questions like these raise important issues relating to the causes of exceptional accomplishments.

We could address these queries in a piecemeal fashion, but a more systematic approach offers advantages. A simple framework provides some needed structure here, helping to identify links between the state of being a child prodigy with its various precursors and possible consequences. We can start by identifying three broad stages in a person's life, early childhood, late childhood and adult. At each of these stages, two possible states can be identified, as follows.

14 This illustration is taken from Dunn & Plomin (1990).

First, in early childhood an individual's family background may be stimulating and supportive or unstimulating and unsupportive. As we have seen, these aspects of a child's early years have considerable impact on a child's early learning and development.

Second in mid-childhood a child may be a prodigy or not a prodigy.

Third, as an adult, the person may be capable or incapable of creative achievements.

By combining each of the two states at any one of these three stages with each state at the other stages, we arrive at eight possible categories of people, as follows:

1 Men and women who did not have stimulating and supportive early upbringings, were not child prodigies and did not produce any creative achievements as adults.

2 Individuals who did have a stimulating and supportive upbringing, but did not become prodigies and never made any creative achievements as adults.

3 People who had a stimulating and supportive early upbringing, were prodigies in childhood, but who, in maturity, did not make any exceptional achievements.

4 Men and women who enjoyed a stimulating and supportive early upbringing, were child prodigies, and did produce major adult achievements.

5 Those who did have a stimulating and supportive early upbringing, but were not child prodigies, and yet did have impressive achievements in adulthood.

6 People who did not have a stimulating and supportive early upbringing, but were prodigies in childhood, and, as adults, made substantial achievements.

7 Men and women who did not have a stimulating and supportive early upbringing, but were nevertheless prodigies in childhood, and, as adults, did not produce any creative achievements.

8 Individuals who did not have a stimulating and supportive early upbringing, and were not prodigies in childhood, but who, as adults, nevertheless produced creative achievements.

Allocating people to these categories is undeniably a somewhat rough and ready procedure, if only because the graduations that exist in each of the three factors involved have to be ignored. Nevertheless, it is a useful exercise, providing useful information about the necessity of certain precursors of genius. The millions of people who belong in categories one and two are of little interest here. Individuals in category three serve mainly to remind us that having a good early start does not guarantee outstanding excellence in adulthood. Billy Sidis belongs in it, although he is untypical both in being relatively well-known and in having had to endure an adult life that was particularly unhappy. There are numerous reasons why not every exceptionally promising young person will have a fulfilling or productive adult life, or be capable of creative achievements. One is that there is no guarantee that a child prodigy will develop all the qualities that are needed in order to make exceptional mature accomplishments possible. A musician, for instance, may be technically outstanding but lack certain of the emotional or intellectual resources that make a performance distinctive. A mathematician may possess a mind furnished with exceptional skills and knowledge but not have the drive necessary to sustain the arduous intellectual effort that is required in order to make progress in the face of difficulties. What is more, as we have seen, in some circumstances influences that accelerate a young person's progress sufficiently to make it appropriate for the individual to be regarded as a prodigy may also work to reduce rather than increase that individual's likelihood of becoming capable of creative adult accomplishments. For example, parents who are anxious for their children to excel at particular skills can all-too-easily deprive them of experiences that help children to become sufficiently independent and self-motivated to make the best of their capabilities.

Knowledge about membership of all the other categories bears on important questions concerning relationships between genius and the circumstances that precede it. Perhaps surprisingly, with none of these five categories is it totally impossible to identify exemplars. It appears, then, that there may be few if any absolutely essential background factors, in the absence of which it would be quite impossible for someone to aspire to being a genius. Less surprisingly, a substantial proportion of those people who are acclaimed as creative geniuses belong within the fourth category, and that is true of a number of Nobel prizewinners (Zuckerman, 1977). Mozart is one name that comes to mind. Others are Yehudi Menuhin, the violinist, and among the other individuals who we have encountered, John Stuart Mill and Norbert Wiener are both members of this category.

Belonging to the fifth category are people who did enjoy a stimulating and supportive early upbringing, but who were not child prodigies, and yet did produce creative adult achievements. Although there are certain areas of achievement in which it is very unlikely that someone will become exceptionally capable unless considerable progress has already been made by the end of childhood, that is not true of all fields of endeavour. Leo Tolstoy, the novelist, and William James, the philosopher and psychologist brother of Henry James, are two examples of people who gave few early indications of the exceptional creativity they were to display as adults. Charles Darwin is another person who belongs in this category. All three of these individuals came from wealthy families. Wealth makes it possible for individuals to make false starts and delay committing themselves to a career without incurring serious penalties, as Tolstoy was able to.

The final three categories include people who did not have early upbringings that were particularly supportive or stimulating. In the sixth group are people who, despite that, were prodigies in childhood and, as adults, did make creative achievements. The lack of a good start in life is clearly a disadvantage for a young person, and in many cases it has ruled out the possibility of becoming a highly creative adult. Nevertheless, it is possible to identify a few individuals who were prodigies and who did produce major achievements despite having had no special advantages in their early years. George Bidder definitely fits into this category, as does James Mill, and Michael Faraday arguably belongs within it. He undoubtedly produced major creative achievements, and he was certainly a bright and precocious child, even if it would be stretching things a little to assert that he was a child prodigy. Another instance of a person who was a prodigy and also a genius, despite not having enjoyed an especially stimulating early background, was J. M. W. Turner, perhaps England's greatest artist.

To belong in the seventh category a person is required not to have had a stimulating and supportive early upbringing, but nevertheless to have become a prodigy in childhood, but without going on to produce creative achievements in maturity. This is one category for which members might be expected to be very rare if not non-existent, and it is certainly not easy to identify individuals who clearly belong within it. All the same, a few can be found. One such person was a talented young American mental calculator, who as a boy entered into a competition with George Bidder. His name was Zerah Colburn, and he was born in Vermont, and his encounter with Bidder took place when Bidder was aged twelve and Colburn probably fourteen.[15] Like George Bidder, Zerah Colburn began attracting attention to himself in early childhood, beginning at the age of six when his father heard him repeating multiplication tables. Colburn, like Bidder, travelled round giving public demonstrations for money. Colburn seems to have been even more precocious than Bidder as a young child. It was reported that at the age of six he could solve problems such as squaring 1,449, multiplying 12,225 times 1,223, and discovering how many seconds there are in 2000 years.

[15] Howe (1990).

Zerah Colburn was reputed to have been an outgoing and intelligent man, and had an interesting life during which he worked an actor, teacher, minister, and also as a mathematician employed to make astronomical calculations. But when he died at the age of thirty-five he was neither prosperous nor happy, and despite his remarkable promise he never made any lasting creative accomplishments.

Like the seventh category, the eight and final one, in which belong individuals who did not have a favourable early upbringing, and were not prodigies, but nevertheless made impressive adult achievements, does not overflow with members. It would hardly be surprising to discover that in the absence of either the advantages of a good early background or any of those early indications of special promise that can bring a child to the attention of individuals who are in a position to provide needed help (as happened in George Bidder's case) the chances of someone producing major adult creative accomplishments have been nil. Nevertheless, this eighth category is not entirely empty, one of its most prominent members being that remarkable engineering genius, George Stephenson. To lack the advantages of a good early background is clearly a disadvantage. Lacking also the benefits that can follow from being regarded as a child prodigy makes a person doubly disadvantaged. But even with that combination of unpromising circumstances, as George Stephenson's life so gloriously demonstrates, genius is not entirely ruled out.

Broadly speaking, child prodigies are young people who for one reason or another seem to have made an unusually good start in life. So far as the likelihood of a person becoming capable of mature creative accomplishments is concerned, the fact that the person has been a prodigy in childhood is important, not because it points to some inherent special gift or talent, but simply because it indicates that unusually fast progress has already been made. Exceptional early progress does not make exceptional adult achievements inevitable, and yet in many cases it does help make them possible. That is especially true in those areas of achievement in which mastery depends upon lengthy and concentrated training.

In fields in which the links between early learning and mature achievements are less straightforward, the advantages of being a prodigy may be fewer. Among novelists, for example, the young Trollope was a daydreamer, the youthful Charles Dickens was an observant young person who was keenly alert to the world he perceived, and the Brontë children created shared imaginary worlds that depended upon the close relationships which existed within a family consisting of intelligent and well-informed individuals. It is true to say that each of these writers had childhood experiences that contributed to their eventually becoming major novelists. However, for them there would have been relatively little added advantage to be gained from their acquiring in childhood the kind of highly specialised expertise that would have led to them being seen as child prodigies.

The fact that it is not essential to have been a prodigy in order to become capable of creative mature accomplishments does not mean that there are no limits to what can be achieved in the absence of a good early start. Stephenson could make himself into a great engineer only because many of the skills an engineer needed in his time were practical ones that he could practise in his everyday life. Modern-day equivalents of George Stephenson are fairly rare, although the ranks of exceptional jazz-players and other non-classical musicians have included some individuals with little formal education in music. But as we perceived earlier, even in Stephenson's era someone with his total lack of school education could never have become a great scientist like Faraday or Darwin, because science cannot be learned from everyday experience. A career like Faraday's is hard to imagine today, with schools providing basic science education and young scientists having to gain a very substantial body of knowledge and skills in order to become prepared for making original contributions. Charles Darwin is a particularly a well-known example of a person who was a genius, but without having seemed at all remarkable as a child, but his career was only possible because his childhood activities did provide him with an invaluable fund of knowledge and skills that he was able to build upon later in life.

7   The expertise of great writers

At first glance the prospect of acquiring expertise and the possibility of becoming a genius seem worlds apart. Gaining expertise takes lengthy periods of practice and training. It requires effortful and repetitive activities, leading to the gradual mastery of skills and accomplishments. Genius, in contrast, is perceived as spontaneous and fluent: it sparkles. Becoming an expert demands powers of doggedness and persistence, but genius appears to spring from inborn brilliance. Expertise is mundane where genius is glamorous. Expertise is a matter of degree, an unexceptional characteristic possessed to varying extents by millions of ordinary men and women. Genius, it seems, is all or nothing, and it only strikes in individuals who possess rare qualities of natural creativity.

But as we have already seen, this picture is largely false. For a start, even geniuses always have to spend at least a decade learning their crafts. There are no valid grounds for believing that those individuals whose eventual achievements have been exceptionally impressive have needed any less effort or any less determination than other people. The fluency that has been remarked upon in thinkers like Einstein and artists like Mozart is real enough, but that is a product of their training and experience, not a quality they were born possessing.

The present chapter explores the circumstances in which certain major authors acquired their expertise as writers. Great writing demands more than mere technical competence, of course, but literature is not possible in the absence of the skills that a writer can only gain through training and experience. It might seem that whilst there are certain fields of accomplishment, such as music, science, or mathematics, in which creative achievements can only be made by individuals who have undergone the thousands of hours of training and practice that are essential in some fields, there are other areas of creativity in which periods of training do not have to be of comparable magnitude. Writing appears to be one. However, we shall discover that evidence about the actual early progress of future authors provides no support for this suggestion. Writers, like other makers of creative achievements, put enormous efforts into the task of acquiring exceptional expertise.

As any recreational tennis player or bridge enthusiast or amateur musician knows, it is possible to spend enormous amounts of time practising an activity without becoming dramatically better at it. If practising is essential for acquiring high levels of skill, it certainly does not guarantee it. Researchers investigating expertise have tried to isolate what it is that is different about the kinds of training and practice activities that do produce high levels of expertise, compared with the kinds of practising that do no more than maintain an amateur's modest level of mastery.

The kind of practice that is necessary in order to acquire exceptional expertise has to be considerably more intensive and much more systematic. Also, the particular practice activities that are engaged in need to be much more closely related to the specific improvements that are being aimed at. For example, where an amateur tennis player wanting to improve a weakness at backhand volleying might simply play more games and look for opportunities to use backhand volleying shots, a professional would be more likely to have training sessions in which the coach made sure that there were hundreds of opportunities to practise the particular actions that required attention. This kind of formal and deliberate practising is liable to be less inherently motivating than the performing activities that people prefer to engage in.[1]

Creative writers, just like those people whose creativity takes other forms, take a long time to master their craft. A reader of someone's 'first novel' would be unwise to infer that the book in the hand represents its author's earliest attempt at serious fiction. A first published novel is almost never its originator's first substantial writing project. All successful authors have been lifelong readers, and the majority gained the habit of committing their thoughts to paper at an early age. It is not uncommon for distinguished writers to have made their first try at writing a book well before the end of childhood. John Stuart Mill did that, as did John Ruskin and H.G. Wells, among others.

Inevitably, these juvenile efforts are often naive, crude and uneven. Nevertheless, as well as displaying their authors' often remarkable precocity they are significant in other ways. First, the manufacture of a whole book by a child signals a devotion to the difficult enterprise of writing that augurs well for an author's future progress. At the very least it demonstrates a willingness to persist at arduous intellectual pursuits for lengthy periods of time. Second, the fact that a child is actually capable of writing

---

[1] Ericsson and Charness (1994).

a book indicates that the young writer has already made a good start at the training at writing that progress builds upon.

The early literary lives of the Brontë family exemplify the capacity for juvenile efforts at writing and the circumstances giving rise to them to influence as well as portend literary careers. Each of the four younger Brontë siblings, whose mother had died when the eldest, Charlotte, was only five, became seriously involved in writing as a recreational activity at around the age of ten. Soon after the deaths in 1825 of the two oldest sisters, Maria (born 1814) and Elizabeth (born 1815), the older of the four surviving children, Charlotte (born 1816) and Branwell (born 1817) started to produce a series of tales about imagined worlds. The earliest compositions were little more than extensions of childish play, bearing all the usual hallmarks of childish writing. They were poorly spelled, largely unpunctuated, and closely modelled upon the stories and newspaper articles that the children had most recently been reading. Remarkably, however, a firm habit of writing about imaginary worlds became established, and it persisted for a decade, making major invasions into the growing authors' time. Over the years the initially childish efforts at writing became more and more sophisticated and adventurous, and they increasingly took verse as well as prose form. A degree of continuity was maintained, however, in the content as well as the form of the narratives, and certain of the story characters that first made their appearance in the early 1830s were still being written about at the end of that decade. For all of the Brontës, their childhood literary activities were immensely important influences on their later capabilities and accomplishments, providing frequent and regular opportunities to practise and extend the writing skills that all authors depend upon.

The imaginary worlds had their beginnings around 1826, when Charlotte and Emily, who shared a bed, invented simple unwritten plays, not unlike those created in many children's imaginary play. The very first of the Brontës' plays took most of the characters from toys, especially their brother Branwell's toy soldiers. The earliest surviving play that was written down, by Branwell, is set in Lorraine and concerns the imaginary intrigues and battles between would-be rulers, in the course of which the events include a rebellion and a siege. As the Brontës' biographer Juliet Barker notes,[2] most of the essential elements of their juvenile writings were already in place at that time, including political rivalries, battles, and rebellions that are played out within fantasy kingdoms. Numerous sources were drawn upon. A particularly important inspiration was *Blackwood's Magazine*, a monthly journal containing a wide mixture of

---

[2] Barker (1994), p. 152. My discussion of the Brontës' early writing activities has drawn heavily upon this excellent book.

articles ranging from fiction to political satire and humour. Branwell's toy soldiers were given names and pressed into service as fictional characters.

The received view that the Brontës led a solitary existence, isolated from the events in the world outside their parsonage home at Haworth, set in the moors of northern England, is far from accurate. The children enjoyed at least two Yorkshire newspapers and had access to a good range of books. Accounts by travellers which the children had read, and various historical descriptions, all found their way into the Brontë juvenilia. The earliest writings were undoubtedly imaginative, but more imitative than original, with little in the way of mature ideas or realistic characters.

From this early stage, the plays and stories were written in minuscule writing, in minute hand-made books. The writing was too small for adults to read without the aid of a magnifying glass. This had the practical consequence of ensuring that the stories were never the subject of grown-ups' censure. So despite their abysmal spelling and often non-existent punctuation, these early efforts never attracted the kinds of comments such as the ubiquitous 'careless: could do better' with which successive generations of teachers have discouraged the creative impulses of their pupils. There was no pressure on the Brontë children to mask their productions with an unnatural veneer of maturity, and no need to make fair copies. All that mattered was that their own brother and sisters could understand the writing, and for them the lapses in grammar, spelling and punctuation created no cause for complaint. On occasions the father, Patrick Brontë, who was a more benign and stimulating parent than Brontë mythology has allowed, as well as being an active reforming churchman, gently remonstrated with his children about the inaccessibility of their written compositions, but to little permanent effect. As late as 1833, when Charlotte was seventeen, his Christmas present to her was a notebook at the front of which he thought it necessary to make the written plea that 'all that is written in this book, must be in a good, plain and legible hand'.[3]

It is clear from their juvenilia that none of the Brontës suddenly or unpredictably arrived on the literary scene as a fully-fledged novelist. Not one of the children gave any indication in these early efforts of having some rare innate talent or natural gift for authorship. As with all children's first attempts at written expression, in every case the earliest of a Brontë sibling's writings are thoroughly childish and naive, and composed of immature sentiments that are inexpertly expressed. The maturity and mastery that are evident in the Brontës' published works only

---

[3] Barker (1994), p. 201.

came much later, following many years during which they constantly gave themselves practice in writing, and experimented at it, their efforts fuelled by the obvious delight that came from manufacturing stories about imaginary worlds.

Understandably, the children were drawn to what they found exotic and dramatic. Toy soldiers newly added to Branwell's collection were quickly shared out among his siblings, given names, and provided with invented backgrounds. One box of soldiers quickly became the 'Young Men', a brave band of twelve young Englishmen who had landed in an African kingdom after an exciting journey that involved dangerous adventures. Once in Africa these heroic young men encountered further dangers, which included 'an Immense and terrible monster his head touched the clouds was encircled with a red and fiery Halo his nostrils flashed forth flames'.[4] From time to time a character would be transformed into an entirely different individual. For instance, a soldier that Emily initially named Gravey suddenly acquired the name of a real person, the Arctic explorer William Perry, whose adventures had recently been described in *Blackwood's Magazine*. But Emily's older sister Charlotte often refused to permit such transformations. After naming one of her soldiers after her current hero, the Duke of Wellington, she insisted on keeping him in the cast throughout a number of plays, until she eventually permitted him to be superseded by his sons.

The character of Perry was not the only borrowing from *Blackwood's*, which had also supplied the African setting. The Brontës had discovered in *Blackwood's Magazine* a lengthy review of a book describing an expeditionary mission from the west coast of Africa into the interior. The stories about the Young Men lifted a number of place names and names of kings from that report. The imaginary land took up a large chunk of western Africa, and included a number of features that were real, including the Gambia and Niger rivers, and some that were based on real places, such as a city at the mouth of the Gambia that was renamed Verdopolis by Branwell and Verreopolis by Charlotte, as well as others that were entirely fictitious. The young authors decided to divide the region into a confederacy of states, each of which was ruled by a soldier belonging to one of the children. Other soldiers ruled over islands situated off the coast. The land as a whole became known as Glasstown. Later, following the destruction of its main city at a later stage in the development of the stories, it was to be renamed Angria. Within Glasstown were to be found a rich range of people, places, events, and buildings, drawn partly from the children's own experiences and partly from things they had read

[4] Barker (1994), p. 154

about in books and newspapers. There were both a fashionable aristocratic society and a lower sphere of life centred around inns and taverns, and buildings similar to ones seen only in biblical paintings as well as others based on Yorkshire wool mills. As in the real world, Glasstown had its share of political and dramatic activities, with wars, revolutions, plots and counter-plots, and a heady mixture of dramatic events.

Sometimes this vivid imaginary world fused with the real world, and a diary entry could switch from everyday life to the imagined land and back again in a single sentence. Thus in one story Charlotte suddenly abandons a description of the island inhabitants of the story constructing a new school to insert an impassioned report of her family's reactions to political changes relating to Roman Catholic emancipation, an issue of the day that aroused strong passions in a clergyman's family.

As the children grew older, the stories became less childish, wittier, and more original, reflecting their authors' increasing sophistication, but no less playful. Irony became more evident. References to drinking and drunkenness in their characters reflected the narrators' increasing knowledge of the real world. Both Charlotte's and Branwell's stories began to demonstrate an impressive and growing knowledge of classical language and literature, with classical references and allusions becoming common. The fourteen-year-old Charlotte had the cast of one story conversing in French.

There was never the slightest doubt that all the authors gained immense enjoyment from the activity of writing. The need to escape or retreat from reality may sometimes have been a contributing influence, and the sheer volume of the production could be seen as evidence of a commitment that seemed at times obsessive, but signs of the authors' pleasure in what they were doing punctuate all the writing. Quite often the different authors, writing under their various pseudonyms, would tease each other or poke fun at their siblings' productions.

The spelling only gradually improved, and punctuation was still getting very little attention even in the stories written in their authors' late teens. In 1829, when he was not yet twelve, Branwell increased his output by starting a magazine that appeared at monthly intervals. It contained articles on all kinds of subjects, mostly written by himself but with a few contributions by Charlotte. Its title, after the model being imitated, was 'Branwell's Blackwood's Magazine'. It was as tiny as the other volumes, being just over two inches high. From the outset, many of the articles appeared under various pseudonyms belonging to characters from the imaginary world of Glasstown, such as 'Captain John Bud', Glasstown's fictitious historian. The complex interweavings of fiction and reality are exemplified by the fact that another of the fictitious contributors to the magazine, the Glasstown poet 'Young Soult' was actually based on a real person, Marshal Soult, a commander under Napoleon Buonaparte. But as was to happen not infrequently in the Brontës' later juvenile writings, a character invented by one sibling might be mercilessly abused by another. Young Soult, for example, whose inventor, Branwell, regarded him with some affection, is fiercely attacked in one of Charlotte's pseudonym's productions, where he is amusingly but sharply caricatured as a pompous poetaster named 'Henry Rhymer'.

Magic and mystery are frequent ingredients in the earlier stories. There were a number of borrowings from *The Arabian Nights* in Charlotte's tales, and she also adapted legends and mysterious tales that had appeared in *Blackwood's Magazine*. Fabulous and exotic locations were favoured, even in connection with characters based on real men and women. For instance, Charlotte situated her Duke of Wellington in a white marble palace among olive trees, palms, and myrtles, and other characters were placed in settings filled with gold and diamonds. The playful author was not too solemn to nudge her readers with an occasional comment on her own facility at creating incongruous mixtures of fantasy and reality. She broke off at one point from a description of the magnificence of a lavishly decorated emerald dome to point out to any reader who might not have already noticed it, that 'you are gazing on the production of a mighty imagination'.[5]

It might have been expected that as the children matured their imaginary worlds would lose some of their allure. But that did not happen until well into adulthood. There was simply no need to entirely abandon the societies that had been invented with the first Glasstown stories, because within the imagined worlds there was ample scope for developments catering for the newer interests and preoccupations of authors who were no longer children. Some of the later creations were complex literary achievements, often scholarly as well as creative, sometimes in verse form rather than prose. The two youngest sisters, Emily (born 1818) and Anne (born 1820) contributed more frequently as time progressed, although the majority of the surviving booklets are by Charlotte and Branwell. Political elements became more prominent. Detailed histories were supplied. Characters were more effectively delineated and developed, with one of Branwell's creations, 'Alexander Rogue', an evil person who had appeared in a number of stories (including some by Charlotte, who calls Rogue 'deceitful, bloody and cruel' as well as 'skilled in all the sleight-of-hand blackleg tricks of the gaming table'[6]) taking centre stage in the first of the books to depart from the miniature form of the earlier ones. The

---

[5] Quoted in Barker (1994), p. 161.   [6] Quoted in Barker (1994), p. 188.

main city of Glasstown was actually destroyed in a revolution (brought on by the actions of the demagogic Alexander Rogue), and replaced by a new city, Angria, but a number of the Glasstown inhabitants remained as characters in the post-Glasstown books. At around the same time, Emily and Anne invented their own independent world, Gondal, situated in the Pacific Ocean.

From the beginning, the depiction of people and events of the imagined worlds had some of the attributes of a soap opera, albeit an uncharacteristically literary and political one. As in modern soap operas, the fictitious societies were depicted as being largely self-sufficient and isolated from the outside world, and successive episodes focused on different characters and situations. In the case of Gondal, unfortunately, although a substantial amount of Gondal poetry and later prose still exists, all the earlier prose narratives have been lost. Gondal was Emily's and Anne's secret world, from which Branwell and Charlotte were excluded. Like Glasstown and Angria, the world of Gondal was one in which warfare and politics alternated with romantic intrigues. Juliet Barker has observed that the women of Gondal are more active and resourceful than those inhabiting the other worlds, as might be expected in a universe devised by only female authors. In contrast with the beautiful but passive playthings who pine for their Angrian lovers, the strong-minded ladies of Gondal take more forceful parts in the stories.

The fact that the creative activity of writing about an invented world was a joint exercise contributed enormously to the authors' enjoyment. It was a marvellous game, in which each participant eagerly ingested and responded to their sibling's latest instalment. Cooperation and competition were equally in evidence. As ever, one Brontë was likely to deal harshly with another's characters. Branwell and Charlotte each constantly reacted to the new developments in the other's fiction, and not infrequently tried to outmanoeuvre the other. Certain of Charlotte's dashing and lovesick young men were transformed by Branwell into cynical politicians. Charlotte retaliated by rewriting the early life of Branwell's anti-hero Alexander Rogue, whom she now revealed to have started off as a handsome young soldier, forced into a life of crime and debauchery only after being unfairly exiled from Glasstown. On one occasion, after Branwell had the gall to kill off a favourite heroine of Charlotte, his sister instantly resurrected her, declaring that the report of her death was simply a rumour designed to arouse the people against an oppressive aristocrat.

As the authors approached adolescence, the love lives and romantic preoccupations of Glasstown's inhabitants came increasingly under the looking glass. By 1831 the fifteen-year-old Charlotte, now an enthusiastic reader of Sir Walter Scott's romances and obsessed with Byron – as were numerous young women at the time – was writing a lengthy poem in which one of the heroines laments her aristocratic lover, a marquis, who has abandoned her for another woman. The latter affair was also described in another story, this time in prose. Love and romance now became the dominant topic of Charlotte's fiction. During this period all the men she writes about are dashing, tall and attractive, and all her heroines beautiful. They are also invariably aristocratic, even if their high birth is sometimes a secret, hidden from all until the final pages. The romantic ingredients of the stories are frequently combined with melodrama. Passionate but unprincipled dark-eyed beauties are besotted with amoral male characters whose scornful sneers betray their wicked natures. But there are also more profound and thoughtful passages, in which serious issues are discussed. Many elements of the Brontë sisters' published novels can be detected in their later juvenilia.

The imaginary worlds continued to engage Charlotte's attention, serving at times as a refuge and a solace, well into the stage of her life at which she was starting to make a serious effort to earn a living from writing. By this time she was learning to use some new techniques, experimenting in her Angrian stories with forms that she subsequently drew upon in her published novels. For example, in an Angrian story written in 1838 she first used the device of narrating a tale through a series of letters between the characters.[7] At around the same time she was also beginning to write about women who were more real and ordinary than the exotically beautiful creations that populate most of the earlier Glasstown and Angria stories. She was starting to depict females with more of her own characteristics, plainer and more lifelike young women who were not unlike the realistic heroine of *Jane Eyre*.

The long-lasting juvenile experiments in which Branwell and his three sisters created and explored their secret worlds hugely influenced the development of their imaginations and the growth of their writing skills. The activities that produced their voluminous early writing equipped each of the Brontës with the technical expertise a creative author needs. Their habit of producing works quickly, without spending time revising their prose, helped to make their writing fluent. The fact that their productions were hidden from potentially censorious adult eyes ensured that the young Brontës were able to explore and extend their literary powers in a kind of protected haven, which allowed their confidence as writers to grow as they matured, unconstrained by thoughts of what outsiders might think. It is virtually unknown for a single family comprising four children

---

[7] Barker (1994), p. 291.

to produce three eminent female authors plus a talented brother who too, but for ill-fortune, might well have been capable of impressive literary achievements. It is hardly conceivable that each of a group of three sisters could have created major novels had it not been for the fact that writing activities played such a prominent part in their early lives.

Charlotte herself was fully aware of the benefits she gained from her early writing. All the same, as Juliet Barker observes,[8] some of the habits that Charlotte picked up in writing about Glasstown and Angria had to be discarded in order for her to become capable of the more realistic fiction of her mature novels. Her juvenile writing is typically exotic, florid, and extravagant. It is dramatic and often highly imaginative, lacking the simplicity and down-to-earth characterisation that was needed in order to produce a novel like *Jane Eyre*. Barker argues that it was difficult for Charlotte to shake off 'her old bad habits of Gothic exaggeration'.[9] She suggests that Charlotte's incomplete success at doing that mars some of her work, including her first serious novel, *The Professor*, which was completed in 1846 when she was just thirty. It was rejected by a number of publishers and did not appear in print until after her death.

Emily and Anne had less to unlearn, because there was not so marked a conflict in either style or content between their juvenile writings and their mature work. Juliet Barker notes that the world of *Wuthering Heights* is in a number of respects similar to the world of Gondal. Both draw on the descriptive passages of Walter Scott as well as moorland life in Yorkshire amid the landscape Emily could see from her own home.[10] Heathcliff has a forerunner in a Gondal character who first appeared ten years before the writing of *Wuthering Heights*, a mysterious doomed outlaw whose sole redeeming feature, like Heathcliff's, is his love for a beautiful woman. Themes revolving around passionate adult love between individuals who have grown up together and then been separated or cast into exile are encountered in Gondal tales and poems. Views about death that are explored in *Wuthering Heights* are presaged in Gondal poetry. Barker points out that the drunken debauchery and casual cruelty that shocked readers of *Wuthering Heights* are common elements in the Gondal tales. The decision of the neglected wife in Anne Brontë's *The Tenant of Wildfell Hall* to nurse her debauched husband in his days of decline echoes a Gondal story in which Zenobia, the long-suffering wife of the unfaithful Northangerland (previously the demagogue and adventurer Alexander Rogue) makes the identical choice.

As a formative influence upon writers' eventual accomplishments, the self-directed shared apprenticeship of the Brontës is unique in its uncon-

---

[8] Barker (1994), p. 500.   [9] Barker (1994), p. 500.   [10] Barker (1994), p. 501.

ventionality and perhaps also in the emotional intensity of its hold over the minds of the young people who created the secret worlds of Glasstown, Angria, and Gondal. But at least as a source of experiences that have nurtured the acquisition of skills and capabilities, other young people's early circumstances have been just as significant. One conventional and not unrealistic image of a successful person's early life, which depicts a diligent and studious but otherwise unexceptional child making the best of excellent early educational opportunities, is more frequently personified in scientists – such as Marie Curie, for example – than in creative writers, as is evident from Harriet Zuckerman's study of the lives of Nobel prizewinners.[11] Nevertheless, there are some writers whose early progress is superior to the average but not altogether extraordinary, and marked more by careful application to learning than by remarkable precocity. The author of *Middlemarch*, arguably the greatest novel in the English language, was such a person in her younger days, although in common with Curie she was to become notably less conventional in the arrangements she made for her adult life.

Mary Anne Evans (later Mary Ann and eventually Marian: the name 'George Eliot' was only a nom-de-plume) grew up in the English midlands. Born in 1819, three months after the infamous Peterloo Massacre – a bloody suppression of peaceful demonstrators against taxes on corn which came to epitomise what was most repressive about traditional British society – she was a contemporary of the Brontë sisters. Like them, she read widely as a child, enjoying the prose of Walter Scott and the verse of Robert Southey, as they did, and later, the writings of Lord Byron. Like them she attended a boarding school. Like them, she lacked close bonds with a mother. In her case this was not a consequence of death but an outcome of her mother's conspicuous failure to establish a warm relationship with her. In common with Charlotte Brontë, Evans was acutely conscious of her lack of conventional beauty. Like the Brontës she was religious in childhood and was affected by the religious controversies of the time. Like them, as she approached adulthood she was oppressively aware of her lack of options for the future. There were few obvious choices available to her, and none of them would have seemed attractive. They included being a governess, or a teacher, or perhaps a spinster devoting her time to the care of an aged parent. In common with the Brontës and (to an even greater extent) with John Stuart Mill, in her first years as an adult she was strongly aware that her education had equipped her with intellectual capacities that she was not at all certain how best to utilise.

In other respects Mary Anne Evans was not at all like any of the Brontë

[11] Zuckerman (1977).

sisters. In sharp contrast to them, until she was a mature woman she did not even consider the possibility of devoting large amounts of her time to writing fiction. At the age of twenty Charlotte Brontë was already making enquiries into the possibility of making a living through writing, and asking for advice from Robert Southey, then the Poet Laureate. In Evans's case it was not until she was already an experienced writer that she began to think seriously about producing novels. What little early fiction she wrote was largely realistic, and it contained nothing comparable to the strongly fantastic elements that are evident in the juvenilia of all the Brontës. Their juvenile writings are often very funny, but there is remarkably little humour in Evans' early efforts: at that time she was invariably serious. Unlike the Brontës she seems to have been habitually earnest as well as diligent, concerned with self-improvement and anxious to transform and reshape herself through her growing intellectual powers. As soon as she could, she removed herself both physically and psychologically from the bourgeois world of her childhood, quite unlike the Brontës, none of whom even considered abandoning their Yorkshire roots. As a young person she was priggish, puritanical and moralistic. Her biographer Frederick Karl asserts that she read more and knew more and thought more than anyone in the mid-Victorian period.[12] That is not an accomplishment that any of the Brontës would have aspired to rival.

These differences ensured that the nature of Mary Anne Evans' training for her career in writing was strikingly different from the Brontës'. And yet it was similar in one vital respect: like theirs, her preparation was extensive, thorough, and long-lasting. The seriousness of her commitment to becoming an especially knowledgeable woman was already beginning to be apparent by the age of ten or eleven. At that time there was nothing ostensibly prodigious about her development: as Frederick Karl remarks[13] she did not sparkle or display quicksilver intelligence. What she did already display to an unusual extent were qualities of gravity and seriousness. Karl suggests that even then she was already looking beyond childhood and anxious to move into an adult life in which she imagined herself becoming more independent and free of the restrictions that children find tiresome. Her reported response at a children's party, when asked why she seemed unhappy, 'I don't like to play with children. I like to talk to grown-up people'[14] points to a profound irritation with the state of childhood.

Her formal education was impressively good. Mary Anne's father, an upwardly mobile and highly successful man who was employed as agent

---

[12] Karl (1995), p. 29.   [13] Karl (1995), p. 23.   [14] Karl (1995), p. 22.

on a large aristocratic estate, went to some pains to ensure that his daughter was given better educational opportunities than were customary for a girl at the time. He was unusually attentive to her in the early years of her childhood, often taking her with him as he made his rounds of the properties that he administered.

At the age of eight she was sent to a boarding school. The school was not in itself remarkable, but it enabled Evans to become acquainted with an intense young teacher named Maria Lewis, who was to be an important mentor for the future novelist, and someone whose own interests and attitudes ensured that Mary Anne would be exposed to various influences that were outward-looking and intellectual, in contrast with the narrowly provincial values that reigned unquestioned within her own family. She was also now exposed to evangelical Christianity, bringing her into a form of religion that was more fervent and more emotional than the traditional kind of worship she was used to. Hence the effects of Lewis' attentions on her young charge were thoroughly subversive, inclining her to question the expectations of a family whose way of life she was already finding irksome. As Karl points out, Robert Evans would have been horrified had he known what was going on. Eventually, Mary Anne would outgrow the tutelage of Maria Lewis and discard the religious beliefs that were so important for her mentor. However, throughout a fifteen-year period Maria Lewis was a significant intellectual influence. She played a key role in enabling the growing child to extend her capabilities and become a woman who had outgrown her conservative early background and developed into a clever and well-informed young person with a mind of her own, and someone whose interests and values were not at all narrow or provincial.

By ten or eleven, there was already a fierce intensity in the way in which she absorbed knowledge from books, to the benefit of her own fast-expanding mental powers. She was already reading Scott's novels. She devoured poetry, and within a year or two would acquire an abiding passion for Milton, whose serious and disciplined approach was to be a lasting influence on her own work. Her father perceived that she was outgrowing her first school, and Mary Anne was moved to an above-average educational establishment where for the first time she was able to receive effective instruction in French, as well as in the traditional school subjects such as history, arithmetic, and English. Characteristically, at the end of her first year she won the school prize in French. The prize was a copy of Pascal's *Pensées*, hardly an obvious choice for a child not yet thirteen, but one that she nevertheless took to and seems to have rapidly mastered. She also learned music. As Einstein was to do some generations later, Mary Anne Evans became a good instrumentalist. The great novelist's expertise at the piano, acquired through years of dogged practice, almost rivalled the great scientist's mastery of the violin.

And she was already becoming a competent writer. Only a few of her compositions at this age remain. They have little in common with the Brontës' earliest writings, lacking their fantastic and imaginative elements but displaying a real understanding of abstract ideas and a promising capacity of self-expression. She was just starting to gain a voice of her own and an independent point of view, albeit one that was somewhat priggish and moralistic.

The seriousness of purpose that was to be Evans' most prominent defining feature was already in evidence in her early teens. By this time she was always busy, diligent, organised, intense and earnest, an avid believer with firm and somewhat intolerant attitudes on social and moral issues. Books filled much of her time, and when she was not reading she would often be writing – poetry as well as prose – or practising at the piano. After her mother died in 1836 she took over the management of the family home. The demands that responsibility placed upon her combined with her intense and puritanical gravity – which made self-denial a virtue – to ensure that her adolescent years were far from being carefree ones.

By eighteen she was consuming scholarly and theological writings, and also histories and biographies, at a pace that even *Middlemarch*'s Dr Causubon could hardly have matched. She studied German and Italian, becoming a fluent reader in both languages, and added to her knowledge of Latin. She started taking a keen interest in the physical sciences, attending lectures on chemistry and reading books on geology and astronomy. At that time she would have enjoyed Faraday's lectures, but she had no opportunity to attend one until about ten years later.

At around this age she was increasingly exposing herself to ideas that were not compatible with her firm religious beliefs. She knew about Lyell's work on geology, which as we have seen, anticipated Darwinism by establishing, with little room for doubt, that gradual change rather than instant creation provided the only viable explanation of how the earth's physical form came about. She was increasingly critical of the published rebuttals of the scientific writings that were challenging religious teachings about the origins of the universe. She was also allowing herself to be moved by Wordsworth's verse and other romantic poetry, such as Byron's, and opening her mind to varieties of spirituality which clashed with the puritanical mindset she had been clinging to. Her doubts about the religious beliefs of her family circle were finally to be made public at the age of twenty-one, when she refused to go to church with her father. She had become friendly with Charles and Elizabeth Bray, a free-thinking brother and sister with strongly humanist interests who profoundly influenced her own thoughts and also brought her into contact with a number of the leading intellectuals and thinkers of the day.

By most standards, Evans was now an exceptionally well educated young woman. Yet between this time and the point at which she began her career as George Eliot the writer of fiction, there was another decade and a half of intense intellectual preparation. Much of this period was devoted to writing and editing activities, which she pursued with the seriousness and diligence that were now customary. The writing she engaged in took various forms. She produced numerous reviews of lengthy books, and wrote scholarly essays on a wide range of topics. Especially in the early years of her twenties, large amounts of her time and energy were devoted to translating, from the German, the immensely long and complicated *Life of Jesus* by David Friedrich Strauss.

Strauss' immensely ambitious 1,500 page work was an attempt to produce a historical account of the events described in the gospels. He treated them not as divine revelations but as narratives with a degree of historical validity. The intention was to demystify the figure of Jesus, preserving his identity as a historical person but without accepting the truth of explanations that resorted to miracles and supernatural causes. Strauss was fully aware of the enormous importance of Christianity, but he adopted a stance in which Christianity was something to be interpreted and commented upon, and to be explained in terms of mythological manifestations and metaphorical meanings, rather than to be straightforwardly believed in.

It is hard to imagine a more difficult task of translation. Finding a capable translator for this important book had proved almost impossible. One other person had been persuaded to try to do it, but had abandoned the book less than a quarter of the way through. The job made huge demands upon even Evans' well-trained capacity for sustained effort and concentration. The work's intricate arguments and convoluted constructions made it hard to understand in the original, let alone translate it into a different language. Mary Anne's German at the time she first confronted this enormous challenge was still fairly limited, and the task was made even more difficult by the fact that the *Life of Jesus* contains numerous quotations in a variety of different languages, including Hebrew, a language which she did not know at all. Yet she set about this intimidating labour with her customary diligence. Evans initially set herself the impossible goal of completing six pages per day, but even she could not keep that up. In the end, translating the *Life of Jesus* took her more than two years. It was an enormous achievement, of course, which increased her own self-confidence as well as strengthening her intellectual muscles. She must have known that remarkably few other people would have possessed the capacity to equal her feat.

The important consequence of Mary Anne Evans' deep and prolonged commitment to a way of life based upon hard work, effort, and an acute awareness of the necessity for self-improvement through education and scholarship, was that by the time she finally began writing fiction at the age of around thirty-five, she was in many respects immensely well prepared for undertaking intellectually challenging work. She had made herself into a writer who was knowledgeable and well-informed and also capable of understanding complex issues and following intricate arguments. She had worked hard to magnify her expressive powers as a writer. Unlike John Stuart Mill, one of her very few contemporaries whose knowledge rivalled hers, she had done it largely through her own efforts. And in common with Michael Faraday, she gained her rare capabilities more through a combination of sustained effort and serious intent than through unusual quickness or inborn facility at learning.

As we have seen, although there are points of similarity between Evans and the Brontë sisters, in many respects their lives and their interests were very different. Her high seriousness and earnestness contrasted with their romantic natures and their perhaps obsessive attraction to worlds of fantasy and imagination. Yet these very different writers are bound together by the fact that they all succeeded, in their contrasting ways, in making themselves formidably well-prepared to be authors of major novels. In each case this preparation was intense and prolonged, taking many years. There is no shred of truth in the suggestion that any of these authors just emerged, chrysalis-like, suddenly and unexpectedly capable of writing novels. All their attainments depended to a very considerable extent upon the training and preparation which the authors gave themselves. It is highly unlikely that any of these writers, or indeed any other major authors, would have written novels of any merit had they missed out on the sustained periods of learning which all of them experienced.

Of course, just as the activities that equipped the Brontës for their creative work and those that made it possible for Mary Anne Evans to become a great author took contrasting forms, the varieties of training experiences that other novelists have been exposed to have been very different from either of these models. Take Charles Dickens, for example. The young Dickens had little of the gravity of the intensely serious Mary Ann Evans, and compared with the Brontës he was less introspective and far more outgoing and alert to his everyday surroundings, constantly observing minute details of the real world rather than inventing ones that were entirely imaginary. One could hardly imagine the painfully shy Emily Brontë pausing as she walked through a local market, as the self-assured young Dickens did, to buy a bag of cherries and pop them, one at a time, into the mouth of a dirty little child who was being carried on the shoulder of a coal-heaver.[15] But there are some similarities, of course. Like the novels of the Brontës and George Eliot, the fiction of Dickens draws extensively upon his own memories of childhood, and it does so in a manner that is more direct, and certainly more obvious, than could be envisaged in the creative achievements of, say, a composer or a scientist. And Dickens' achievements, like those of the other novelists, drew upon skills and capabilities that had been gradually and painstakingly acquired. Like the others, Dickens gave himself a thorough training, and worked very hard at becoming a writer.

As a preparation for a future novelist, Dickens' childhood had been rich in two kinds of experiences. First, there was a strong family tradition of story telling, and he had plenty of opportunities to absorb the knack of putting together narratives that kept an audience in suspense. Second, at an early age he gained the habit of reading regularly, a habit which lengthy bouts of illness helped to instil. Yet there was little in Dickens' childhood that prepared him for writing as such. As a boy he was certainly alert, sensitive, and unusually observant, and especially after his months in the blacking factory and his father's period of imprisonment as a debtor he was sharply aware of the value of striving for qualifications and the material security they could bring. But in comparison with other future authors such as Mary Anne Evans and the Brontës he had far less actual experience at expressing himself in written language, even though he had been known to send occasional reports to newspapers while he was still at school.

Strangely enough it was his father, whose way of life Charles Dickens regarded in many respects as something to avoid rather than emulate, who inspired his first serious training as a writer. After retiring from the Navy Post Office and at the age of forty-one, John Dickens surprisingly and uncharacteristically took it upon himself to master shorthand, in order to increase his chances of getting himself a post in journalism. At fifteen, already working as a law clerk, Charles took it into his head that if he too learned shorthand he could become a reporter and earn much more than he was currently getting, and it also struck him that a job in a newspaper could be considerably livelier than his own position in a law firm was turning out to be.

He found that learning shorthand was a difficult challenge, and one

---

[15] Hibbert (1983), p. 153.

that he did not enjoy at all, but he persisted at it doggedly and before reaching the age of seventeen was ready and prepared to work as a reporter. From this time onwards, working initially as a freelance court reporter and later in a series of increasingly demanding journalistic posts, his way of life encouraged him to concentrate on extending his skills at communicating in writing. He was anxious to improve on his education, demonstrating his devotion to self-improvement by applying at the earliest possible time – his eighteenth birthday – for a ticket of admission to the British Museum Reading Room. He used that ticket productively, recalling in later years that his hours of study there had been some of the most valuable of his life.

From his court reporting job he soon moved to a better position as a parliamentary reporter for a periodical. This gave him more opportunities to shine as well as enabling him to learn how Britain was governed at the time. He took on occasional other assignments, succeeding to the extent that by the age of nineteen he was sometimes earning as much as twenty-five guineas in a week, which compared remarkably well with the six shillings a week that he had been paid for working in the blacking shop. At twenty-five he moved to a secure post with the *Morning Chronicle*, where his job involved reporting on political meetings and elections in the provinces. There was a good deal of travel, making for a busy and exciting life that suited an energetic young man. He found numerous opportunities to add to his income and his writing skills by undertaking additional assignments, and by this time he had also begun to write short stories. At the age of twenty-one he sent one of these to the *Monthly Magazine*. It was accepted and quickly published.[16] He was asked for more, and they were soon pouring out of him. By the summer of 1834 he was writing under the pseudonym 'Boz' and making himself a reputation, and fame and wealth were just around the corner.

Even those major Victorian authors whose autobiographical statements have suggested otherwise put plenty of effort into gaining training and experience at writing. Elizabeth Gaskell was constantly reading and writing from an early age, keeping journals, making notes, recording stories and conversations. Anthony Trollope, despite his self-depiction of having been a dunce at his school, Harrow, won an essay prize in English and kept a continuous journal for a ten-year period starting at the age of fifteen. The fact that he had a literary mother would have encouraged him to perceive the possible value of expertise at writing. He did acknowledge the contribution to his development as an author of his early writing activities, which he said 'habituated me to the rapid use of pen and ink,

---

[16] Hibbert (1983), p. 155.

and taught me how to express myself with facility'. [17] Being an awkward and unhappy child, the young Anthony Trollope became a great day-dreamer, endlessly making up stories that provided a refuge and a comfort. Together, his journals and his daydreaming activities played a part in his growth as a writer, functioning not unlike a modest version of the imaginary worlds of the Brontës.

Like ordinary men and women, major authors have had to invest large amounts of time and effort in order to become unusually skilled. Their heavy dependence upon training and preparation is one of the many aspects of human experience that creative geniuses share with other people.

[17] Glendinning (1992), p. 40.

8   Inventing and discovering

This chapter explores some of the circumstances that immediately precede the major inventions and discoveries that make human progress a reality.

It would be wrong to think of advances typically occurring as consequences of single acts of discovery. The conventional notion of a creative discovery or invention is most accurately seen as a somewhat misleading social construct,[1] and in fact it is usually impossible to identify precise defining moments at which discoveries are made. Even the assumption that there is always one particular inventor or discoverer to whom an advance can be attributed can be called into question. Typically, the actual circumstances in which advances take place are complicated and untidy, and usually involve a variety of contributions being made over substantial periods of time, often by a number of different people. It has been convincingly argued that the contrasting traditional or conventional depiction of creative inventions, according to which discoveries take the form of sudden and dramatic insights by particular individuals, stems from rewritings of scientific history. Such accounts, it is claimed, misrepresent reality to the point of being seriously misleading, by making the chains of events that lead to human advances appear to be far simpler, more sudden, and considerably more dramatic than they really are.

For example, George Stephenson and James Watt have both been credited with inventing the steam engine, although neither of them actually did. Nor, strictly speaking, did Thomas Newcomen, who made the first practical steam-powered machine with moving parts. Newcomen built upon earlier developments by Thomas Savery, in which air pressure produced a vacuum that was utilised to pump water from mines. Savery's innovations, in turn, were preceded by the written description of a steam turbine made sixteen hundred years earlier by the Greek mathematician Hero. Doubtless Hero too was able to benefit from the efforts of his predecessors. In short, there was no single act of inventing the steam engine:

---

[1] See, for example, Schaffer (1996).

it was more a matter of a variety of problems being successively solved by a number of different individuals, each of whom made good use of previous advances. That alternative depiction of the events surrounding new advances is usually more realistic than the conventional one, even in those instances of invention in which the period of time needed to create effective devices and improve them was considerably shorter than the lengthy period over which effective steam engines were perfected. So, for instance, the invention of powered flight, and the development of the internal combustion engine, each depended on contributions being made by a number of individuals.

The discoveries of steam power, powered flight, and the internal combustion engine are far from being the only innovations which popular accounts have described in ways that misrepresent and oversimplify the actual circumstances. Another instance is the introduction of the cotton gin, which is often reported to have been invented in 1793 by the American inventor Eli Whitney. Whitney's advance was certainly a major innovation. It made the large-scale production of cotton in the United States immensely more economical, by replacing the use of human labour for the lengthy chore of removing the seeds from cotton with machines that did the same job fifty times faster. The gin (an abbreviation of 'engine') pulled the cotton along a roller through a kind of comb, which trapped the seeds, separating them from the cotton fibre.

However, as Robert Weisberg has pointed out,[2] the true story is not one of a sudden discovery or invention. Whitney was by no means the only inventor to have developed mechanical methods for removing cotton seeds. Cotton gins were already being used in the United States at the time when Whitney first encountered the activity of producing cotton, and similar machines had been working for hundreds of years in a number of other places where cotton was grown, including Italy and India.

Whitney's contribution was undoubtedly a very important one, because his devices, unlike earlier ones, worked with those kinds of cotton that could be most profitably grown in the southern areas of the United States. Previously existing machines only worked with finer cotton varieties that were not so economical to produce, because their rate of growth was slower. But Whitney's achievement, just like the advances of Watt and Stephenson, involved working with machines that were already in use and adapting them for particular tasks, rather than creating or discovering an entirely novel device that had not previously existed at all.

Even those popular reports that include detailed descriptions of how a

---

[2] Weisberg (1993), p. 131.

discovery was made are prone to be inaccurate. It is conceivable, if unlikely, that Archimedes did once leap from his bath shouting 'Eureka', but it is certainly not true that Newton discovered gravity by experiencing a sudden insight on seeing an apple fall to the ground. Newton did not actually arrive at the concept of universal gravitation until more than twenty years after the apple incident is said to have happened. In the intervening period, Newton's views about the reasons for bodies falling to the ground were broadly in accord with those of other thinkers among his near-contemporaries, such as Descartes.[3] Similarly, the well-known story that Galileo discovered that the time a pendulum takes to swing is independent of the angle after he had watched a swinging lamp in Pisa Cathedral in 1583 cannot possibly be true, if only because Galileo's work on pendulums only began ten years later.[4] And if the young James Watt really did have thoughts about mechanical engines after noticing that steam rattled the lid of a kettle, as British children are regularly told, that incident must have taken place a considerable time after Newcomen had already constructed an engine which made use of the power of the vacuum that is produced by condensing steam. Newcomen's first steam engine had been built in around the year 1712. Watt was born only in 1736. Watt, who started out as a maker of scientific instruments, did indeed succeed in making steam engines that were considerably more efficient than Newcomen's. However, that was achieved not by a sudden discovery but as an outcome of gradual technological improvements that made it possible to produce engine parts which were more precisely manufactured than the ones available at Newcomen's time.

Because of the limitations of people's memories, distorted recollections of the stages of thought that lead to scientific discoveries are not at all uncommon, and perhaps unavoidable. Charles Darwin had become convinced by the time he wrote his autobiography in old age that his thoughts about evolution had been influenced by a book by Thomas Malthus which he had read in 1838. Malthus argued the theory that the growth in a population tends to outpace increases in food supply. Darwin came to believe that the Malthusian notion of struggle for existence had suggested to him the idea of variations being selectively preserved or destroyed. However, examination of the notebook entries written by Darwin around the actual time of reading Malthus indicates that the book was just one of many influences that shaped his thinking. The ideas put forward by Malthus fitted in with ones that Darwin was already developing for himself, and they were not the unique source of any dramatically new or sudden insight.

---

[3] See Schaffer (1996), p. 14.   [4] Schaffer (1996).

In certain instances, the massive task of tracing the sequence of thoughts and intuitions that have led an individual creative thinker or artist towards insights or discoveries resulting in major advances has been attempted with considerable success. For instance, Howard Gruber[5] has made substantial progress towards mapping the steps of reasoning via which Darwin burrowed his way towards the insights that gave rise to some of his most important ideas. Other scholars have made progress towards delineating the thought processes underlying the insights of other scientists such as Faraday and Einstein, as well as a number of creative thinkers and artists. My aim in this chapter is the more modest one of demonstrating that the challenges involved in accounting for the creative activities of major thinkers belong in the category of problems rather than mysteries, by showing that even if the detailed mental processes that enabled, say, Shakespeare to write *Hamlet* or Mozart to compose *Don Giovanni* remain largely untraced, there is no reason to believe that the creative processes involved are inherently mysterious, or miraculous. I suggest that the intellectual accomplishments of even the greatest genius are in principle no less explicable than those more mundane achievements of creative problem-solving that are regularly accomplished by individuals who are definitely not geniuses.

Taking that view does not mean questioning either the awesomeness or the originality of a genius's accomplishments. That geniuses are different from other people in the magnitude of their achievements is not being disputed. Yet there are strong grounds for believing that the mental operations that geniuses depend upon are not qualitatively distinct from the ones used by individuals whose expertise is not exceptional, and that mental processes underlying the creative acts of geniuses follow broadly the same rules and principles as the mental processes that lead other men and women towards more mundane creative achievements, and involve no added magic ingredient. In earlier chapters I argued that geniuses do not substantially differ from creative people in their dependence upon preparation and training. Here the aim is to demonstrate that geniuses are not totally different from non-geniuses in the ways in which, in maturity, they introduce and make effective use of those mental activities that lead to substantial creative attainments.

Brief examinations of four aspects of creative activities will serve to highlight the similarities between geniuses and other people. I begin by drawing attention to the fact that virtually all discoverers benefit from standing on the shoulders of previous thinkers. Second, I observe that collaboration between creative workers is more common than is usually

[5] Gruber (1981).

supposed, especially (but not only) in the sciences. Third, I point out that even when highly creative people work alone they are usually building upon earlier accomplishments by themselves and their contemporaries, rather than starting completely from scratch. Fourth, I draw attention to the fact that, geniuses, like everyone else, habitually see the creative activities they engage in as being difficult and arduous. Together, these observations contribute firm backing for the conclusion that the problem-solving activities involved in the most remarkable creative achievements and accomplishments are not fundamentally distinct from those that contribute to the everyday accomplishments of people whose expertise would not be regarded as being extraordinary.

On giants' shoulders

That the shoulders of one's predecessors can provide an artistic or intellectual voyager with an advantageous viewpoint has become something of a cliché, but it is a telling observation all the same. Many factors can affect the way in which a creatively active individual makes use of earlier thinkers' contributions. Reverence for previous discoverers' efforts – as is evident in the remark by the twelfth-century writer, John of Salisbury, that we are like dwarfs who see further than the giants of the past, but only because we are raised up by their superior size – can be judicious and healthy, so long as it does not stand in the way of change and innovation. Conversely, a degree of disrespect or even contempt for the accomplishments of earlier generations – as is illustrated in the remark about Newton that he did not just stand upon the shoulders of giants but stamped on them[6] – need not be disadvantageous provided that it does not lead to crucial insights being ignored.

The giants' shoulders metaphor is a fitting one, and it is not easy to think of counter-examples. It is doubtful whether there are any geniuses who have *not* greatly profited from the efforts of their predecessors. There have been remarkably few cases of innovators whose contributions were unanticipated and original to the extent that it has proved impossible to detect contributing influences. Significantly, such instances are not only rare but almost always refer to individuals in connection with whom our knowledge of the actual background circumstances is very sparse, such as Archimedes. Even the most original discoveries and inventions have had crucial antecedents. Turing's Universal Machine, a fair candidate to be considered as the first 'real' computer, drew inspiration from Babbage's nineteenth-century design for a computer, and Babbage in turn, built on previous developments.

[6] Bragg (1998), p. 96.

Consider the case of Archimedes. He did make scientific and mathematical advances that do not appear to have been anticipated by any achievements of previous thinkers. However, remarkably little is known about the advances that immediately preceded his, and so it is entirely possible that our ignorance of insights that might have stimulated Archimedes' thoughts indicates no more than a hiatus in our own knowledge. We do know that Archimedes shared a number of qualities with more recent geniuses. Like Newton and Einstein, he was remarkably single-minded in his pursuit of solutions to the problems that obsessed him. Like them he would spend days at a time thinking about nothing else, ignoring other people and neglecting even the most basic everyday activities like eating and dressing himself.[7] It would be surprising if Archimedes had not been able, in common with those other great scientists, to draw upon sources of inspiration in the form of thoughts put forward by his most immediate predecessors. The fact that no evidence of such ideas survives is no justification for inferring that they never existed.

Collaborating with others

In popular mythology the typical genius is a thoroughly solitary individual. Yet scanning the ranks of geniuses in an effort to locate individuals who have worked in complete isolation is a noticeably unfruitful exercise. Unsurprisingly, creative thinkers do tend to be unsociable during the periods when they are most heavily engaged on their work. A few, like Newton, have been seen by others as not simply uncongenial but positively unpleasant. But any solitariness apparent in scientific geniuses is as likely to have been a consequence as a cause of their intense commitment to the struggle to make progress. Michael Faraday came as close as anyone to epitomising the notion of the solitary scientist, and he combined a strong preference for working alone with a habitual reluctance to talk about his thoughts until he had resolved the problems he was engaged upon. And yet even Faraday had a strong sense of obligation to others – as his tireless lecturing activities demonstrated – as well as strong social instincts, granted that the latter were exercised mainly within circles comprising his own family and his co-religionists.

As we saw earlier, even the supposedly reclusive Darwin was in fact constantly in contact with others, and that is evident from the ten large volumes of his correspondence that survive. He cooperated with other scientists and collectors energetically and also profitably throughout his long career. His effectiveness at what we would nowadays call

[7] Bragg (1998), pp. 19–20.

'networking' contributed immensely to his success at mustering an impressive body of empirical support for the theory of evolution. It also helped to ensure that his scientific reputation at the time when the theory was published was solid enough to deter many who would have mocked at or ignored the theory had it not come with the backing of an already distinguished scientist.

Of course, science in previous centuries was not quite so much of a joint exercise as it is today. But even at the beginning of the nineteenth century Humphry Davy felt impelled to take (in the company of his young assistant Michael Faraday) a prolonged tour of Europe in order to meet with other active scientists, despite the fact that the state of enmity between France and Britain at that time made parts of the journey hazardous in the extreme. And by the end of that century Thomas Edison was demonstrating that a capacity for managing and coordinating investigative activities was a valuable prerequisite for success as a scientific inventor.

Collaboration between scientists in its relatively modern forms is seen in the activities of Marie and Pierre Curie, and also in the productive scientific partnership of James Watson and Francis Crick. The Curies met when Marie was a student at the Sorbonne, where Pierre was already a prominent physicist. They married in 1895. They worked together on radium and discovered radioactivity, and in 1903 jointly won the Nobel Prize for Physics. Their joint work ended only when Pierre was killed in a traffic accident in 1906. Watson and Crick met in 1951, just two years prior to their discovery that DNA has a double helical structure. That discovery revolutionised understanding of the way in which organisms genetically reproduce themselves, as a consequence of the replication of information carried in the genes. Other scientists cooperated with them, notably Maurice Wilkins, who shared the Nobel Prize with Crick and Watson, and Rosalind Franklin, who perhaps deserved to have done. The discovery of the structure of DNA also depended on recent progress by a number of other people, including the chemist Linus Pauling. Pauling had played a crucial role by developing methods for identifying the structure of proteins, and had also demonstrated the applicability of helical models.

Among non-scientists there may be fewer advantages and more disadvantages to be gained by cooperating closely with others. But even in those arts in which the creative person habitually works alone it is easier to locate examplers of sociable musicians (like Schubert) and convivial painters (like Renoir) than of creative artists who have lived as hermits, except when blindness, deafness, and other infirmities have intervened. Even among writers, whose creative activity is inescapably solitary by its very nature, a degree of cooperation and co-dependence has been commonplace. The popular depiction of the Brontë sisters as eccentric isolates penning lonely thoughts from their moorland retreat is throughly misleading, as we have already seen. They were constantly reading and reacting to each other's efforts. Mary Anne Evans (George Eliot) was always looking for reassurance from those she depended upon and trusted. Charles Dickens, a sociable extrovert, spent much of his time planning entertainments and putting on plays.

Building on recent progress

Whether or not discoverers and inventors actively collaborate with others, they often make considerable use of their own earlier work and they also take advantages of the advances being made by their contemporaries. This bootstrapping process can give access to a mass of relevant existing knowledge, adding to any insights and revelations that have already been gained by making observations from the vantage point of past giants' shoulders. That an innovator has taken pains to make careful and extensive use of what is already known becomes evident from close inspection, even when (or perhaps especially when) first impressions may suggest otherwise. The circumstances surrounding the development of powered flight by the Wright brothers provide a good example of this. The Wright brothers have been seen as uneducated lone pioneers who suddenly discovered how to make aeroplanes that actually worked. Their invention seems to have come from out of the blue, as a result of some experiments conducted during the brief intervals of leisure that the brothers were able to steal from their everyday work as bicycle mechanics.

The reality, however, was nothing like that at all. As Robert Weisberg[8] and other scholars have explained, the Wright brothers conducted their experiments into powered flight at a time when there was acute interest in the possibility of flying, and scientific knowledge of aeronautics was expanding fast. They made sure that they were extremely well informed about all the current developments that could be incorporated into their own efforts. By their early twenties the brothers had carefully studied a number of reports of recent attempts to make flying machines, by several able inventors. One such inventor was Otto Lilienthal, an engineer who built a number of gliders and published some useful tables, enabling estimates to be calculated of the size of wings needed in order to achieve given degrees of lift. Lilienthal died when one of his gliders crashed in 1896. Other inventors who were already at work when the Wright broth-

[8] Weisberg (1993).

ers turned their efforts to flight included Samuel Langley, who began by testing a series of model planes in order to help discover the optimal dimensions. In 1896 a steam-powered model he had constructed reached a height of 100 feet. Yet another able pioneer was Octave Chanute, an engineer like Lilienthal. In common with Lilienthal, Chanute experimented with gliders, and one of his planes stayed aloft for ten-second periods, travelling about 250 feet.

All three of these inventors produced published accounts of their endeavours, and these were carefully studied by Wilbur and Orville Wright during the period when they were beginning to develop their own flying machines. So the Wright brothers were definitely not starting from nowhere, and their ideas did not generate in any kind of vacuum. And far from being either uneducated or unprepared, the Wrights had grown up in a home environment that was rich in opportunities to learn about machines. Their first introduction to powered flight had taken place when the older brother, Wilbur, was no more than eleven, at which time the boys were given a rubber-powered toy helicopter. By the time they became seriously interested in the possibility of trying to construct an aeroplane, they were already trained mechanics who understood trigonometry and algebra and had had some success at developing new techniques for manufacturing bicycles. Their subsequent work involved the efficient exploitation of their carefully acquired knowledge and expertise, over a lengthy period of time. They worked on a series of problems, always drawing upon any relevant data that other inventors had made available, and they proceeded in a highly organised manner. Their strategy involved making detailed plans and setting themselves intermediate targets that formed stepping stones leading towards their eventual goal.

Of course there were dramatic moments, of which the most spectacular took place in December 1903, when one of the Wright brothers' flying machines took flight and stayed in the air for almost a minute, in which it travelled not quite half a mile. Yet the invention of powered flight was characterised less by sudden breakthroughs or spontaneous insights than by rigorous planning, careful analysis, and much trial-and-error experimentation. The Wright brothers' eventual success only appears sudden or unexpected to those who are unaware of the efforts that preceded it. The single moment at which powered flight can be said to have been invented is just as elusive as the precise time at which steam engines arrived.

Creativity in the arts is not entirely different. Sudden insights and 'aha' experiences figure prominently in many accounts of artistic advances, and a number of writers and other artists have sincerely believed that their own work was created from thoughts and ideas that have suddenly presented themselves, perhaps after swimming around for some time in the unconscious mind. Coleridge's account of the writing of *Kubla Khan*, according to which, on awakening from a dream-filled sleep, 'he appeared to himself to have a distinct recollection of the whole, and taking his pen, ink, and paper, instantly and eagerly wrote down the lines that are here preserved'[9] is especially dramatic, although it is but one of a number of similar accounts by literary authors. Dostoyevsky made similar claims, and insisted that 'a creative work comes suddenly, as a complete whole, finished and ready, out of the soul of a poet'[10]. But whenever it has been possible to find evidence about the real circumstances in which creative achievements have been made, it turns out that they are not at all like that. Coleridge's story, which reports events supposed to have taken place almost twenty years earlier, is contradicted by evidence that he deliberately drew upon various sources. Some of these suggested the poem's images; others provided actual phrases that appear in the poem as published. Contrary to his statement that he immediately wrote down the poem in its final form, Coleridge made a preliminary version which he subsequently altered. In the case of Dostoyevsky, his claim that creative works appear suddenly in a finished completed form is firmly refuted by an analysis of the notebooks he filled when undertaking his work.[11] These reveal, for instance, that when he was getting ready to write *The Idiot* he worked on no less than eight plans for the first part of the novel, that he speculated at length about possible ways in which the narrative might develop, that he thought about the ways in which other authors had resolved problems similar to the ones he was confronting, that his characters drew upon various models known to him, and that his themes and narratives frequently made use of events he had experienced or read about.

Musicians and painters are just as likely as writers to engage in substantial preparatory work and to repeatedly revise their initial attempts. For instance, Beethoven's Ninth Symphony drew heavily upon reworked versions of compositions that had been made during the preceding ten years or so: Beethoven's notebooks demonstrate that large amounts of time and energy were devoted to planning, preparing, developing and elaborating the work. Even with Mozart, who is often said to have written out compositions from scratch, in their final form, the records firmly contradict this, providing plenty of evidence of corrections and alterations, and abandoned false starts.

Just as scientists have exploited the advances made by others, writers, artists and musicians have habitually borrowed themes and ideas from

[9] Quoted in Perkins (1981), p. 10.   [10] Quoted in Weisberg (1993), p. 231.
[11] Weisberg (1993), p.230.

their contemporaries and predecessors, as well as recirculating themes used earlier by themselves. Bach, for example, often borrowed themes from other composers, including Vivaldi, and that practice was considered entirely acceptable at the time. Moreover, in literally hundreds of instances Bach re-used melodies or ideas from his own earlier compositions. Borrowing from one's own works or those of others was just as frequent in other eighteenth-century composers, including Handel. It is not at all rare for a number of composers to have often drawn on a common source, and many of the melodies that occur in Mozart's compositions can also be found in the music of his contemporaries. Stylistic and technical borrowings are equally common. Mozart's earliest symphonies were greatly influenced by the compositions of J. S. Bach's son Johann Christian Bach, as was noted earlier, and some of Mozart's other compositions contain extensive stylistic borrowings from Haydn.[12]

Struggling against difficulties

One of the most common misconceptions about the creative achievements of geniuses is that they are made effortlessly and without strain or difficulty. Certain autobiographical accounts drawing on a person's recollections years after the work was done, such as Coleridge's anecdote about the writing of *Kubla Khan*, appear to confirm that belief. However, numerous other statements by geniuses about their own working practices, including ones made at around the time that they were actually engaged in their most important work, suggest that activities accompanied by feelings of ease or effortlessness have played only a very small part in the manufacture of creative achievements.

Reports of having to make sustained and arduous efforts are much more common. 'The only secret I have got is damned hard work,' was the British artist Turner's response to a request for advice about painting.[13] The philosopher Bertrand Russell said that he was made ill by the sheer difficulty of the work that went into producing his *Principia Mathematica*. Even Mozart, whose fluency and apparent ease of composition is often commented upon, chose to emphasise the arduous toil that went into his compositions.[14] Newton, Darwin, and Einstein all commented on the exhausting mental struggles that their work involved. Einstein complained about the amount of rewriting and amending his work required.[15] Faraday repeatedly exhausted himself as a result of the continuous concentration his efforts demanded. He was forced to stop work for months at a time.[16] Indeed, experiences of exhaustion brought upon largely by the

[12] Weisberg (1993) p. 224–30.   [13] Quoted in Hamilton (1997), p. 28.
[14] Weisberg (1993), p. 225.   [15] Fölsing (1997).   [16] Williams (1965), p. 102.

effortfulness of their intellectual activities were remarked upon by the majority of the creative individuals whose early lives we have been examining.

To conclude, extraordinary as the creative activities of geniuses undoubtedly are, they do not seem to be fundamentally distinct from those that many other people are capable of. In the present chapter, as in the previous ones, we have encountered many indications of similarities between geniuses and other men and women and no firm indications of inherent differences between them. A number of psychologists have suggested that the differences between creative problem-solving and ordinary thinking are ones of degree rather than kind.[17] Investigation of the actual circumstances surrounding the achievements of geniuses has yielded little support for the view that exceptional human accomplishments call for explanations invoking mechanisms or processes that are totally different from the causes of more mundane human attainments.

[17] Weisberg (1993).

Everyone has heard it said of somebody or other that he (or she) was born to be a genius. Can such an assertion ever be correct? A simple 'yes or no' answer has to be negative, because sophisticated inborn capabilities simply cannot exist. Outside mythology, nobody begins life having proclivities that can guarantee the emergence of high abilities.

That does not necessarily mean that the idea of being born to be a genius must be entirely false. People are not born identical, and some of the ways in which they differ at birth can have consequences that affect the course of their whole lives. One widely accepted view is that certain individuals begin life possessing innate gifts or talents that predispose a person towards exceptional attainments in a particular area of ability. Another common belief is that a person's intelligence level, which has a major role in determining the likelihood of substantial achievements, is largely fixed at birth. This chapter examines some of the evidence that has a bearing on the possible involvement of innately-determined influences on variability, among the numerous contributing forces that combine to enable certain individuals to become exceptionally capable.

All human individuals are affected in many ways by the particular combination of genetic resources they inherit. That the influences of genetic differences between people can extend to the manner in which lives are experienced is easily verified. Just watch the contrasting ways in which people at a party react to the entrance of a spectacularly beautiful individual and to a man or woman of ordinary appearance. Those differing responses will certainly affect the individuals who elicit them. Indeed, the manner in which others react to people can have an impact on many of their experiences. One beautiful woman has her education enriched as a consequence of influential people being drawn to her company; another fails to make the most of her opportunities because of repeated experiences of getting her wishes without having to make an effort. An ordinary-looking man loses out because the teacher who might have been able to help him prefers to spend time with other pupils. Another plain man eventually thrives because his failure to gain attention fuels his determination to do well. It is not at all uncommon for the degree of success a young person experiences to be partly decided by genetic characteristics even when the genetically influenced characteristics that are crucial are ones that have no direct effects on the person's capabilities as such. In the performing arts, for example, it is not unknown for stage directors to select the prettiest of a group of equally competent young ballet dancers for a starring role.

Those examples illustrate just a few of the many ways in which our lives are affected by the particular genetic material we happen to inherit. Note, however, that the eventual nature of the influences that originate in genetic variability is typically unpredictable and far being from straight-forward. It is easy enough to see that people's appearances can affect how others respond to them, but it is not usually possible to predict the long-term consequences of that. That unpredictability is highly significant, because in order to establish that there was something real in the notion of a person being 'born to be a genius' it would be necessary to go a stage beyond merely confirming that individuals are influenced by their genes, and demonstrate that a consequence of people's differing genetic compositions is to affect their abilities in a clearly predictable manner.

Do differing genetic materials have predictable influences on individuals' attainments, or not? In the first part of this chapter I examine evidence relating to the frequent claim that such direct influences stemming from people's genes do indeed exist, and take the form of innate talents or gifts. These, it is often claimed, are possessed by some young people but not others. A common assumption is that a person must possess gifts or talents in order to be capable of reaching the highest levels of expertise. Afterwards, I investigate the related possibility that innate variability in general intelligence makes a big contribution to the likelihood of individuals gaining exceptional capabilities. Finally, I take a broader look at the issues, and reach some conclusions concerning possible genetic influences on the likelihood of someone becoming a genius.

In the minds of many people it is a clear and simple fact, not to be questioned, that certain men and women have been born with innate talents that make them capable of high attainments. I call that viewpoint 'the talent account'. Someone who subscribes to it takes it for granted that geniuses, in common with many others who achieve unusually high levels of expertise, do so at least partly as an outcome of being born possessing a special mental capacity of some kind.

The talent account is widely accepted and rarely challenged. It is not hard to understand why. It agrees with our commonsense impressions. It is consistent with numerous everyday observations. There is no denying that from an early age young people do differ in their patterns of ability. One child does well at arithmetic but appears incapable of learning to play a musical instrument. Another youngster is hopeless at both music and arithmetic but has a flair for new languages. Even within the same family there may be striking differences between siblings: one daughter takes to the task of learning to play the piano with apparent ease, while her older sister struggles to master a few elementary pieces. In some cases these differences between individuals appear to be present from very early in life. Often it is evident that differences in ability cannot be explained in terms of children's differing experiences of formal training. And sometimes children make contrasting amounts of progress even when they are equally keen to do well.

In short, young men and women differ in their capabilities even when there seems to be an absence of those causes of variability that arise from differing opportunities to gain skills and knowledge. Not surprisingly, the apparent lack of alternative explanations for such differences has led many to conclude that there must exist inherent differences between individuals in their potential to excel, with some children but not others possessing innate gifts or talents. So the talent account continues to be accepted, even in the absence of any positive evidence in support of it, because it appears to provide an explanation of a kind for differences that are otherwise inexplicable. Intuitively, it seems right.

But is the talent account actually correct? Its agreement with common-sense beliefs, combined with the seeming lack of alternative reasons for differences between people in their levels of expertise, makes it a plausible theory. Yet there is a big gap between a plausible explanation and a proven one, and in the case of the talent account there are compelling grounds for questioning it.[1] One serious weakness is the fact that for most people who accept the talent account their only justification for doing so is the apparent lack of alternatives. An explanatory theory requires positive evidence if it is to be convincing, and the fact that people have failed to discern alternative causes of variations in progress hardly amounts to a compelling case for the view that other causes do not exist. If I am anxious to persuade others of the correctness of my personal explanation of particular events, my observation that I have not been able to come up with a better explanation is unlikely to be perceived as reinforcing my claims.

In some cases alternative possible causes of variability become evident just as soon as a serious effort is made to look for them. In the case of musical skills, for instance, even when two children do not differ at all in the amount of formal instruction they have been given, it takes little effort

---

[1] A detailed examination of the evidence relating to the talent account is provided by Howe, Davidson and Sloboda (1998).

to realise that there may well have been large (if unnoticed) differences in the extent to which they have enjoyed musical experiences and formed preferences that would have affected musical development by sensitising a child to certain patterns of sounds.

Does it greatly matter whether the talent account is true or false? It matters immensely, not only because efforts to explain creative achievements can never succeed if they depend upon faulty assumptions about the origins of a person's unusual capabilities, but also because important practical issues are involved. The fact that the talent account is widely believed in has consequences that affect the lives of numerous young people. Within certain fields of expertise, such as music, unquestioning acceptance of the talent account is almost invariably accompanied by the belief that excellence is only attainable by those children who are innately talented. A frequent result of teachers and other influential adults having this combination of beliefs is that when scarce educational resources or opportunities are being allocated they are likely to be directed exclusively towards those young people who are thought to possess a special talent. Young children who are believed to lack innate talents are denied resources that are vital in order for a child to gain any chance of succeeding.

If the talent account was shown to be correct, it might be argued that a selection process that is based upon it makes sense, because it directs limited resources towards those individuals who are most capable of taking advantage of them. But if the talent account is wrong, and innate talents are fictional rather than real, a policy of denying facilities to young people because they are deemed not to possess such talents is clearly wasteful and unjust. It could still be argued that those children who are selected as being talented are the ones who are most likely to succeed anyway, since their above-average early progress still may be a good predictor of eventual success even if the inference that such progress points to an innate talent being present is wrong. It makes sense, in other words, to have a selection policy that favours young people who have already done well. Even so, a policy of totally denying learning facilities to any child who (because he or she has not yet made unusual progress) is thought to lack a vital innate talent can hardly be justified unless there are convincing reasons for assuming that such talents do indeed exist.

There is no item of evidence that single-handedly confirms or refutes the talent account, but various kinds of information have a bearing on the issue. A number of findings have been seen as offering support. First, for instance, there is some evidence that appears to show that skills appear inexplicably early in a few children. Second, some other findings seem to point to the possible existence of special inborn capacities in a small number of individuals. Third, various scientific results appear to indicate the involvement of biologically transmitted mechanisms in exceptional skills.

A number of reports of extraordinarily precocious development in early childhood have appeared. These accounts are certainly consistent with the possibility that some children are born possessing special qualities that raise the likelihood of their becoming exceptionally capable. Of course, the sheer fact that a particular child turns out to be a prodigy does not in itself demonstrate that there must have been anything unusual about that child at the time of birth. However, if unusual capabilities were seen to emerge in the very earliest months of life, it would be hard to see how the child could possibly have acquired them through the kinds of learning that ordinary children are capable of. In that event the conclusion that some special innate causes were involved would seem unavoidable.

The published reports include some accounts of quite remarkable development in the first year of a child's life. One boy is reported to have begun speaking at five months of age and to have gained a fifty-word vocabulary by six months and the capacity to speak in three languages by the age of three years.[2] Another child is said to have begun to speak in sentences at three months, hold conversations at six months, and read simple books by his first birthday.

However, the reliability of these accounts as sources of evidence is doubtful, because they are all retrospective and anecdotal. In the case of the boy who was reported to speak in sentences at three months, he was not actually seen by the psychologist who wrote about him, David Feldman, until reaching the age of three. The parents told Feldman that they had been amazed by their son's progress in his first year, and yet Feldman himself confessed to being just as astounded by the parents' absolute dedication to accelerating the child's development and their unending quest for ways to stimulate him. In all likelihood the child's early achievements were indeed exceptional, but strong doubts about the likelihood of their emerging spontaneously and without any parental prompting are raised by the fact that all that we know about the actual circumstances comes from the testimony of parents who were extraordinarily committed to stimulating their child's progress.

Further pointers to the possible involvement of inborn qualities have been provided by findings indicating that a minority of very young children possess special capacities that can facilitate the acquisition of a skill. The field of music provides the clearest indication of the possible pres-

---

[2] Howe, Davidson, & Sloboda (1998).

ence of a special innate capacity, possessed by only a few individuals, and which can help a young child to make good progress. Certain young children are found to have 'perfect' or absolute pitch perception. This enables them to name and sing specified musical pitches without needing to be provided with the kind of reference pitch that other children and adults have to depend upon. Having such a capacity can be an advantage for a child who is learning to play a musical instrument.

Ostensibly, perfect pitch perception provides a clear exemplar of innate talent. It facilitates progress in a specific skill area, it is possessed only by a minority of individuals, and it appears early in life in the absence of deliberate efforts to gain it. However, the fact that perfect pitch is not acquired deliberately does not necessarily mean it is unlearned. A pertinent fact is that perfect pitch can be gained through deliberate learning, even by older individuals, although not without considerable time and effort. The reason why perfect pitch perception usually appears early in life rather than later may simply be that children are more likely to acquire the skill at an age when their attention is directed to single sounds, rather than being captured by the combinations of sounds that form melodies and musical phrases. Moreover, the case for perceiving perfect pitch as an example of an innate talent is weakened by the uncomfortable fact that whilst perfect or absolute pitch perception does indeed give a young learner certain advantages, it is less helpful at more advanced stages. So even if there had existed firm grounds for regarding the capacity to perceive absolute pitch as being innate, the fact that most adult musicians do not regard the possession of perfect pitch as being essential or even especially beneficial would weaken the argument for that capacity being seen as evidence of the presence of an inborn gift or talent that makes its possessor capable of special accomplishments.

Additional information that has been seen as providing support for the talent account is encountered within a body of research findings demonstrating links between exceptional skills and various indicators of brain activity. It has been established that high abilities may be related to numerous biological and physical indicators, including blood flow, allergy, and uric-acid measures, levels of testosterone, glucose metabolism rates, laterality, neurohistology, immune disorders, myopia and left-handedness. In other words, assessments of ability levels are linked to various indications of the physical operation of the human brain. The fact that such links exist seems to give credence to the claim that geniuses and other exceptionally able and creative people are inherently different from others, just as the talent account asserts.

But here again, although the evidence is not inconsistent with the talent account, it provides no firm support for it. A limitation of the findings that indicate possible links between physical indicators and ratings of ability is that they all take the form of correlations, or numerical relationships. Such findings merely demonstrate that high levels of one of these two tend to be associated with high levels of the other. There are no grounds at all for deducing that those physical qualities that have been measured in the research investigations necessarily play any part in actually *causing* the high abilities. In most instances, there are a number of alternate possible reasons for two variables being correlated with one another.

It is certainly possible that biological differences between people do contribute to differences between them in their abilities. However, the reverse could also be true. That is, experiences may affect a person's physical form. Alternatively, in many cases a separate influence can have a similar affect on a skill marker and on a biological indicator, and in that event the two will be found to be correlated even when there is a complete absence of a cause-and-effect relationship between them. Merely establishing that a correlation exists does nothing to help decide between these alternative possibilities.

Another shortcoming of the evidence from physical indicators of brain functioning as a source of support for the talent account is that whilst ratings of some of these indicators are indeed related to high ability, hardly any physical or biological indicators *selectively* predict high performance levels at particular kinds of accomplishment. Typically, a biological indicator is correlated with various different kinds of high-level mental functioning, and very few biological markers generate the selective predictions about specific attainments that ought to be possible if physically based talents really do exist. Moreover, in the few exceptions, the observed physical differences between individuals appear to be outcomes rather than causes of their differing attainments. For example, amongst violinists and other string players, in whom it has been noticed that the particular part of the cerebral cortex that is responsible for controlling the digits of the left hand (which fingers the strings) is larger than in non-musicians,[3] it is also observed that the extent to which a string-player's physical brain structure is unusual depends upon the age at which the individual started to learn the instrument. This additional information points to the conclusion that the observed physical differences are outcomes of musical training rather than contributing influences upon musicianship.

In sum, convincing empirical support for the talent account is conspicuously lacking. Moreover, there are various items of evidence that seem to positively contradict it. For instance, the author of a study of outstanding

---

[3] Schlaug, Jäncke, Huang, & Steinmetz (1995).

young adult American pianists unexpectedly failed to locate the early indicators of future excellence that are widely supposed to be present,[4] and that same finding was repeated in some further investigations examining the early progress of successful young muscians that were undertaken by John Sloboda, Jane Davidson, and myself.[5] We made serious efforts to detect early signs of progress that might have formed effective predictors of high musical attainments, but none of the possible indicators we looked at yielded valid predictions. There was simply no trace of the early indicators of future expertise that we would have expected to find, had the talent account been correct.

The case for the talent account has been further weakened by other discomfirmatory evidence. Some additional research findings that are especially hard to reconcile with the talent account have emerged from studies in which it proved possible to train a random sample of quite ordinary adults to reach extraordinarily high levels of competence at a variety of skills. The standards these individuals achieved, solely as an outcome of intensive training, were so much beyond what most people regard as being possible that those who witnessed the skills being displayed were convinced that the individuals involved must have had a special innate gift or talent.[6]

In other studies researchers have looked for, but failed to observe, differences in performance between ordinary children and ones thought to be innately talented. The findings point to a lack of differences between supposedly talented and supposedly untalented children at various indicators of progress, including the length of the training period necessary to reach high levels of competence[7] and the gains achieved following a given amount of practising.[8] The sheer amount of training and practice a person has undertaken turns out to be the best available predictor of high levels of expertise. That is so despite the fact that the measures of practising that have been used in the investigations have been somewhat crude ones. In most cases these assessments are retrospective, which makes their reliability questionable, and they take no account of important factors such as the person's motivation to practise or the quality and appropriateness of the practising activities. And yet in spite of all these limitations, assessments of practising have turned out to be good predictors of future success.

When all the observable reasons for people differing in their capabilities are taken into account, including variations in practising and in the quality of training and motivation, and commitment, as well as all the

[4] Sosniak (1985).   [5] See, for example, Howe, Davidson, & Sloboda (1998).
[6] Ericsson & Faivre (1988).   [7] Hayes (1981).
[8] Sloboda, Davidson, Howe, & Moore (1996).

numerous other ways in which individuals' differing experiences can affect their progress and development, the notion of innate talents may turn out to be entirely superfluous. In other words, the talent account may be an explanation for something that does not need explaining, because all the differences that the talent account is supposed to account for can be explained quite satisfactorily in other ways. It may be simply unnecessary to assume that there exist certain unobservable entities possessing the forms and functions that innate talents are believed to have. So even though the idea that innate talents provide a mechanism via which genetic differences between people have impacts on their capabilities is widely accepted and commonly believed in, there are good reasons for thinking that such talents are mythical rather than real.

Even if the talent account is wrong, it is still possible that there are other ways in which inborn differences between people may have predictable influences on the likelihood of individuals becoming capable of major creative attainments. Inherent differences in general intelligence could be crucial here. That possibility seems to gain credence from the fact that it is often assumed that a person's intelligence level is largely fixed at birth, and from the widespread belief that intelligence has a major role in making substantial achievements possible.

Both of these assumptions are questionable, however. The belief that a person's intelligence is largely fixed has been forcefully promoted by experts on intelligence testing, but there has never been convincing supporting evidence for it. That is not to deny that there are some findings that are consistent with the idea of a fixed intelligence. For instance, it has been demonstrated that individuals' IQ (Intelligence Quotient) test scores tend to be stable, as is evident from the observation that if someone is tested on successive years, the person's two scores are usually similar.

However, the observation that in most cases a person's score does not greatly change does not justify our inference that it *cannot* change. To claim that the presence of stability proves change to be impossible is rather like saying that the fact that most people live in the same house from one year to the next and keep the same telephone number means that these are unalterable. But it is easy to see that when there are good reasons for altering either of them, change can and does occur. Similarly, when there exist substantial reasons for intelligence levels changing, they too do alter.

The idea that a person's intelligence is largely unchangeable is also contradicted by evidence from each of a variety of different sources.[9] For

---

[9] For a survey of the evidence, see Howe (1997).

example, a number of investigations studying the effects on a child of being adopted by a family who provide a good home environment have yielded evidence of massive increases in intelligence. Additional evidence of such improvements has come from studies evaluating educational intervention programmes that were designed to provide compensatory experiences for young children whose home environments failed to provide good opportunities to gain important mental skills. Also, investigations in which the effects of variations in the amount of schooling received by children have been measured have provided yet more results demonstrating the changeability of intelligence test scores. Finally, a large body of findings has been accumulated demonstrating the changeability of intelligence by showing that in a number of separate nations average intelligence test scores have improved very considerably from one generation to another.

Nevertheless, a few writers on intelligence and intelligence testing have continued to insist that a person's intelligence cannot be substantially altered. They have put forward a number of claims which, they believe, invalidate the evidence indicating that intelligence can change. First, they point out that in some of the investigations in which young children's intelligence levels were found to improve as a consequence of attending compensatory learning programmes, the improvements faded or decayed over a period of years. Second, they note that even the initial increases in children's IQ levels resulting from attendance at such programmes have not invariably been large.

Both of these objections are easily refuted. It is certainly true that fading or decay is sometimes observed in newly acquired intellectual skills, but fading only takes place when there are good reasons for it. Those circumstances in which improvements that followed remedial education have eventually faded have been ones in which the children concerned were living in educationally deprived circumstances (typically in urban ghettos), in which they had little or no encouragement to practise or use their newly acquired mental abilities. It is noteworthy that fading only sometimes occurs. There have been instances of improvements in intelligence that have not faded at all.

It is also true that some of the reported changes in IQ levels following attendance at intervention programmes designed to extend a child's mental capabilities have been relatively small. But that observation does not amount to a convincing case against intelligence being changeable. The fact that certain interventions have not made a large difference in children's intelligence levels is not hard to explain. One obvious reason is that many of the interventions have simply not been substantial enough to make a real impact on children's mental capabilities. Consider, for

example, the case of some early intervention programmes that were introduced under the 'Head Start' initiative in the United States. In 1969 the
psychologist Arthur Jensen made a widely-cited claim that these programmes had failed to achieve the intended outcomes. However, he
neglected to point out that many of those programmes had been meagrely
financed and had lasted no longer than two months on a part-time basis.
For a typical child participant the total duration of time involved would
often have been appreciably less than a hundred hours. That amount of
time may appear fairly substantial, but it is actually quite puny in comparison with the periods of time needed to make major changes in young
people's acquired capabilities, even ones that are much narrower than
those assessed in intelligence tests. As we have already observed, around
3,000 hours of concentrated training and practice is required in order for
a higly motivated young person to reach the standard of performance at a
musical instrument such as the pianoforte that would be expected in a
good amateur player. Achieving professional standards of expertise
requires considerably longer, around 10,000 hours. And comparable
periods of time are necessary to achieve high levels of expertise in other
areas of attainment, such as chess, various sports, and foreign languages.

Moreover, in those kinds of capabilities at which children from varying
backgrounds are found to differ, it is usually found that there have been
massive differences between the children in the extent to which they have
enjoyed positive everyday experiences. Recall, for instance, the findings of
the study by Betty Hart and Todd Risley that examined the possible
reasons for the differences between three-year-olds from different social
classes in the size of their spoken vocabularies.[10] It was discovered that
even by that age those children who came from professional families had
already heard more than thirty million words directed towards them. In
contrast, the children from working-class families had only heard around
about twenty million words, and for the children from families on welfare
the comparable figure was around ten million words.

In short, behind the observed variability in language performance were
literally enormous variations in the children's actual experiences of language. In the light of the evidence that differences of that kind of magnitude in children's experiences lie behind differences in their capabilities,
the investments of time that have been devoted to early intervention programmes have been so tiny as to make it seem highly unlikely that they
would have large effects. In the circumstances it is remarkable that in
many cases the effects of such interventions have nevertheless been substantial. There is sufficient evidence of large alterations taking place in

[10] Hart and Risley (1995).

children's intelligence to make it seem likely that those mental qualities that are assessed in an intelligence test are no more fixed or unchangeable than those acquired capabilities which, unlike intelligence, are widely acknowledged to be acquired as an outcome of experience and learning. Efforts to refute that evidence have been unconvincing.

Turning now to the second of the assertions about intelligence that I mentioned, namely that intelligence plays a major role in making substantial achievements possible, that initially appears to be less open to dispute than the assertion that a person's intelligence level is largely fixed at birth. However, the role of the kind of human intelligence that is assessed in intelligence tests is not quite so clear or straightforward as is often assumed. One discovery that many people find surprising is that, at least at the highest levels of achievement, there is little or no relationship between people's performance levels and their scores on intelligence tests. It is undeniable that high achievers are usually intelligent people, but it is equally true that within a group consisting of individuals who all gain high scores at intelligence tests, those who have the loftiest test scores of all are no more likely than the others to produce exceptional creative achievements.[11] Exceptionally high scores on an intelligence test are not good indicators of the likelihood of a person producing the kinds of creative achievement that lead to their maker being called a genius.

Predictably, there are some relationships between intelligence-test scores and intellectual achievements. Substantial mental accomplishments in individuals whose IQ test scores are below average are unusual, although not entirely unknown. But within a group of people who all have high test scores, links between their assessed intelligence and their actual attainments are less evident. The relationships between the two, indicated by correlation levels, are insufficiently substantial for it to be possible to make useful predictions about someone's success in making exceptional achievements on the basis of a knowledge of their intelligence test score. And at anything approaching genius levels of expertise, there are no correlations at all between people's test scores and their actual attainments.

Findings emerging from a huge study of human intelligence that was initiated in California by the psychologist Lewis Terman at the beginning of the twentieth century indicated that individuals who were identified as being unusually intelligent in childhood often did go on to have highly successful adult careers. That result seemed to confirm the predictive value of intelligence testing. However, it was later demonstrated that had the children been selected on the basis of their family backgrounds and school records, without paying any attention to their intelligence test

---

[11] Howe (1997).

scores, equally accurate predictions could have been made about their attainments in later life.

The belief that certain individuals can be said to have been born to be geniuses is not one that is supported by firm evidence, and the innate gifts or talents that are commonly believed to be possessed by a minority of individuals who are thereby imbued with a capacity to excel in particular areas of expertise are probably mythical rather than real. The idea that an inherent quality of intelligence plays a role in determining an individual becoming a genius appears to be equally groundless. And yet, as we have seen, people's experiences are undoubtedly influenced by the particular combinations of genes they inherit. If that is true, is it not inevitable that someone's inherited genes strongly affect the likelihood of that person becoming capable of exceptional achievements? And in that event, might it not be possible at some stage in the future to 'read' the genetic informa- tion that is present in the organs of a newborn baby, and make accurate predictions about the child's future attainments? We cannot be certain, but in my judgement the answer to both those questions is likely to be negative, and I think that the reasons why many people believe otherwise are rooted in misconceptions about the manner in which genetic influences actually contribute to human variability.

When pondering about genetic inheritance, which involves a number of complex issues that are not fully understood, we naturally lean upon metaphors that we hope will help link the abstract complexities of genetic science to the more familiar territory of our own existing knowledge. But although metaphors can indeed be helpful, at least up to a point, they can also mislead, and some of those that people have introduced in relation to genetic causation have been definitely misleading. Genes are often regarded as providing the function of 'blueprints', or 'instructions', or 'recipes' which do their work by telling human cells how to construct individual human beings. Unfortunately, although none of these charac- terisations of the functioning of genetic information is totally incorrect, each considerably oversimplifies the true state of affairs. That is not the way it works.

What is particularly deceptive about the above metaphors is their implication that genetic materials invariably exert their influence by initiating a fixed causal chain and, in consequence, largely determining various outcomes. The reality is more complicated. Genetic resources certainly make vital contributions, but they can do so at various stages in an organism's development. The choices that an organism makes con- cerning if, how, and when there will be a contributing input of a particular item of genetic material, and concerning precisely what the form of that input will be, depend upon numerous other factors that affect the organism's development, including various environmental inputs that are mediated by the organism's experiences. In humans, to complicate things even more, the manner in which genes contribute to psychological functioning is considerably less direct than is implied by any of the above metaphors. In reality, rather than thinking of a gene exerting some influence that directly affects a complex psychological characteristic, it would be more accurate to imagine the relatively immediate effect of genetic inputs being to affect, say, the production of some or other hormone. Genes are sequences of DNA base pairs, and their direct effects take the form of contributions being made to the structure of proteins. That is achieved by affecting the structure of amino-acid sequences.

Depending on the particular circumstances, those relatively immediate effects may help trigger off other influences, whose effects may influence occurrences at successively more distant future stages. Eventually, following what may be a lengthy chain of physical activities, there may be consequences that take the form of psychological acts or events. Note, however, that because at each of a number of subsequent stages the actual influence of a particular item of genetic information will also depend on various other factors, the long-term influence of a particular item of genetic information will be largely unpredictable. So even when it is indisputable that genetically based influences upon human variability have been among the contributing influences determining the rate and direction of an individual person's progress, it would be wrong to conclude that any traits or activities that have been affected by those genetic inputs have been straightforwardly determined by them.

Hence the simplistic notions of genetic causation that come to mind whenever one sees newspaper accounts of the search for 'the gene for intelligence, or 'the' gene for any other complex psychological attribute, are, to say the least, misleading. They reflect a model of genetic causation that is far too simple to represent what actually takes place, and is not based upon anything approaching a realistic understanding of how genetic differences between individuals actually contribute to people's differing psychological lives. There are no direct one-to-one relationships between genes and psychological characteristics, and the popular idea that there are genes 'for' complex traits is simply wrong.

And yet, however misleading they may be, statements about 'the' gene for this or that will continue to be made, partly for the simple reason that they are easy to understand. This misuse is to some extent encouraged by occasional newspaper reports of investigations in which certain gene abnormalities are found to have predictable effects. Yet it needs to be registered that these reports almost invariably refer to circumstances in which genetic defects cause malfunctions, or prevent something happening. It is quite true that missing or defective genes can have powerful effects, just as a loose connection can bring a large computer to a halt or a missing sparking plug can stop a car. But the fact that a single gene can cause a serious mishap does not legitimise the inference that a single gene can make a person intelligent or more thoughtful, any more than a single connection can make my computer more powerful. As Stephen Pinker remarks in his book *How the Mind Works*, quoting a politician, 'Any jackass can kick down a barn, but it takes a carpenter to build one.'[12]

The fact that the influences of genetic resources are indirect rather than direct and may become activated in ways that partly depend upon unpredictable environmental inputs has various practical implications. The actual effects of being or not being genetically endowed in a particular manner will depend upon a variety of other circumstances. By way of a rather loose analogy, we can compare the possible effects of a person's being supplied with a particular genetic resource with those of an individual nation happening to have a particular mineral resource. What, we can ask, have been the effects of, say, Britain possessing abundant resources of coal? The answer will depend upon the historical period being examined. Prior to the industrial revolution, opportunities to benefit from that resource were restricted, because transportation was expensive and the machines that would later optimise the value of coal had not been invented. By the nineteenth century, the situation had radically changed, and coal had become a hugely important component of the nation's prosperity. However, before the end of the twentieth century, the importance of coal had receded, largely as a consequence of the increasing availability of power from alternative sources. In short, then, at any particular time the actual impact of coal has depended upon various other circumstances. Broadly similar considerations apply when one enquires into the likely effects of genetic variability. The actual influences will depend on various other circumstances. That is true even with relatively simple physical attributes, let alone complex psychological ones. For example, there are people who, because of their particular inherited genetic resources, tend to be fatter than the average when the level of nutrition is high but thinner than average when little nutrition is available.[13]

It has been claimed by psychologists and educators that even if genetic resources and environmental inputs are equally vital ingredients of human development, it can nevertheless be meaningful to enquire whether differences between people in their genetic endowments are more or less influential, as determinants of characteristics such as intelli-

---

[12] Pinker (1997), p. 34–5.   [13] Lewontin (1982).

gence, than differences between them in their experiences of life. So despite the fact that this question wrongly implies that genes and experiences represent separate influences that interact with one another in a relatively simple manner, it might still be reasonable to ask whether or not genetic differences between people invariably lead to differences in their psychological functioning. It might also be reasonable to ask whether genetically different individuals brought up in similar environments are more or less alike than genetically similar individuals brought up under contrasting circumstances. However, providing straightforward answers to questions like these is made difficult, and perhaps impossible, by the fact that individual variability under one set of circumstances may depend mainly upon genetic differences, but in a different set of circumstances is more strongly affected by environmental resources. Stephen Gould provides a hypothetical example relating to the circumstances affecting individuals' heights in a poor Indian village.[14] In one generation, affected by nutritional deficits, the average height is around 5 feet 6 inches and even the tallest individuals are no more than 5 feet 8 inches. Height is highly heritable, and the height of sons in the village is closely related to their fathers' height. Yet a few generations later, despite the fact that height is highly heritable, the average height has risen to 5 feet 10 inches. So despite the marked heritability of height, changed circumstances of life have led to a situation in which the heights of even the tallest individuals from the first generation are exceeded by many individuals.

A related assumption is that investigations based on identical twins can shed light on the question of whether the effects on people's mental capacities of genetic differences are greater or less than the outcomes of raising individuals in differing environments. In principle at least, by comparing identical twins reared together and apart, it certainly ought to be possible to estimate the extent to which genetic and environmental sources of variability have affected mental capabilities. In practice, there are enormous and perhaps insurmountable difficulties. For instance, in order to be absolutely certain that twins do not have shared environments it would be necessary to separate them soon after conception. But that simply cannot be done, and in reality the best that can be achieved is to select twins who have been separated at birth. Unfortunately, however, even that is virtually impossible, for a number of reasons. First, since identical twins are somewhat rare it is extremely unusual to encounter circumstances in which it has been necessary to resort to the undesirable (for various reasons) step of separating them at the time of birth. Second, in the very rare event of that happening, social and ethical considerations

---

[14] Gould (1984).

would normally dictate that steps would be taken to ensure that some contact between the twins could be maintained. In the majority of cases they would be brought up within the same family. Just imagine the kinds of circumstances that were sufficiently grave and desperate to make it unavoidable that identical twins were not only separated at the time of birth but were also brought up in circumstances that permitted no contact between the twins to be maintained. It is almost inconceivable that in circumstances as dire as those it would nevertheless be possible to undertake all the activities that would be necessary in order to keep accurate records of what had transpired. And yet in order for a properly controlled research study to be undertaken it would be essential for accurate and detailed records to be available.

These difficulties combine to make it extremely difficult to locate properly documented cases of identical twins who have been separated at birth in numbers that are sufficient to conduct properly designed research investigations. Nevertheless, some studies of identical twins reared together and apart have been reported, and evidence has been collected from around a hundred such individuals. On close examination, however, it transpires that these reports are not actually comparisons between twins reared together and ones separated at birth. In fact they are comparisons between twins who have been reared entirely together and ones reared partly apart, and the latter category includes pairs of twins who have spent as much as four years together, typically the earliest and most crucial formative years. Also, the reports lack detailed information on crucial variables such as the exact dates at which the twins were first separated. In view of the rare and difficult circumstances surrounding the early separation of identical twins these defects may be inevitable. But they are crucial defects all the same, and because of them it may never be possible to arrive at firm answers to questions about the inheritance of intelligence on the basis of the findings of twin studies.

It is currently becoming less necessary to depend on twin studies in order to acquire information about the possible effects on mature capabilities of differences between people in their genetic materials. Direct mapping of genetic information will make it possible for a fuller and more detailed picture to emerge, and it may well prove possible to identify certain genetic features whose presence adds to the likelihood of their possessor acquiring impressive mental capabilities. But it will never be possible to identify individuals who, by virtue of their genes, are born to be geniuses. One-to-one relationships between genetic differences and ability differences are ruled out by the complexity and indirectness of genetic contributions to human activities.

It tends to be assumed that if there do exist qualities that make some people more capable than others and have an inherited component, those qualities are ones that are closely related to a person's cognitive attributes such as cleverness or creativity. However, it is just as likely that those – conceivably largely inherited – human qualities that make the largest contributions towards setting geniuses apart from other people are ones of temperament and personality rather than being narrowly intellectual ones. The finding that assessments of a child's capacity to resist distractions and avoid impulsive actions are better predictors of later success than measures of early intelligence is consistent with that view. As we have seen, the particular qualities that contemporaries most frequently remarked upon in geniuses such as Newton and Mozart were broadly temperamental. Doggedness, persistence, the capacity for fierce and sustained concentration, as well as intense curiosity, are the attributes that others have noticed, and geniuses themselves have concurred with that emphasis. A number of geniuses, including Darwin and Einstein, have disclaimed having superior inherent intelligence, but no genius has ever denied either possessing or relying upon a capacity for diligence or a healthy curiosity.

One of the reasons for people being reluctant to let go of the idea that geniuses are a race apart, distinct from everyone else by virtue of their inherent qualities as well as their marvellous accomplishments, is the fear that geniuses will be diminished if we remove the magic and mystery surrounding them. I do not share that view. On the contrary, it is not until we understand that they are made from the same flesh and bones as the rest of us that we start to appreciate just how wonderfully remarkable these men and women really are. They show us what humankind is capable of. And it is only when we acknowledge that geniuses are not totally unlike other people that our minds open up to all that we can learn from them.

Appendix: Personalia

Archimedes (287–212 BC) Greek mathematician and physicist, considered to be one of the most original of all the great mathematicians.

Bach, Johann Sebastian (1685–1750) The great German composer.

Bach, Johann Christian (1735–82) Composer, and one of the three sons of J. S. Bach to be a musician. He helped and influenced the young Mozart.

Balzac, Honoré de (1799–1850) French novelist, the author of an important sequence of novels which included *Eugénie Grandet* and *Le Père Goriot*, and were collectively known as *La Comédie Humaine*.

Banks, Joseph (1743–1820) Wealthy botanist and explorer who accompanied Captain James Cook on an important voyage on the *Endeavour*.

Bidder, George Parker (1806–78) Engineer. He gained minor fame as a child prodigy, and became a friend and associate of George and Robert Stephenson.

Blenkinsop, John (1783–1831) Pioneering railway engineer. In 1812 he produced a successful early locomotive.

Brontë, Anne (1820–49) Novelist and poet. The youngest of the Brontë sisters, and the author of *The Tenant of Wildfell Hall*.

Brontë, (Patrick) Branwell (1817–48) Only brother of the Brontë sisters. Although he never had much success in adult life he was an important influence on his sisters' early development.

Brontë, Charlotte (1816–55) Novelist, and the eldest of the three Brontë sisters to survive childhood. Her *Jane Eyre* was an immediate success and has always been widely read.

Brontë, Emily (1818–48) Novelist and poet, and the author of *Wuthering Heights*.

Brontë, Patrick (1777–1861) The father of the Brontë sisters. He was born in Ireland and became a Yorkshire curate. Although sometimes depicted as a grim and domineering parent, he had strong literary interests and was an enthusiastic fighter for good causes and a benign influence on his children.

Burton, Sir Richard (1821–90) Explorer, translator and scholar, who enjoyed a varied and colourful career.

Cook, (Captain) James (1728–79) Explorer, navigator and map-maker, who came from humble origins. He made numerous discoveries and charted much of Australia.

Crick, Francis (1916–) With Maurice Wilkins and James Watson he made important discoveries relating to DNA.

Curie, Marie (1876–1934) French physicist, born in Poland, who made major discoveries relating to radioactivity.

Dante Alighieri (1265–1321) Italian poet, and author of *The Divine Comedy*.

Darwin, Erasmus (1731–1802) The grandfather of Charles Darwin, and a thinker whose botanic poems include speculations on evolution.

Darwin, Charles (1809–82) Biologist, whose theory of evolution by natural selection has continued to have an impact on thinking about the origins of life ever since it was published, in 1859, in *On the Origin Of Species*.

Davy, Sir Humphry (1778–1829) Prominent chemist, and the employer and mentor of Michael Faraday. Davy's invention of a safety lamp for miners at the same time as a rival lamp was developed by George Stephenson led to a bitter controversy.

Descartes, René (1596–1650) French philosopher, scientist, and mathematician.

Dickens, Charles (1812–70) Author and editor whose many novels, beginning with *Pickwick Papers* which appeared in his early twenties, were widely acclaimed and have had an enormous readership.

Einstein, Albert (1879–1955) He was born in Germany, but his earth-shattering work on relativity and other early discoveries were conducted while he was living in Switzerland. He became an American citizen in 1940.

Eliot, George, see Evans, Mary Anne.

Evans, Mary Anne (also known as Mary Ann, Marian, or George Eliot) (1819–80) English author and scholar, whose *Middlemarch* is considered by many to be the greatest novel in the English language.

Faraday, Michael (1791–1867) Major British scientist who despite leaving school at thirteen to become an apprentice bookbinder, carried out numerous important experiments and prepared the way for the practical application of electrical power.

Fitzroy, Robert (1805–65) Captain commanding the *Beagle*, which carried Charles Darwin on its five-year voyage and played an important part in his development as a mature biologist.

Galileo Galilei (1564–1642) The great Italian astronomer and physicist.

His observations confirmed the theory of Copernicus that the earth rotates around the sun, and his work greatly extended the understanding of gravity.

Galton, Francis (1822–1911) A second cousin of Charles Darwin who put forward theories about the inheritance of human intelligence and was an advocate of eugenics.

Gaskell, Elizabeth (1810–65) English author whose novels included *North and South*. She also wrote a biography of Charlotte Brontë.

Gladstone, William Ewart (1809–98) British politician and statesman.

Grant, Robert (1793–1874) Anatomist and naturalist. He helped Charles Darwin at Edinburgh University and was one of his most important mentors.

Henslow, John (1796–1861) The Cambridge botany professor and mentor of Darwin who was influential in making it possible for Darwin to participate in the voyage of the *Beagle*.

Hope, Thomas (1766–1844) Chemistry professor whose lectures at Edinburgh University were among the few to be highly rated by Charles Darwin.

Huxley, Thomas (1825–95) Scientist and disciple of Charles Darwin. He had an important role in promoting the theory of evolution by natural selection and shielding Darwin from much of the hostility that the theory aroused.

Jameson, Robert (1774–1854) Mineralogist and professor at Edinburgh University. Charles Darwin, unlike some his contemporaries, was unimpressed by Jameson's lectures, but he benefited from studying the collections in the natural history museum that was directed by Jameson.

Kant, Immanuel (1724–1804) German philosopher, whose *Critique of Pure Reason* examines how knowledge depends upon the manner in which our sensory experiences are categorised and organised.

Lyell, Charles (1797–1875) Geologist, and a friend of Charles Darwin. Lyell's *Principles of Geology*, part of which Darwin read at the beginning of his voyage on the *Beagle*, convincingly established that the inanimate world reached its present form as a result of gradual change rather than sudden creation.

Malthus, Thomas (1766–1834) English scholar whose writings on the growth of population influenced Darwin by showing the likely effects of influences similar to natural selection.

Maxwell, James Clerk (1831–79) Scottish physicist who built on the work of Michael Faraday and others and extended understanding of electricity and magnetism.

Mendel, Gregor (1822–84) Austrian biologist, and an ordained monk.

The findings of Mendel's experiments on plant breeding formed the basis of the modern science of genetics.

Menuhin, Yehudi (1916–99). Violinist, who was born in New York but lived mainly in England. He first became famous as a child prodigy.

Mill, James (1773–1836) The father of John Stuart Mill, whom he carefully tutored in childhood. James Mill was also a substantial scholar in his own right, and produced a monumental *History of British India*.

Mill, John Stuart (1806–73) Partly as a result of the intense early education provided by his father, Mill was intellectually precocious as a child and went on to become one of the greatest social and political thinkers of the nineteenth century.

Mozart, Leopold (1719–87) The father of Wolfgang Amadeus Mozart and an ambitious music teacher who played an active role in training and promoting his son.

Mozart, Wolfgang Amadeus (1756–91) The great Austrian composer was trained as a musical performer by his father, and first attracted attention through his prodigious childhood feats.

Newcomen, Thomas (1663–1729) Inventor of the first practical steam engine with moving parts.

Newton, Isaac (1642–1727) Great mathematician and physicist, who also devoted much of his time to alchemy. Before Einstein, our basic understanding of the laws governing the physical universe depended heavily on the work of Newton.

Paganini, Nicolò (1782–1840) Italian violinist of extraordinary virtuosity.

Pascal, Blaise (1623–62) French scientist, mathematician and theologian, whose inventions included an early calculating machine.

Ruskin, John (1819–1900) English social reformer and writer on art, whose writing was influential in sensitising the British public to the art of the renaissance.

Russell, Bertrand (1872–1970) English philosopher, mathematician and social critic, and a godson of John Stuart Mill.

Satie, Erik (1866–1925) Composer of highly distinctive works for the piano.

Savery, Thomas (c.1650–1715) English engineer who invented a device which used a vacuum to raise water. This incorporated a number of features that made possible the invention of steam engines.

Schubert, Franz (1797–1828) Austrian composer, who produced a substantial number of major compositions in his short life.

Scott, Walter (1771–1832) Prolific and widely read Scottish novelist, whose works include a series of historic stories known as the Waverley novels.

Shakespeare, William (1564–1612) The dramatist and poet, whose achievements strongly influenced the English language as well as its literature.

Shostakovich, Dimitry (1906–75) Russian composer.

Smiles, Samuel (1812–1904) Best known as the author of *Self Help*, a collection of brief lives which was intended to open ordinary people's eyes to the benefits of study and perseverance, Smiles also wrote the first biography of George Stephenson, who epitomised some of the virtues Smiles admired.

Stephenson, George (1781–1848) The great railway engineer who made steam locomotion for travellers possible, having acquired the skills that made him an outstanding inventor by his own efforts, following a childhood characterised by poverty and the complete absence of formal education.

Tolstoy, Leo (1828–1910) Russian writer, whose important novels include *War and Peace* and *Anna Karenina*.

Trollope, Anthony (1815–82) Following an unhappy childhood Trollope thrived at a responsible post working for the newly developed postal service, and at around the same time began writing the first of a substantial number of novels.

Turner, Joseph M. W. (1775–1851) The son of a London barber, and perhaps the greatest of English artists. His remarkable and innovative paintings formed a strong influence on the Impressionists.

Twain, Mark (1835–1910) The name Twain was the pseudonym of Samuel Clemens, an American author whose prolific and often humorous writings included *Tom Sawyer* and *Huckleberry Finn*.

Watson, James (1928–) American biologist who worked with Francis Crick and Maurice Wilkins on the structure of DNA.

Watt, James (1736–1819) Scottish instrument maker and engineer. His important improvements to steam engines made them sufficiently efficient and reliable for steam locomotion to become possible.

Watts, Isaac (1674–1748) An English pastor who is best known as a writer of hymns, but was also the author of *The Improvement of the Mind*, a book which strongly influenced the intellectual development of the young Michael Faraday.

Wells, Herbert G. (1866–1946) English novelist and man of letters. He wrote numerous novels, including *The Time Machine*, and was also influential as an educator who produced books that brought subjects such as science and history to a broad audience.

White, Gilbert (1720–93) English naturalist and curate, whose *Natural History and Antiquities of Selborne* has influenced numerous amateur naturalists including the young Charles Darwin.

Whitney, Eli (1765–1825) American inventor, best known for his cotton 'gin' which greatly improved the efficiency of the cotton industry in the United States.

Wiener, Norbert (1894–1964) American mathematician, and an outstanding prodigy in childhood. He contributed towards the early development of computers.

Wright, Wilbur (1867–1912) and **Orville** (1871–1948) The American pioneers of powered flight.

References

Barker, J. (1994) *The Brontës*. London: Weidenfeld & Nicolson.

Barlow, N. (Ed.) (1958) *The autobiography of Charles Darwin*. London: Collins.

Bowlby, J. (1990) *Charles Darwin: a biography*. London: Hutchinson.

Bragg, M. (1998) *On giants' shoulders: great scientists and their discoveries from Archimedes to DNA*. London: Hodder & Stoughton.

Brannigan, A. (1981) *The social basis of scientific discoveries*. New York: Cambridge University Press.

Brent, P. (1981) *Charles Darwin*. London: Heinemann.

Browne, J. (1995) *Charles Darwin: voyaging*. London: Jonathan Cape.

Burkhardt, F., & Smith, S. (1985) *The correspondence of Charles Darwin, Volume 1, 1821–1835*. Cambridge University Press.

Burkhardt, F., & Smith, S. (1994) *The correspondence of Charles Darwin, Volume 9, 1861*. Cambridge University Press.

Chi, M. T. H. (1978) Knowledge structures and memory development. In R. Siegler (Ed.), *Children's thinking: what develops?*. Hillsdale, New Jersey: Erlbaum.

Clark, E. F. (1983) *George Parker Bidder: the calculating boy*. Bedford: KSL Publications.

Colangelo, N., Assouline, S. G., Kerr, B., Huesman, R., & Johnson, D. (1993) Mechanical inventiveness, pp. 160–70 in G. Brock & K. Ackril (Eds.), *Ciba Foundation Symposium 178: The origins and development of high ability*. Chichester, England: Wiley.

Conroy, Frank (1995) *Body and Soul*. London: Penguin.

Csikszentmihalyi, M., & Csikszentmihalyi, I. S. (1993). Family influences on the development of giftedness. In G. R. Bock and K. Ackrill (Eds.), *CIBA Foundation Symposium No 178: The origins and development of high ability*. Chichester, England: Wiley.

Davies, H. (1975) *George Stephenson: a biographical study of the Father of Railways*. London: Weidenfeld & Nicolson.

Desmond, A., & Moore, J. (1991) *Darwin*. London: Michael Joseph.

Dunn, J., & Plomin, R. (1990) *Separate lives*. New York: Basic Books.

Ericsson, K. A. (1985) Memory skill. *Canadian Journal of Psychology*, 39, 188–231.

Ericsson, K. A., & Charness, N. (1994) Expert performance: its structure and acquisition. *American Psychologist*, 49, 725–47.

Ericsson, K. A. & Faivre, I. A. (1988) What's exceptional about exceptional abilities? In L. K. Obler & D. Fein (Eds.), *The exceptional brain: neuropsychology of talent and special abiliites*. New York: Guilford Press.

Ericsson, K. A., Krampe, R. T., & Tesch-Römer, C. (1993) The role of deliberate practice in the acquisition of expert performance. *Psychological Review*, 100, 363–406.

Fölsing, A. (1997) *Albert Einstein*, translated by Ewald Osers. New York: Viking.

Fowler, W. (1981) Case studies of cognitive precocity: the role of exogenous and endogenous stimulation in early mental development. *Journal of Applied Developmental Psychology*, 2, 319–67.

Gardner, H. (1997) *Extraordinary minds: portraits of exceptional individuals and an examination of our extraordinariness.* London: Weidenfeld & Nicolson.

Glendinning, V. (1992) *Trollope.* London: Hutchinson.

Gould, S. J. (1984) *The mismeasure of man.* New York: Norton.

Gruber, H. E. (1981) *Darwin on man: a psychological study of scientific creativity*, second edition. University of Chicago Press.

Hamilton, J. (1997) *Turner: a life.* London: Hodder & Stoughton.

Hart, B., & Risley, T. (1995) *Meaningful differences in everyday parenting and intellectual development in young American children.* Baltimore, Maryland: Brookes.

Hayes, J. R. (1981) *The complete problem solver.* Philadelphia, Pennsylvania: The Franklin Institute Press.

Hibbert, C. (1983) *The making of Charles Dickens.* Harmondsworth: Penguin Books.

Howe, M. J. A. (1990) *The origins of exceptional abilities.* Oxford: Blackwell.

Howe, M. J. A. (1997) *IQ in question: the truth about intelligence.* London: Sage.

Howe, M. J. A., Davidson, J. W., & Sloboda, J. A. (1998) Innate talents: reality or myth? *Behavioral and Brain Sciences*, 21, 399–442.

Howe, M. J. A., & Godfrey, J. (1977) *Student note-taking as an aid to learning.* Exeter University Teaching Services.

Jones, B. (1870) *The life and letters of Faraday*, Volume 1. London: Longman, Green, & Co.

Kagan, J. (1989) Temperamental contributions to social behaviour. *American Psychologist*, 44, 668–74.

Karl, F. (1995) *George Eliot: a biography.* London: HarperCollins.

Knight, D. M. (1985) Davy and Faraday: fathers and sons, pp. 32–49 in D. Gooding and F. A. J. L. James (Eds.), *Faraday rediscovered: essays on the life and work of Michael Faraday, 1791–1867.* New York: Stockton Press.

Lehmann, A. C. (1997) The acquisition of expertise in music, in Deliege, I., and Sloboda, J. A. (Eds.), *Perception and cognition of music.* Hillsdale, New Jersey: Elbaum.

Lehmann, A. C., & Ericsson, K. A. (1998) The historical development of domains of expertise: performance standards and innovations in music. In A. Steptoe (Ed.), *Genius and the mind: studies of creativity and temperament in the historical record.* Oxford University Press.

Lewontin, R. (1982) *Human diversity.* New York: Freeman.

Mazlish, B. (1975) *James and John Stuart Mill.* London: Hutchinson.

Mill, J. S. (1971) *Autobiography*, (edited by Jack Stillinger). Oxford University Press. [Originally published in 1873.]

Morris, P. E., Gruneberg, M. M., Sykes, R. N., & Merrick, A. (1981) Football knowledge and the acquisition of new results. *British Journal of Psychology*, 76, 415–25.

Murray, P. (1989) Introduction. In P. Murray (Ed.) *Genius: the history of an idea.* Oxford: Basil Blackwell.

Newsome, D. (1997) *The Victorian world picture.* London: John Murray.

Norris, C. (1989) Deconstructing genius: Paul de Man and the critique of romantic ideology. pp. 141–65 in P. Murray (Ed.) *Genius: the history of an idea.* Oxford: Basil Blackwell.

Packe, M. St. J. (1954) *The life of John Stuart Mill.* London: Secker & Warburg.

Perkins, D. N. (1981) *The mind's best work.* Cambridge, Massachusetts: Harvard University Press.

Pinker, S. (1997) *How the mind works.* London: Allen Lane.

Radford, J. (1990) *Child prodigies and exceptional early achievers.* London: Harvester Wheatsheaf.

Rolt, L. T. C. (1960) *George and Robert Stephenson: the railway revolution.* London: Longman Green.

Schaffer, S. (1996) Making up discovery. In M. A. Boden (Ed.), *Dimensions of Creativity.* Cambridge, Massachusetts: MIT Press.

Schlaug, G., Jäncke, L., Huang, Y., & Steinmetz, H. (1995) *In vivo* evidence of structural brain asymmetry in musicians. *Science,* 267, 699–701.

Simonton, D. K. (1994) *Greatness: who makes history and why.* New York: Guilford.

Skidelsky, R. (1983) *John Maynard Keynes.* Volume I, *Hopes betrayed.* London: Macmillan.

Sloboda, J. A. (1985). *The musical mind: the cognitive psychology of music.* Oxford University Press.

Sloboda, J. A., Davidson, J. W., Howe, M. J A., and Moore, D. G. (1996) The role of practice in the development of performing musicians. *British Journal of Psychology,* 87, 399–412.

Smiles, S. (1881) *The Life of George Stephenson* (Centenary Edition). London: John Murray. [The book was originally published in 1857.]

Sosniak, L. A. (1985) Learning to be a concert pianist. In B. S. Bloom (Ed.), *Developing talent in young people.* New York: Ballantine.

Spoto, D. (1983) *The dark side of genius: the life of Alfred Hitchcock.* New York: Ballantine Books.

Sulloway, F. J. (1985) Darwin's early intellectual development: an overview of the *Beagle* voyage (1831–36), pp. 121–54 in D. J. Kohn, (Ed.), *The Darwinian heritage.* New Jersey: Princeton University Press.

Summerside, T. (1878) *Anecdotes, reminiscences and conversations of and with the late George Stephenson, Father of Railways.* London.

Wallace, A. (1986) *The prodigy: a biography of William James Sidis, the world's greatest child prodigy.* London: Macmillan.

Watts, I. (1801) *The improvement of the mind: or a supplement to the art of logic:* (containing a variety of remarks and rules for the attainment and communication of useful knowledge in religion, in the sciences, and in common life. To which is added, Discourse on the Education of Children and Youth: two parts, complete in one volume.) Printed by J. Abraham, Clement's Lane, Lombard Street, London.

Weiner, N. (1953) *Ex-prodigy: my childhood and youth.* New York: Simon & Schuster.

Weisberg, R.W. (1993) *Creativity: beyond the myth of genius*. New York: Freeman.

Weisberg, R. W. (1998) Creativity and knowledge: a challenge to theories. In R. J. Sternberg (Ed.) *Handbook of creativity*. Cambridge University Press.

Westfall, R. S. (1980) Newton's marvellous years of discovery and their aftermath: myth versus manuscript. *Isis*, 71, 109–21.

Williams, L. P. (1965) *Michael Faraday*. London: Chapman & Hall.

Wilson, E. (1941) *The wound and the bow: seven studies in literature*. Cambridge, Massachusetts: Houghton Mifflin.

Witte, K. H. G. (1975) *The education of Karl Witte*, translated by Leo Weiner. New York: Arno Press. [Originally published in 1914 by Thomas Cromwell.]

Wolpert, L. (1992) *The unnatural nature of science*. London: Faber & Faber.

Zuckerman, H. (1977) *Scientific elite: Nobel laureates in the United States*. New York: Free Press.

Index